NEGOTIATION: FROM THEORY TO PRACTICE

Also by Jacques Rojot

COLLECTIVE BARGAINING: An Analysis and Case Study for Europe
COMPORTEMENT ET ORGANISATION
LABOUR LAW AND INDUSTRIAL RELATIONS IN FRANCE

Negotiation: From Theory to Practice

Jacques Rojot

Professor of Management
University of Paris I – Sorbonne

palgrave
macmillan

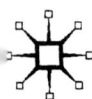

Published by
PALGRAVE MACMILLAN
Houndmills, Basingstoke, Hampshire RG21 6XS and
175 Fifth Avenue, New York, N.Y. 10010
Companies and representatives throughout the world

PALGRAVE MACMILLAN is the global academic imprint of the Palgrave
Macmillan division of St. Martin's Press, LLC and of Palgrave Macmillan Ltd.
Macmillan® is a registered trademark in the United States, United Kingdom
and other countries. Palgrave is a registered trademark in the European
Union and other countries.

ISBN-13: 978–0–333–52210–3
ISBN-10: 0–333–52210–9

This book is printed on paper suitable for recycling and
made from fully managed and sustained forest sources.

A catalogue record for this book is available from the British Library.

Printed and bound in Great Britain by
Antony Rowe Ltd, Chippenham and Eastbourne

For Elisabeth ROJOT-ANDRE
and Camille ROJOT

Contents

Contents

List of Figures

Acknowledgements

It is a pleasure at this time to acknowledge the precious help of many colleagues and friends. I am particularly in debt to Professors Susan Schneider, Stephen Weiss and Hoyt Wheeler who have provided many greatly helpful comments on earlier drafts of this work. They will find their suggestions embodied in the text. I am also extremely grateful to Professor Sam Bacharach who encouraged me to publish what was at the time a very tentative manuscript.

It should also be noted that this book is the final outcome of a course in negotiation. This course has been given on numerous occasions and with varied spans of time over more than ten years. It has been attended by managers as well as students and it has taken place in universities, business schools and in-company programmes in several countries.

Like most books this one could not exist without much that has been written before on the subject. It borrows largely from two sources: research which has been published before, and negotiation folklore arising from discussions with students, participants and practitioners. Reference is made in the body of the text to the work of authors which has been used here and is drawn upon. For lack of space no reference can be made individually to all those who have attended the course or who have kindly agreed to share their experience with me but their contributions are gratefully remembered. Without them this book would not exist and they contributed generously.

Finally, it must be mentioned that some of the material presented, mostly in the last two parts, was developed and taught jointly by the author and Mr A.W. Gottschalk. The author regrets that Mr Gottschalk could not take part in the actual writing of the book. Without him also, this book would not exist. His contributions are explicitly mentioned in several places. Notably, I am in debt to him for the developments on tactics, in particular the classification of tactics in categories and subgroups, the developments on the four bargaining styles and the presentation of the assumptions, concessions and information under the 'box' model in Part III.

Introduction

A large number of books have been written about negotiation. They fall mostly within two categories: theoretical treatises, and 'how to' books containing recipes and tactics for training negotiators.

Both types of books are useful and many, in both categories, are excellent within the limitations of their type. However, theoretical treatises fall short of giving any practical guidance, and 'how to' books lack flexibility. By giving only advice, which can be often quite useful and sensible, they leave the reader alone with a set of tactics, of rules of conduct, which are not always compatible, and which he is left to use blindly in all situations, without any guide, or any map, to help to decide which one to select and whether they are still appropriate to a given, new, specific case.

This book attempts to bridge the gap between the two categories. It is firmly grounded in theory because of a strong belief in the truth of the saying that 'there is nothing as practical as a good theory'. A relevant theory provides a conceptual framework, a guide to understanding, a map which can be used to analyse and understand what should be done in a real life situation.

However, the category of theoretical books is itself divided into many sub-categories along the lines of different disciplines and schools of thought. For instance, Zartman[1] distinguishes, according to the approach used, seven different schools of study of negotiation, and an eighth one cutting across the methodologies of several: historical, contextual, structural, strategic personality types, behavioural skills, process variables and procedural; the latter using experimentation and simulation. From the standpoint of the disciplines, the very large number of works from scholars interested in negotiation, much too numerous to be listed, let alone quoted here,[2] have come from many fields and many traditions, within which, understandably, only a few key examples can be given.[3] The main strands are, possibly economics,[4] decision theory and games theory,[5] social psychology and, to a somewhat lesser extent, psychology.[6]

All these contributions have provided a large amount of knowledge. However, we wish to place ourselves in a different position and begin from a different standpoint. The theoretical

1

contributions from decision theory and the theory of games have recently, in a remarkable book, been linked with and put to use in the daily practice of negotiation;[7] it is therefore unnecessary to try to review them once again here. On the other hand negotiating cannot be reduced to a purely economic activity or to a bilateral monopoly. This has been widely recognised and the contributions of social psychology and psychology have been acknowledged. However, negotiation can no more be limited to the psychological encounter of individuals, be they alone or placed in social situations. Negotiating is also essentially a social activity, in the sense that it takes place in a socially determined setting. This is why sociological theory should be used as a basis for its understanding, and, more precisely, the sociology of organisations. We shall therefore begin with an outline of the body of sociological theory out of which we shall derive the main building blocks of the negotiation structure and process.

However, our goal is also to try to bridge the gap between theory and practice. We must therefore recognise the fact that if negotiation occurs within the framework of social determinants which, to a large extent, shapes it, it also ends up with individuals facing each other. In other words, negotiation can be conceptualised at three levels. It is in fact a three stages concept, from the more general down: (1) it occurs in a given environment, it has a pre-established stucture; (2) it is a process, it pits opposite interests, activities against each other; (3) it is the actual interaction of people, individuals. As we move down the stages we move more and more from the domain of knowledge to the one of know-how. At the first level, it is necessary to understand the environment as it is set and as it forms the structure of negotiation. It is the domain of concepts, understanding and analysis, of bargaining power. At the second level, we move from structure to process. It is the domain of technical skills, of procedures, of strategies and tactics. At the third level, we deal with the actual encounter of persons. It is the domain of social skills and interpersonal behaviour, of styles and management of a situation.

Therefore, obviously, because of this conceptualisation of negotiation, and because we attempt to move from structure to behaviour, in the discussion of the two latter stages we shall need to add to our sociological framework some of the contributions of social psychology. This field itself, as noted by Pruitt,[8] contains two main traditions for research: field studies based on case studies, sets of interviews and statistical surveys and experimental studies in laboratory settings. Apparently, the experimental method offers the advantage of establishing a cause-effect relationship. However, it has been noted that nearly all experimental studies of negotiation have failed to investigate directly the process itself.[9] Often, also, the experimental designs are very abstracted, simplified models with many limitations.[10] Besides, Morley and Stephenson[11] have pointed to the amount of uncertainty involved in experimental research, questioning the reliability of the research findings, their generality across different experimental procedures and different tasks assigned in the experiments, and their generality across different subject populations. On the latter point, Rubin and Brown[12] call attention to the danger of gearing bargaining research to the 'social psychology of the college sophomore' and the need to work with other subjects. Also they note the fact that most experimental researchers have been interested in different parameters. It seems sometimes as if each researcher had selected his own experimental set-up and research parameters without regard to what was done by others. Finally, sometimes, because, no doubt, of this diversity, some results seem difficult to reconcile. All this is not meant to be a criticism of the discipline. Social psychological experiments have largely, if incompletely, expanded the knowledge about bargaining. Besides, the cost of full-scale, real-time experiments, with controls for all the variables, would be prohibitively expensive in the present condition of resources devoted to research in higher education. The above remarks are probably more of a comment on the present sad condition of funding of social science research than a reflection on the validity of the results of experimental social psychology. Experimental design becomes a function of the chance availability of means for subjects instead of the other way around.

These considerations will lead us to use the experimental studies as a source of insights into negotiation, which can be extremely powerful as noted by Zartman,[13] but not to go over them in detail. Excellent reviews of these studies have been carried out, by Rubin and Brown, Mageneau and Pruitt, and by Druckman *et al.* among others.[14]

We shall also use the results of case studies and rely very largely – outside the realm of social psychology properly speaking – upon some of what Pruitt calls 'looser sets of ideas based on unsystematic observations', such as the work of Stevens[15] and Walton and McKersie, and Schelling. The latter's contributions are extensively discussed and quoted below. We have found these studies particularly perceptive and insightful as well as extremely helpful in bridging the gap between our conceptual framework issued from organisational sociology and practical issues.

However, the main postulates and assumptions on which we shall rest our theoretical analysis are grounded in sociology. Strauss[16] had already called attention to the necessity of taking into account the setting of the negotiations to understand better the negotiating process. However, we want to go further, and consider the structural setting, the environment of the negotiations – how it is perceived and the limits on that perception – as the fundamental feature of negotiating. The wider theoretical reference is found in the French School of organisational sociology as it is referred to below.

When these theoretical assumptions are established, we shall cover the path between theory and practice by moving towards strategy, tactics and behaviour in a bargaining situation, using inputs from social psychology and field studies as well as work in related fields.

The goal of this book therefore is twofold. First, to give an understanding of the roots of negotiating, what it really consists of, and then to provide from there some practical guidance useful for negotiators who can better understand and apply it because it is placed within a consistent theoretical framework. This framework will be described in simple but theoretically accurate terms.

It has already been pointed out that 'a critical task for bargainers is to translate the environmental resources and constraints into tactical action at the bargaining table',[17] and this is precisely the path that this book will attempt to follow.

Part I
Analytical Background

The potential for conflict is present everywhere. It is particularly visible in organised situations, although it is also very often present in informal, chance happenings.

As soon as there are two individuals in contact, particularly, but not only, when there is also collective action, or when the impact on a collective situation or an individual's action can be foreseen, there is almost always a divergence of opinion, a variety of vested interests, of differing beliefs involved. The examples are innumerable, but a few can be put forward as they are obviously present in the settings of everyone's daily life: labour and management clash within the plant, marketing and production disagree at corporate headquarters, seller and buyer haggle over a variety of contracts ranging from complex multimillion-dollar deals down to ten-cent so-called 'collectors" items at a flea market. This includes examples so present in day-to-day life, such as a used-car purchase, the rental of a house or flat, or a family discussion, that we may tend to forget that they can be analysed as textbook examples of opportunities for developing raw confict. But, if we pause to think about it, landlord and tenant disagree about almost everything, from who should pay for what share of the cost of utilities, to the condition of the premises before and after moving-in. In the same way, parents and children are locked in endless disputes about wages (understood as allowances), hours (for evenings out, dinner time), quality of working life (for each other). Also spouses may be of a different mind regarding a whole set of items including which television programme should be watched, what should be the purpose of an evening out, whose in-laws should be visited first, or where to spend the holidays. Even drivers who have never met each other before will battle for the right of way at a remote, badly-marked road junction, the rule of the road notwithstanding.

Most people, practically every day, are locked in situations where elements of disagreement are built-in, and display varying degrees of conflictual violence. Furthermore, from a managerial standpoint, it should be underlined that most decisions in an organisation, or a business, are the object of conflict, particularly at managerial level, because the stakes are high, both for the organisation as a whole and for the individuals concerned, in terms of their personal interests and careers.

1 Understanding Conflict

The ubiquity of conflict has often been perceived and has given rise to several schools of thought. At the risk of oversimplifying both a complex reality and the worthy contributions of many theorists and social scientists, they can be summarised in three categories.[1]

These three categories illustrate the three basic attitudes which have been prevalent among social scientists confronted with conflict: try to suppress it for it is bad in itself; try to cure it, for it is an organisational disease; acknowledge it and try to manage it. This, in turn, has led to three types of methods for the analysis of conflict: mechanical, human relations, and managerial. The latter implies an understanding of organisations as a network of negotiations. But before getting into the topic of negotiating directly, it is useful to review the first two categories of theories, as the assumptions on which they are based are instructive and will assist an understanding of what can and cannot be expected of negotiating.

SECTION I – THE TRADITIONAL THEORIES

(a) The Mechanical Theories and their Assumptions

The mechanical theories are part of what has often been called the classic theory of organisations. One can trace their origins to the research of Weber on bureaucracy, understood in the sense of the rational and efficient mode of organisation of collective actions. Taylor is the universally-known theorist of the scientific analysis of production engineering and Fayol is the early theorist of administrative organisation. Their work has given rise to a wide current of thought, still very much in evidence today.[2]

Again it should be very strongly pointed out that the remarks which follow are not meant to be criticisms and do not aim to detract anything from the gains in knowledge and understanding as well as the very tangible benefits that these theories have brought us: Taylorism has given us mass production and its benefits. It is still the rule of organisation at most production operations worldwide, the

movement for quality of working life notwithstanding. The classic
school of administrative organisation has probably allowed for the
growth of the large business organisation, and is still also very
dominant in large administrative and industrial structures, public or
private, today. The major benefit of these approaches should, and
are, acknowledged, only their claims to universality are questioned
thereafter. In other words, they are very useful, but cannot be
considered as the definitive answer to all organisational problems
everywhere.

The main assumption behind the classic or mechanical theory is
that conflict can be suppressed. If one designs and sets up the right
type of organisation, one suppresses conflict between all the interested parties within the organisation. Once the 'right man' is in the
'right place' everything should work smoothly. If some degree of
conflict remains then either the rules of organisation or some of the
individuals concerned are at fault; therefore, if one improves the
rules and/or trains or eliminates the individuals concerned, harmony
should be restored.

The basic hypothesis on which this assumption rests is that, once
the right organisational scheme is devised, after systematic study,
according to 'scientifically' established principles, and is correctly
implemented, things will always work as they should, as they were
meant to work initially, and as it was planned that they would. Four
secondary assumptions flow from the main one.

First, there is one best way to organise and to do things and one
only. The scientific study of the organisation of the process of work
will bring out this correct way and consequently will outline the
correct organisational design to be followed. Variations are only a
waste of time at best and generally disruptive. Second, people are
changeable at will within the right design of organisation. When job
definitions have been established they can be filled interchangeably
with anybody possessing the right qualifications who has been
correctly trained and has learned the detailed tasks to be performed.
Third, the only kind of power is legitimate power. Power is a function
of the position of an individual in the organisation and of the
hierarchical level of his position in relation to all others. Fourth, the
only motivation is money: once the correct tasks and the correct
procedures have been designed and implemented in the right organisation and the right individuals selected and trained, the way to
obtain a satisfactory performance is to pay each man in each job at its
rate, also scientifically arrived at.

Unfortunately the four assumptions are not always sustained in practice. In fact things very seldom work consistently in the way that the mechanical theories imply that they should. Again this is not meant to imply that the mechanical or classic theory is useless or invalid, only that it has a limited view of reality. However, even though these limitations are obvious, as it will be pointed out below, the assumptions we reviewed are still generally widely held to be valid, to the present day.

(b) Criticism of these Assumptions

If it were true that there is one right way to do things, which is the one best way, and therefore only one right way, it would presumably be embodied within successful, or even simply surviving, organisations' rules.

But then how is it possible that almost nobody in practice does things according to rule in most organisations? The infinite variety of situations that one meets in the world, and the more so in complex organisations, builds up a need for initiative, for finding out and carrying out innovative solutions at all levels of an organisation. As a matter of fact, by insisting on the application of the rule, and the officially sanctioned best way to do things, subordinates, if they do wish, can efficiently frustrate the intentions of their superiors and hamper the efficiency of the organisation that the rules were precisely intended to maximise. Examples abound: for instance, a caretaker may refuse to accept an urgent registered letter on behalf of the company he works for on the eve of a long weekend because 'it is not in his job description', while his superior is momentarily attending to other tasks. Also, an army private on duty can keep out of the barracks superior officers who are urgently needed and want to get in, but cannot follow the step-by-step procedure or supply the password, even though they are obviously who they claim to be. Actually the more authoritarian the organisation, the more frustrating to management is the strict application of the rule by subordinates without any leeway. To further prove this point, 'work to rule' has become, in many cases, a more efficient tool of disruption than work stoppage or strikes to compel management to give in to employees' demands in labour disputes. Airline controllers who insist on strictly following the prescribed safety regulations wreak havoc on airline traffic; customs officers who insist on checking the contents of every truck crossing a border can bring to a standstill international traffic.

This is not to say that the rules and procedures are not useful or necessary in organisations, but it shows only that the principle of the one best way obviously suffers numerous exceptions.

Besides, it contains a very critical implicit hypothesis: if there is really a one best scientific way to perform a given operation, and, if once told, some people do go on doing otherwise in their own way, they can be assumed to be either stupid or ill-willed. If they appear stupid they should be trained again, if they still do not understand and comply, they must be assumed to be unfit to understand simple things and therefore put away. If they understand but do not comply, they are ill-willed or vicious and therefore they should be punished. One often sees this implicit consequence of the 'one best way' belief work its way into political arguments at all levels.

The second assumption is that people can be shifted around in organisations without major changes and consequences. It also flies in the face of rich contrary evidence: the rumours, expectations, and the subsequent shift in habits, power, responsibility, acquired 'rights' by workplace 'customs', which occur in any large organisation when a head of department is replaced by a new man, is a good case in point to demonstrate its fallacy.

The third assumption also requires some qualifications. Many theorists since Barnard[3] have demonstrated that legitimate power cannot be the only source of power for somebody needing to assert authority. Very easily we can see around us that different people apparently holding similar positions or titles, will, through individual relationships, charisma or some other reason, yield very different amounts of actual power. For instance, the respect commanded in the classroom by teachers assigned identical status varies widely in practice within the same school. Also, conversely, the head of an organisation, even if gifted with a fairly authoritarian personality, is not all powerful. As a matter of fact, very often the power to act concretely, to really have an impact on the environment and the public or the customers or suppliers, does not belong to the official head of the organisation, but to the individual subordinates on its lower rungs, who are the ones who actually are in contact with them, through a complex network of rules setting up a hierarchy and set of duties. The former, lacking the relevant operational knowledge, issues either ill-informed, and therefore unenforceable, narrow orders, or broad guidelines, in both cases subject to many wide interpretations, one of which is selected at the will of the subordinates.

The fourth assumption, just as the preceding three, quickly finds its limitations. Money, certainly, acts as motivator but it is also certainly not the only one. Other incentives do exist and may be just as powerful. For instance, analysis of voluntary job mobility has clearly demonstrated that there are many reasons other than a wage increase, everything being equal, for an individual employee to change jobs.[4]

(c) The Human Relations Theories

The original human relations theories tend, by and large, to consider conflict as an organisational disease to be cured. These theories often rest mainly on the analysis of individual characteristics and traits. The basic hypothesis at play behind them is that conflict exists because people misunderstand each other. Most of the versions find their roots in the dual sources of the work of Kurt Lewin and of the experiments conducted at the Hawthorne Plant of General Electrics under the leadership of Elton Mayo in the late 1920s. One of the goals of the latter researchers was to verify some of the assumptions behind Taylor's theory, and therefore the research was carried into motivation to work. The experimental design was based on experiments accompanied by observations and interviews with the employees. The now well-known result of the research, which was later followed by in-depth interviews, was to discover that individuals were not motivated by money and by money only, but mostly by affectivity.[5] Power was discovered to be no longer a function of the hierarchical positions within the organisation, but of the network of relationships of affection, respect and other sentiments between individuals, irrespective of their relative rank. The relevant picture of the organisation was not an organisational chart, but a sociogram. People are not interchangeable because the informal organisation made of reciprocal links between individuals is the truly important organisation as opposed to the formal picture made of ordered job descriptions.

Interestingly enough, the human relations theories keep nevertheless one basic assumption in common with the mechanical model: The implicit assumption of the existence of a 'one best way'. Therefore both kinds of theories share a deterministic view of the world. The focus has changed from the design of a formal organisation and precise work procedures to the design of an informal organisation fitted to the individual's psychological and social needs inside the work group. However, the same basic principle remains underlying: One satisfies the psychological and social needs in the right way, just as one designed job contents in the best way, and one obtains a smoothly working organisation. With proper training of the leadership in the recognition and satisfaction of the affective needs among subordinates, instead of training in work methods, conflict is eliminated. Goldthorpe[6] has clearly demonstrated long ago the limits of applying only the Human Relations analysis of conflict in his pioneering study of foremen's training in British coal mines and of the programmes aimed at the prevention of industrial conflict. He clearly pointed out the existence of an unavoidable structural conflict which pre-exists before other potential conflicts due to either misunderstandings or human relations differences appear.

Again it should be underlined that our brief summary does not do full justice to the theories whose bases are roughly outlined above. Goldthorpe himself was careful to distinguish between the actual results of the Hawthorne experiments and their later interpretation by others. The present developments aim only at pointing out their limits regarding the interpretation of conflict within organisations. They must be recognised to have brought usefully to the attention of social science many important features which before were the object of little or no interest, such as, for instance, the role of the informal organisation and the small group in phenomena relating to leadership, motivation and so on. A very influential school of research to be known under the general and sometimes misleading name of Human Relations developed directly from that research and from the work of Kurt Lewin.[7] The elements of theory later on brought by McGregor, Maslow, Herzberg, Argyris, and many others were extremely influential on managerial thinking, both in the United States and later in Europe. Lewin himself, as well as some later theorists, had been careful to point out the relative, or contingent, character of his findings, therefore attenuating the deterministic outlook of the theory. Nonetheless, this type of human relations theory has its limits, outlined originally by Gouldner's work and later by other sociologists. For instance, Crozier, after analysing the leadership patterns of supervisors in charge of work groups in an insurance company, found out that, where the leaders were shifted around among work groups, 78 per cent of them changed their leadership style and adapted to the new circumstances by adopting the one of their predecessors at the head of the group. This experiment outlines the limits of an explanation of behaviour rooted only in psychology and points towards the characteristic of contingency to the environ-ment of behavioural patterns: The same individual with the same psychological make-up will adopt different behaviours in different situations. Psychology alone does not determine all aspects of the behaviour of individuals within groups. Individual behaviour varies according to structural features present or not in specific situations and which relate to it. Therefore psychological methods cannot suppress all conflicts or all of conflict but only the part of it which comes from the fact that individuals may have different perceptions of the same reality. Nevertheless, where this is done, the situation presented by reality itself may still be the object of conflict.

SECTION II – ORGANISATIONS AS A NETWORK OF NEGOTIATIONS

This approach is at the root of our analysis of negotiation and it will be presented more extensively than the precedent ones. It rests upon two assumptions which are critical and should be made clear at the outset.

(a) Basic Assumptions

1 – The prevalence of conflict
Our first assumption holds that conflict is not pathological, contrary to what is held by the human relations theories, and that it is not an accident or a result of a faulty organisation, contrary to what is held by the mechanical theories. It is present and unavoidable in most, if not all, social situations and interactions. It is unavoidable in the sense that it cannot be suppressed or totally eliminated; nevertheless it can and should be managed, channelled and contained. Rather than open conflict, or fight, into which it can nevertheless easily turn, it is more accurate to think of a state of potential conflict of interests, activated or not. We started above by noticing that this condition is prevalent in today's society. We now present the reasons why this is so.

It is present and unavoidable for several reasons. First, because individuals or groups, in or out of organisations, are faced with a limited amount of resources, in terms of goods, services or power, whilst their demands, expectations or aspirations are, if not limitless in the same terms, at least far exceeding the size of available goods, services or power. Second, because social situations are situations of exchange. Individuals involved bring a contribution and expect a retribution, in some terms: material, status or other. They will generally tend to maximise the retribution that they expect in regard to the value that they assign to their contribution. Third, because in any system of organisation, formal or informal, there is a permanent opposition which exists between those who manage and take decisions or allocate input, throughout and output of the organisation and those who produce, handle or use them, carrying out the plans decided above. This opposition may be implicit or explicit but it is always present. Also it is clear that individuals as well as organisations, have latent as well as manifest objectives. Those who manage organisations will be the ones who are generally assumed to act for the best interests of the whole organisation. Undoubtedly they will act also simultaneously for their own good according to their own purposes. For instance, managers of a large company aim to bring a large profit for the satisfaction of the goals of the stakeholders: shareholders, employees, eventually consumers. They also have in mind their own career goals. A more concrete example may clarify better this point. It can be assumed to be in the interest of the whole of a large organisation that the decision-makers who run it receive all kinds of privileges allowing them to save time in avoiding menial tasks in order to devote it to the strategic issues that they are supposed to be alone able to resolve. For example they should not waste their valuable time hunting for a parking space in a parking area with a limited capacity while momentous issues await their wisdom. Consequently reserved parking spaces are provided conveniently for them near the headquarters' entrance access. There is also no doubt that these reserved parking spaces, as well as other privileges, are also quite convenient for the personal comfort of those who hold them, as well as probably coveted status symbols. Those who do not benefit from them are likely also to share the view expressed by Townsend,[8] who considers that if these exalted decision-makers are so useful and so indispensable to the organisation, they should arrive before, and leave after everybody else, and therefore are not in need of reserved parking spaces anyway.

Fourth, and more seriously, some degree of discipline is necessary for the smooth running of an organisation. However, it is a source of conflict: for instance, what seems a perfectly logical and acceptable rule of behaviour to be enforced from the management's standpoint, such as having all employees report to work at 8.0 a.m., in order to insure that a consistent work force be allocated to the amount of work planned, may well constitute a constraint difficult to accept for the employees concerned who may have also some important needs of their own to attend to between 8.0 and, say, 9.30 a.m. Fifth, and finally, a theory recently developed for explaining industrial conflict,[9] but which can be applied to all social situations, holds that there are biological reasons for conflict in human societies. It applies Darwinian theory to deduce that natural selection has produced in man an innate trend to pursue social dominance which now belongs to human nature. This trend to social dominance is reinforced for it brings rewards, material and otherwise, in the present society. Therefore it is also perceived as being instrumental, and also it is socially learned in western educational systems. From there follows a condition of status tension by which man is naturally pushed to create hierarchies and to look for a dominant role in them.

Therefore conflict is prevalent in our societies.

2 – Conflict and negotiation

Our second assumption is derived directly from the first one, but needs some elaboration.

On the one hand there are two possible definitions of conflict in any given context. Generally, there exists what can be called latent conflict, which is the permanent condition of opposition between two or several parties with divergent interests in the production, allocation or exchange of scarce resources. For instance, consumers are opposed to producers regarding the price of goods, labour is opposed to management regarding the division of profits between wages and retained earnings/dividends or duration of work, two national states are in conflict regarding their reciprocal rights on areas of land. But there also exists open or active conflict, which is the actual interplay of the parties around specific problems, when the general condition of latent conflict takes an acute character: for instance, the actual purchase of a given quantity of goods, a wage dispute and/or a strike, an international war or invasion of an island or of a border zone.

On the other hand we can also note that there are apparently many ways other than negotiation to resolve conflicts. For instance, one can consider the following alternative means.

COMBAT : as in fight, war
CHANCE : as in tossing a coin
CONTEST : as in a competitive exam

> VOTING   : as in an election, a committee
> DEFER TO AUTHORITY   : as in court proceedings
> DECISION BY FIAT   : by a superior
> ADHERENCE TO NORMS   : internalised by both sides

These means of solving conflict, of course, do not fall within the scope of a restrictive definition of negotiation. Conversely, the declaration or open recognition by opponents that they enter negotiations applies often only as a means to solve open, active conflict. Nevertheless two points are immediately evident: First, elements of negotiation are very often, if not always, present in situations of latent conflict. For instance, parties 'test' each others' willingness to acknowledge a state of open conflict. They also try to establish power positions ahead of time relative to each other. They also may 'feel' each others' positions.

Second, all other means of solving conflict, besides a declared condition of negotiation itself, which are listed above, also involve, contain, or drive to negotiation with a more or less marked degree of formality. For instance, war seldom ends by total annihilation of the adversary but often in negotiating a peace treaty. It can also be considered, borrowing from the famous line written by Clausewitz, as a bargaining tool in a pre-existent negotiation of a larger scope. Also when in conflict, the parties have to first agree to the principle to resort to any given means of conflict-solving as well as to the selection of the rules to be applied. To that end they have to negotiate to some extent. Such is the case for chance, the parties have to negotiate in advance, for instance, to agree to settle by throwing a coin and which of them wins if heads comes up. It also applies to contest, voting and deference to authority: in order to establish the rules of the contest, the type of poll and the selection of the referee or the judge. If a party is compelled to submit to decision by fiat, or to a pre-established system of deference to authority, it still can try to negotiate its compliance with the award, in exchange, for instance, for its agreement not to try to get the decision undermined or overturned by another process. Finally, there is often room for interpretation and argument as regards the exact meaning and scope of jointly-held norms.

Our second assumption, therefore, rests in the fact that, if conflict is so prevalent, and if, aside of formal, declared negotiation, all other means of solving conflict include more or less informal aspects or elements of negotiation, then most, if not all situations are to some extent negotiating situations. It follows that, at the level of the organisation, any organisation can be analysed as an interwoven grid of conflictual situations and therefore be understood as a network of interrelated negotiations, as Crozier points out.[10]

It has been argued that this pervasiveness of negotiation is a new factor in our societies and that we now live in the 'age of negotiation'.[11] Other scholars like Strauss[12] have maintained that, on the contrary, negotiation was always present in traditional societies but was less visible because it was not the object of attention of scientific thought. We may add that, possibly, in authoritarian systems, it was 'hidden', for cultural reasons, under the guise of other processes, giving mostly as a result forms of what we shall define immediately below as being 'informal negotiation'. The developments which will follow later, when we discuss bargaining power, will show that we tend to share the second view, contrarily to Pruitt,[13] who adopts Zartman's position. The discussion is however mostly of theoretical interest and with limited practical impact: the point on which all agree is that, presently, negotiation is a central concern in all aspects of our lives, outside and within as well as in-between organisations.

3 – Definition of negotiation

Therefore negotiation is even more prevalent than it was seen to be at first glance. This is particularly the case if we do not limit ourselves to an analysis of formal, declared negotiation and to its use in open or active conflict situations and if we consider it also in its informal aspects or elements, Of course in the developments which follow we shall concern ourselves with, as far as possible, the most extended and largest meaning of negotiating.

However, we need to distinguish the negotiating situations that we address from other cases. To that end we need a definition gathering together the elements of negotiation.

Some may consider that this endeavour constitutes a relatively matter-of-fact and minor task. For instance, Bartos,[14] before proceeding himself to a major effort to formalise the concept of negotiation, notes accurately that 'it is not too difficult to state what most men think of when they speak of negotiation. They usually have in mind a process through which two teams try to resolve their differences and arrive at an agreement'. However, to endeavour to go beyond the obvious is more difficult.

First, a point of vocabulary must be cleared. Some scholars attempt to make a distinction between negotiation and bargaining.[15] Given the scope of this book, which attempts to deal with practice as well as theory, we shall not adopt this semantic distinction and follow the line of those, who like Rubin and Brown[16] consider the two terms synonymous. We believe that common usage now holds them so and that their various dictionary definitions are so close as to be identical for practical purposes.

Second, many definitions have been offered, by many theorists, more or less formalised depending upon the purpose of the researcher. Obviously the fields of game theory, decision theory, and, to a somewhat lesser extent, sociology and experimental social psychology require relatively restrictive definitions. The former two fields are too remote from practice and therefore require definitions too narrowly formalised to be of help to us here. The other ones might be more useful, because, although not as restraining, they keep a level of precision sufficient to allow us to recognise the elements of negotiation and identify it when it takes place by itself or is present within other different processes, such as the ones listed above; all the while allowing us to keep it separate and not to confuse it with these processes.

If we review a few definitions of negotiations in this framework, we quickly find that they have many elements in common.

For instance, Rubin and Brown[17] define bargaining as 'the process whereby two or more parties attempt to settle what each shall give and take, or perform and receive, in a transaction between them'. McGrath[18] considers it as: 'A process in which the representatives of two or more parties come together explicitly in search of an agreement on an issue about which they were divided'. For Hammer as well as for Yukl,[19] bargaining is the interaction that occurs when two or more persons attempt to agree on a mutually acceptable outcome in a situation where their orders of preference for possible outcomes are negatively correlated'.

We could accumulate such definitions and analyse the minor variations among them. However, we find it more fruitful to follow the example of Zartman[20] or Cross[21] and list the elements common to many definitions, allowing us to identify negotiation and separate it from other processes of conflict solving and at the same time provide an operational concept consonant with practical experience.

Therefore, we consider negotiation as a process. That is to say, a dynamic situation, on-going, involving moves and countermoves, and not a static one. It is a joint process which occurs between one or several parties, or their representatives. No one negotiates alone, but negotiation is not reduced to dyadic situations. The parties can, but do not have to, interact directly, verbally or otherwise. They can also do so through representatives or not at all. In that sense we include what Schelling calls 'tacit bargaining'[22] which is considered as one of two forms of bargaining by Mageneau and Pruitt[23] and we imply a larger definition than the one that many social psychologists hold. From the above developments it is obvious that for us the parties are in conflict, active or latent; they have, to some extent, but not compulsorily, inherently opposite interests and in that sense we are more restrictive than some other researchers. Young,[24] for instance, following another lead from Schelling, also includes situations of pure co-operation. Not surprisingly, in the light of the conceptual elements that we presented above in our framework, we exclude these situations. However the parties attempt to resolve their conflict and search for an agreement explicit or tacit, they do not primarily seek to destroy each other. The capacity to fail to reach agreement is present in variable degree but significant. The issue about which they are divided has value for both of them, failure is not unconsequential. Finally, they operate under constraints of time.[25] Clearly, if it does not matter when we agree, it does not matter if we agree.

(b) Rejection of the Hypothesis of the 'One Best Way'

We have now arrived at a definition of negotiation within the framework of our conception of the theories of conflict. However, there are implicit conclusions in this position and we need to elaborate on them. The rejection of the hypothesis of the one best way has important consequences on how the parties in a negotiation relationship, understood as defined above, are going to interact:

1 – Individuals are rational
If there is no 'one best way' to set up a formal organisation or to arrange affective relations, it means that individuals, one way or another, cannot be completely manipulated. They always keep the possibility of making decisions for themselves. They cannot be pre-determinated: therefore they act rationally.

In other words, people are not only hands or hearts as it is assumed in both mechanist and human relations theories with their deterministic characteristic. They are also a brain. Therefore they cannot be as simply understood as these theories assume. The simple scheme – one applies the correct stimulus (money or affectivity) and then people are motivated, then act according to plan – is erroneous.

In fact. the behaviour of individuals follows much more complex rules. Whatever is the type of organisation they belong to, and whatever are the constraints and stimulus applied to them, people almost always keep a degree of freedom in deciding how to act. Except in some very exceptional cases, such as the one of a person sentenced to death and marched in front of the firing squad, the organisation in which one finds oneself and the stimulus applied are not totally constraining. In almost all situations, individuals keep a degree of freedom granted to them by the possibility of choice between several courses of action. Of course, different benefits and cost to the individual are associated with each course of action. Each one will analyse them in his own terms. These terms vary from individual to individual.

The fact that people have a choice between different courses of action and weigh the benefits and costs associated with each course in their own particular terms makes their behaviour at least partly unpredictable. It cannot be totally determined or forecasted in advance because there exist, at least potentially, several different courses of action opened. An individual selects one amongst several possible others and does so according to his own specific preferences. Therefore there is almost always a margin of choice for an individual facing any situation. Consequently there cannot be simple tricks or easy recipes to make individuals act in a given way with certainty.

This is the case even in very tightly controlled organisations. For instance, it can be said that subordinates negotiate obedience. They may select one of several courses of action which include disobedience, and prefer it to the ones which involve obedience, if, in their eyes, the cost to them of obeying outweighs the risks involved in disobeying. The more constrained the situation, the more risky and costly the courses of action which include the option of not following the rules and/or disobeying. But they always remain open potentially if the pressures coming from the organisation and from following the rules become too overwhelming. Examples can be taken from the military or the prison world. Soldiers are expected to obey their superiors and are punished if they do not. Nevertheless an officer who resorts too often too strongly to harsh punishment as compared with his peers will either attract the attention of his own superiors and eventually be sanctioned himself and given another assignment or will recognise the problem by himself and change his behaviour. Therefore, at the cost of being repeatedly and harshly punished, if the 'leadership' style of the officer becomes unbearable in their opinion, his subordinates can eventually have him removed, or have him change his methods. This is achieved by willingly and deliberately adopting a behaviour which causes repeated sanctions to be applied to them. They 'negotiate' their obedience in doing so and consequently will ultimately receive a leadership style that they consider roughly acceptable to them in exchange for abandoning their behaviour. In the same way inmates can, and sometimes do, resort to jail riots, when imprisonment conditions worsen too much, by overwhelming the guards in a concerted action. Sometimes at the cost of the lives of some of their own and generally at the risk of additional prison time. In not doing so they also in some sense negotiate the orderly running of the jail against sufferable detainment conditions. A most extreme case can be illustrated by the horrible example a few years ago of Brazilian jail inmates, who, fearing that an open revolt from their part would be drowned in blood, proceeded to the killing of one among them every day until they obtained satisfaction for some of their demands under the pressure put upon the authorities by an increasingly alarmed national and international public opinion.

However, the existence of different courses of action open to an individual in almost all cases, each of which is assorted with different costs and benefits, does not mean that individuals or groups always have totally coherent and clear projects and strategies. They may react on the spur of the moment without planning or even coherently reviewing the situation. But they react by following a course which, at this specific time they consider to be, under their view of the circumstances, the most favourable to their own interest. In writing that they are rational, we only mean that they are active agents, following a course set by themselves, and not predetermined by motivations, not simply passively responding to adequately selected stimulants. In that sense they are pro-active. They try to fulfil some combination of their own expectations or goals which is most satisfactory to them.

The notion of goals calls for some clarification and elaboration. Personal goals of an individual may include achievement, promotion, income, recognition, self-improvement, as well as many other items. He then shall strive for a given combination of them which is the most satisfactory given the situation he is in. But, even if several individuals are in the same situation, each individual's set of goals is uniquely his own, for each may have an entirely different perception of the situation.[26] An individual may not even have consciously spelled the goals out for himself explicitly. Therefore, even though his behaviour has always a meaning, it is a meaning for him only, more or less formally conceptualised. It cannot be totally outguessed by somebody else for several reasons. First, it depends on a person's own understanding or perception of the situation, the opportunities that he sees available to him, in his eyes, and this differs with different individuals. Second, it depends on the way that this person operates to satisfy his many different expectations or goals and/or to improve the situation in a way deemed favourable, and this is also specific to an individual, to some extent. Therefore, this implies that individals always have a strategy based on their premises and according to which they interact and negotiate with their superiors, subordinates and equals. Even if it cannot be totally outguessed, this strategy is present. Within the limits of a more or less formal conceptualisation on their part, the behaviour of individuals is always rational for them and on their own terms.

The present analysis raises two issues: on the one hand, the extent and nature of an individual's rationality in determining his strategies, and, on the other hand, how he carries them in order to achieve his goals. This second point will be dealt with in the next chapter; it concerns in fact the nature of power. However, the first one will be dealt with immediately below because of its close links with the present discussion.

2 – Bounded rationality
The concept of bounded rationality has been elaborated and pro-posed by Simon[27] and expanded upon by Crozier and Friedberg,[28] who analyse the constraints which shape decisions criteria and within which rationality gets into play.

'Roughly speaking rationality is concerned with the selection of preferred behaviour alternatives in terms of some system of values whereby the consequence of behavior can be evaluated'.[29] However, individuals cannot be expected to be perfectly and totally rational and to behave accordingly. For instance, it is not possible for an indi-vidual to define or even guess at all possible behaviour alternatives when faced with a given situation; there are too many avenues for action potentially open for him to be able to discover them all. Neither is it possible to consider together the subset of those which have been discovered because they are too cumbersome for the processing capabilities of a man. Nor is it feasible to apply fully the weights of a stable and consistent value system to the alternatives selected in all their aspects because any situation is too rich in details and not enough is known about each alternative. Finally, it is totally impossible, in practical terms, to outline the possible chain of consequences of all alternatives because the future is fraught with too much uncertainty. In sum, the world is simply too complex and unpredictable. Too many alternatives are open and constantly changing with unforeseeable consequences. The understanding or guessing of consequences is always fragmented, never complete. In other words, 'The limits of rationality derive from the inability of the human mind to bring upon a single decision all the aspects of value, knowledge, and behavior that would be relevant'.[30]

Thus individuals cannot be perfectly and 'objectively' (in Simon's sense) rational, and we have also just pointed out that they cannot be predetermined. However, this should not be construed as meaning that they are going to act randomly or irrationally. Within the framework of their limited knowledge, capacities, and means of action, they are going to try to select a preferred alternative. Therefore they are not irrational, but their rationality is limited, bounded. That is to say, individuals cannot be considered as totally rational, but not because they do follow a line of behaviour which is irrational. On the contrary their behaviour is almost always rational. But it is not objectively and totally so because they act within a framework bounded by their limited capacities facing too rich and too complex a world.

This framework is bounded in two dimensions: Perfect rationality would drive us to assume a synoptic and maximising attitude. Synoptic in the sense that all possible alternative courses of action would be considered together, and maximising in the sense that they could be considered in all their potential consequences and that then the one maximising the satisfaction and minimising the dissatisfaction of the individual concerned would be selected. All costs and benefits incurred would be considered by him. We know that this cannot be the case for there is not enough time or information to register, and even less consider, all likely courses of action opened, and the human mind is too limited to analyse them, were they to be available. Additionally the world is too uncertain and turbulent to allow one to assess all the potential consequences of a course of action with any degree of foresight. Thus, instead of being synoptic, the consideration of alternatives is sequential, and, instead of maximising, the selection of one is only satisfying.

This means that, when placed in a given situation, an individual will consider, one after the other, several alternative courses of action which come to his mind. Each is considered and weighted separately in its turn against criteria of minimum satisfaction of his objectives, implicit for the individual. The first one which satisfies these criteria is accepted without further consideration; until then, the ones which do not are rejected and another potential course of action is generated and sequentially considered. Alternative courses are rejected until one satisfies the minimum criteria or until the criteria are modified downwards. Therefore the behaviour of the individual is not to try to maximise his satisfaction, but to fulfil his minimum criteria for satisfaction. Then the process stops. This process is illustrated by the analysis of a decision which curiously enough has been examined by several analysts of negotiation,[31] although in very different terms: the one of the Cuban missile crisis. The analysis by Crozier is most illuminating. He uses Allison's historical description of the decision-making process which culminates in the selection of the blockade alternative to demonstrate the characteristics of bounded rationality. The course of action selected was considered sequentially and not synoptically with the other potential alternatives. For instance, the blockade was not even considered at first and this alternative was generated later during the discussion which started by considering and rejecting successively an invasion, an air destroy mission, and so on. It was satisfying and not maximising, for as soon as a course of action satisfied minimum criteria imposed by the President and was acceptable to the other individuals and organisations involved, it was accepted and carried out without further research or discussion. Crozier also points out that the decision process was in fact a negotiation between interested parties, each one trying to satisfy criteria set according to its own interests.

These criteria, of course, result from the objectives of each individual. Nevertheless the term 'objectives' should not be misleading. Individuals more or less know what it is that they prefer: they have expectations, aspirations. But this does not mean that they have a perfectly spelled out set of precise goals. Their objectives may be, but often are not, totally clear, not completely formulated, as we pointed out just above. Besides, they change with time, according to varying levels of aspirations. They are diffuse and very often plural and may even be incompatible with each other to some degree. At different points in time, the same individual may well successively entertain incompatible or even contradictory opinions and goals. For instance, an airline pilot on the way to his work may well entertain two different opinions about the merits of unionism: he may try to build up the strength of his own union and at the same time may well wish the disappearance of the union of airport employees which pickets the entrance to the car park and delays him. Therefore often goals are more likely to be directions for action, clouds of expectations rather than well-defined and clear-cut objectives. Nevertheless they do exist and are the reasons behind the behaviour of people at a given point in time. It is in order to satisfy these expectations that people act. Their behaviour is therefore rational, even if submitted to the limits of bounded rationality and the relative fuzziness or incompatibility of their own goals.

The complexity of the ideas and the objectives of the individuals is even more accentuated by the fact that one should distinguish between latent and manifest objectives. Even in the simplest case, when an individual is perfectly conscious of his relatively well-defined objectives, he may not want, dare or be able to put them forward. For instance, the shop steward who leads a strike for the manifest objective of an 'across the Board' wage increase may have the latent objective of being re-elected to his union position, or he might have his eye on a job within the union structure as a permanent union officer. A store salesman has a quota to fulfil but also might have been told by his boss to 'sell at least one unit today or else . . . ' The buyer may not so much want a good deal for his company than to outdo colleagues and get promoted to a recently opened vacancy in management. Of course in a negotiating situation both latent and manifest objectives are often hidden to avoid giving an early advantage to the opponent.

3 – Consequences of bounded rationality

The concept of bounded rationality is important for the understanding of negotiation. Foremost, it will be the implicit guiding thread to all our subsequent analysis of the negotiating process in the sense that it must be clear that all negotiators, in all situations, operate in a situation of bounded rationality. This has direct consequences on all three stages of the process: analysis of the environment, strategies and tactics, actual interaction of the individual bargainers.

Besides, this concept gives us immediately three very useful insights to remember:

First it helps us realise that everybody behaves rationally in their own eyes, according to their own set of objectives, however more or less well-defined they are, within the framework of their own bounded rationality as we described it above. Our opponent in a negotiating situation behaves according to his own perception of the situation and to criteria which may be more or less dimly outlined for himself but of which we ourselves are certainly much less aware than he himself will be. Therefore it can be assumed that his behaviour always makes sense for him, as a result of his own set of objectives, expectations and as his preferred path of action. But his behaviour may not make sense at all for us because we observe 'from the outside', without the benefit of the knowledge of his objectives, expectations and the bounds on his rationality. This does not mean that we can conclude that he is irrational, unreasonable, idiotic or vicious, it only means that we do not know the limits on his rationality and therefore that we need more information.

An example may help clarify this point. A firm was undergoing an acute case of the classic state of conflict between production and sales. It was subcontracting parts to another industry directly serving the consumer. Its market consisted of a single large customer, representing more than 50 per cent of sales and a large number of very small accounts. Urgent orders from the main customer came suddenly and had to be satisfied immediately in order to keep the critical amount of business from this essential source. In turn, this caused conflict with the production department because it wrecked the scheduling for standing orders from small firms. A feasibility study concluded that the implementation of a computerised production programme could alleviate to a large degree scheduling conflicts. It was established, tested, found to work satisfactorily and implemented plant-wide. Within a few weeks the first incidents of malfunction appeared in practice in the programme, and within a few months the new system had to be abandoned. Further analysis demonstrated that its malfunctioning and subsequent fall into disuse were due to its meeting with hostility from all concerned on the shopfloor. From the standpoint of top management this seemed totally irrational, for theoretically everybody would have been able to benefit from this new system. Its early application had put two points in evidence. First, there was about one-third excess slack time on the part of workers to produce the final output. Second, the company could have raised the wages by more than a third. It may seem irrational that these benefits were not tapped, but the old system was actually beneficial to all parties concerned in their own eyes, except top management: the foremen, aware of the existence of the labour slack, negotiated its continuing existence against some degree of flexibility in work pace and workers' mobility to accommodate schedule changes and assert a degree of power in setting schedules. The shop stewards, by resisting excessive speeding of the pace, maintained a degree of influence and power, and workers were able to benefit from the status quo in terms of workload and flexibility. The behaviour of each party concerned was rational from its own standpoint, but not understandable by top management within its own rationality without a consultant's analysis and further study.

A second useful conclusion to draw from the condition of bounded rationality is that we should not assume that the other party sees a situation in which both of us are involved as we ourselves see it. In other words, there is no reason for people engaged in a negotiating relationship to accept a common definition of their situation, a common frame of reference. Indeed, one party may not even see himself within a bargaining relationship at all. He may, for instance, assume that he is going to get his way without obstacles of any kind, or even reach his goal by violence.

Furthermore, even if the parties involved agree that they are within the framework of a negotiating relationship, there is no reason to assume that they agree implicitly or explicitly on a code of behaviour, on a common set of rules defining what should be acceptable or not, fair or not. It is possible that they implicitly do so but it would be dangerous to assume that this is automatically the case.

In other words, the definition of the situation and the relation in which the parties stand are themselves to some extent the object of negotiation. Of course many situations are to a large extent more or less clear-cut, but there is often some degree of leeway which provides for the possibility of several different sets of rules of order, of various modes of action for the parties. Therefore the rules themselves may be the object of bargaining, before bringing out the issue of negotiating for stakes itself. In a preliminary step, the rules become the stakes.[32] Then the stakes themselves have to be shaped out and defined. The parties may first have to find a way of 'agreeing about what it is that they disagree upon'. The process may not be easy or fruitful when the parties start from vastly differing assumptions, attitudes and preconceptions. For instance, delegations from the USA and mainland China met yearly in Warsaw after World War II long before the recognition of the People's Republic of China by the USA in the 1960s. Even though these meetings took place regularly, the parties, during this span of time, had not yet begun to define the rules of negotiation, much less agree about what they were disagreeing upon, even less start to negotiate.

Finally, there is a third important conclusion to be drawn from the recognition of the limits issuing from bounded rationality: Persuasion, the action of talking somebody into a change of attitude through logical reasoning will very often not work in negotiating. Clearly, this is because, however logical or rational and clear is our reasoning, for ourselves, our logic will not work to persuade somebody to step out of the bonds of his own rationality and logic. He himself is following his own rationality without imagining that it can be not as obvious to others as it is to himself. What is evident for us derives from our own set of goals and our own understanding of the situation. This may very well not be so evident, or it may even not be conceivable, to the other party, constrained by his own set of goals and his own analysis of the situation. In order to be persuasive, our reasoning and demonstration would have to fit the bonds of the other party's own rationality, about which, in a given situation, at first we know nothing. If this is not the case, however clear it is for us, our reasoning will simply look like hollow and prejudiced argument towards our side as far as the other party is concerned. This is the case even if we believe deeply in the merits of our case and even back it with facts and figures. This is also partly because, as we shall discuss below, the same facts can be looked at, perceived and understood in very different lights by different people according to the limit of their bounded rationality. Here again examples are multiple. For instance, if one is convinced that all used-car salesmen are crooks, one will never believe, after acquiring a used car, that one was given a fair deal by the salesman. If the car is satisfactory and reasonably priced, one will rather think that one has outnegotiated the salesman, got the best from him, or that the salesman made a mistake. Another clear illustration is the way racial or social prejudices taint perceptions of the action of the groups discriminated against in the eyes of the members of the dominant group. Whatever they do they lose because their actions are interpreted automatically in an unfavourable light, whatever they are. For instance, a well-dressed member of a minority is seen as 'putting on airs', while one who is casually dressed is considered 'sloppy'.

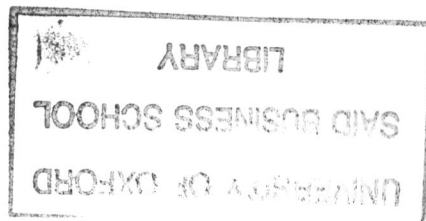

2 The Parties, the Environment and Bargaining Power

This chapter is devoted to building upon the elements outlined in Chapter 1. In other words, it draws the practical conclusions to be inferred from the prevalence of conflictual situations and from bounded rationality as they are seen to apply to a negotiating situation.

We are still concerned for the present time with the first of the three conceptual levels in negotiation described in the introduction: the knowledge and understanding of the structural features of any bargaining situation. It is only after having dealt with it that we shall turn towards the process and the interaction of the negotiators. A negotiation is structured by the relationship between the parties, the resources and constraints within the environment and bargaining power.

SECTION 1 – THE PARTIES AND THEIR RELATIONSHIP

We shall define in the next section how to identify who are the relevant parties concerned within a given bargaining situation which need to be considered for the analysis of the process of negotiation. But we are concerned here with some of the general features of the parties as elements of the structure of a negotiation and the following developments aim to identify and discuss some characteristics applicable to all parties involved in all negotiations.

A situation of negotiation may take place within very different types of relationships existing between the parties. It is necessary to understand and analyse clearly that background before deciding on any kind of moves.

(a) The Degree of Permanence of the Relationship

The relationship can range from the permanent to the casual. Its degree of permanence runs a whole gamut between situations when the negotiating parties are locked in a very long term relationship, be it amiable or conflictual, down to 'one shot' types of encounter. Examples of the former are East–West political relationships. Whether concerned with 'Cold War' or '*Détente*', the parties in the relationship, on both sides of the Iron Curtain, have been the same nations since 1945. Any negotiations between both sides, whether they concern disarmament, the status of Berlin or the maintaining of the Spandau prison, will take place within the framework of that permanent relationship. Negotiations may be run by different individuals, but it will be the same parties, in the sense of interested nations, before, during and after each negotiation. This of course is not fixed forever and can and will change in the long term, but the given condition prevails for extended periods of time. A commercial example can be found in the relationship between a major multinational oil company which has exploration, production, manufacturing and marketing operations in one country, and the host government.

At the other extreme of the range are one-shot negotiations; this type of casual or chance encounter negotiation is well exemplified by the tourist buying a souvenir or gift in a foreign country just before returning home. In this case the two parties are unlikely ever to see each other again and are meeting for the first time.

Clearly the element of permanence has direct consequences. In commercial negotiations the situation is obviously different as, for instance, between established customer and supplier, or between first time negotiators. The degree of permanence of the negotiating relationship has a number of key impacts. In the chance encounter, a one-off or one-shot situation, the incentive towards conflict or to 'compete' can be assumed to be stronger. The parties have no expectation of ever meeting each other in the future, no goodwill to maintain. The absence of norms is obvious. One or both parties may lie. Where the relationship is more permanent a degree of co-operation may be induced. The parties will have to see each other again and to live not only with the agreement that they have reached but also with the consequences of their behaviour towards one another during the negotiating process. That influence of the degree of permanence of the relationship can be seen in labour as well as commercial negotiating. In labour negotiations, at one point, whether after open conflict or not, work is going to resume with largely the same work force under the same management as before. However, the fact that a relationship within which a negotiation takes place has some character of permanence does not compulsorily preclude high incentives to conflict or competition, up to possible instances of intimidation or violence if the negotiation includes open conflict. For instance, either a degree of calculated intimidation can be introduced by one party – strikebreakers, threat of competition – or the negotiation can involuntarily slip into it – riot on the work premises or argument degenerating into a shouting match. This element, in fact, points toward a second important characteristic of the relationship.

(b) Attitudes of the Parties towards Each Other

The objective of a negotiation is to negotiate specific items. This may at first seem to be a statement of the obvious. However, if we think for instance of labour negotiations, numerous are the cases where untrained negotiators do not really bargain labour wages, working conditions and relative power positions, but really argue about the management and the nature of the global social system. Issues such as 'exploitation of the proletariat', 'freedom of enterprise', 'class warfare' or 'creeping socialism' have nothing to do really with items under discussion in a labour negotiation. As an otherwise left wing continental European union puts it very clearly in a training manual for its militants: The goal of a negotiation is to bargain specific demands not social or class relationships. Again in labour relations terms and in other words, within the given framework of the existing economic and social systems of production, that one may like, accept to live with, hate or want to transform, the objective is to negotiate items – in the short term and independently of long term objectives.

This of course should not be construed as meaning that collective bargaining processes and results have no effect in the long term and upon the global social system. Also it certainly does not mean that long-term consequences of present negotiations should be ignored. But it definitely does mean that in collective bargaining one should negotiate for an agreement satisfactory to him on the items which are discussed and definitely not in order to protect the last bastion of Western Christiandom or to help bring about the immediate arrival of the classless society.

The same remarks can be made regarding a commercial negotiation where bargaining for prestige, winning the best of somebody one does not like, demonstrating one's skill, impressing colleagues, neighbours, family, instead of concentrating on the issue at stake can have disastrous results. Many people who went to buy second-hand cars from dealers accompanied by their families and friends can bear witness to that fact. Again it does not mean that the result of the negotiation will have no bearing on the prestige of the negotiators, but only that, in the short term, it is not what the negotiators should concentrate on.

(c) Individual and Collective Negotiations

It must be recognised that parties in the negotiating process can be individuals but may as well be groups. However, any kind of a crowd of individuals, for example, does not constitute a group and is unlikely to be taken seriously as a negotiating party by any potential opponent. Groups are defined as something different from a haphazard assembly of people. As stated by Sayles,[1] in order to be stable and interested enough to take part in negotiating, a group must fulfil the following conditions: The possession of a common interest, the capacity to act in a coherent and co-ordinated way and the opportunity to do so. Examples of such groups can be found, for instance, in a plant in categories such as the union section, the maintenance men, management, legal fictions such as corporations, or bodies without a corporate existence such as a group of companies, a plant, or a similar entity.

In cases where one or several groups are involved as parties the negotiation becomes collective. Therefore, prior to formulating a negotiating strategy, an important question is whether the negotiations are individual or collective. For our purpose we shall define individual negotiations as those in which a person negotiates on his own behalf without having constituents. Responsibility and accountability are located with the principal involved. It is a relatively extreme case except for the examples drawn from daily life and illustrated above. A clean-cut example in commercial negotiations would be the one of a small builder negotiating for the purchase of land singly-owned on which he will subsequently build houses. He will be aware of the resources at his disposal to fund the phases: from initial purchase, to design of the houses, procurement of materials, payment of staff and potential revenue arising out of sales of the completed houses. Although he may make trade-offs between costs, for example, if a higher land price can be recouped through increasing the density of housing, he is the only person essentially concerned with the result. In more complex commercial organisations the two negotiators are likely to be salaried employees operating on behalf of their corporate employer but located within a corporate hierarchy.

1 – Most negotiations are collective
Many negotiators, the people who actually are going to interact, then operate on behalf of parties. Even in daily life transactions people often negotiate on behalf of their family, team, or a group of friends. This is even more clearly put in evidence when we look at labour negotiations where people at the bargaining table negotiate directly for parties made of large groups and where many other parties, although not directly belonging to the direct interaction, are nevertheless interested in the results of the negotiation. Besides, within each party there may exist several different constituencies. If we look in more detail at a labour bargaining table we can consider that it is indeed collective bargaining. If we look first at the labour side we can assume that the negotiators represent directly quite a few separate constituencies. The following ones can be pointed out: blue collar workers, who can be unskilled, semi-skilled or skilled and highly-skilled, white collar workers who can be hourly paid or salaried and belong to different grades, professional employees, technical staff, supervisory staff. The constituencies may actually be drawn according to lines other than skill opposing, for instance, young workers and older workers. Or the work-force can belong to several different unions according to craft or ideology depending upon the country. Also some workers or employees may be non-union. Even within the union several constituencies may co-exist between shop stewards, officers, militant members and the membership at large. It is obvious that all these constituencies have different if not divergent goals, interests and objectives. For instance, highly-skilled workers will aim to maintain the wage skill differential, while unskilled ones will aim for a lump-sum wage increase; older workers are more interested in retirement benefits while the younger ones want the money now. Female employees may be more concerned with equal opportunity. Besides, often it is not only the local union which is represented at the bargaining table. Representatives of the national union, or the union federation, according to the case, are present or stay close in the background, with a policy which can vary from extracting maximum

capacity to pay from the employer to setting industry-wide equivalent wages. Of course we should add other interested parties watching the negotiation from outside: political interests; the public interested in knowing if the result will be a strike depriving them of a service or a commodity or a settlement meaning an increase in prices of such; other local unions looking for a potential pattern-setting trend; the media; the list is almost endless.

In much the same way within management, if, for instance, the negotiation takes place at plant level, one should take care to distinguish the goals, interests and objectives of corporate management, company-wide, from the plant managers. One may fear establishing a company pattern, while the other wants to settle. At plant level, if business is good, one may imagine that the sales management presses for a settlement at almost any cost, while, because of past schedule disruptions the production manager wants to set an example, but the personnel manager is concerned about his relationship with the union. Therefore there also exist constituencies within the managerial party. Also, in the same way, other interested parties around, but not in the negotiation, include not only the media and the public, but also the employers' association, other local employers, middle management within the company, unorganised employees, and so on.

The key factor is that as soon as negotiations involve more than single individuals bargaining on their own account we are concerned with situations in which groups and organisations bargain collectively with one another. In that sense, bargaining becomes collective because it pits collectives, groups, themselves made of constituencies, and not only individuals, against each other. It becomes then of essential importance that, prior to any further action, the relevant and interested parties and the constituencies within these parties are identified and distinguished from the negotiators who shall carry out the representative activities and actual negotiations.

It should be underlined here that, in the case of collective negotiations, the relationship between the parties must be conceptually distinguished from the relationship between the negotiators. The parties are collective entities, the negotiators are the individuals who are going to interact generally physically or through the intermediary of some other medium such as the telephone, except in the extreme case of tacit bargaining. Both must be understood as having each a different specific relationship. For instance, a company may be the supplier of another one for a long time but a new buyer may meet a new seller in both companies for the first time. Sometimes the negotiators will mirror the relationship between the entities represented by the parties. Sometimes the negotiators may have a privileged relationship of trust of their own, born of habit or mutual confidence, independently of the relationship between the parties. Conversely the negotiators may let themselves slip into a conflictual spiral of their own, jeopardising what was a formerly good relationship between the parties. Morley and Stephenson[2] point to the importance of the distinction between the two relationships.

2 – Intra-party negotiations
Another essential feature characterises collective negotiations. They are not constituted only of the interactions of the negotiators at the bargaining table, but they are constituted of much more complex sets of interactions between the groups of constituents present in each party and represented through the negotiators. Consequently what happens in a meeting does not involve only the actual behaviour of the negotiators; it has to take into account the interactions between groups of constituents. Both prior to the negotiations and during the process itself a considerable pressure can and does develop not only between the negotiators but also among the parties themselves and also between each party and its own negotiators which represent it at the bargaining table.

This point has a number of important consequences in theory and in practice. In fact, each negotiator or team of negotiators is bound in a network of constraints which are more or less tightly drawn by the constituencies existing within the party that he represents and which reduce his freedom of manoeuvre. In practice, each team of negotiators represents sets of diverse, divergent and even contradictory interests. Thus they see their power of decision-making while bargaining severely curtailed to the margin which exists between what each of their constituencies wish and what each may accept. Of course sometimes they have to answer to constituencies which have incompatible and contradictory goals. But if the power to negotiate is vested in the negotiators, the real power, the power to give and take, to bind oneself to an agreement, often remains with the constituents and not with the negotiators. For instance, in labour negotiations the power to resume or to continue working rests with the work-force, not with the union bargaining team. In the same way, ultimately, it is senior management who decide to concede an increase or to maintain the level of employment in the plant, not the bargainer on management's side. In international negotiations Parliament may or may not ratify treaties, entered into by diplomats.

Therefore there is also a whole process[3] of bargaining within each party, within each negotiator's own organisation, which takes place around internal issues. The process takes place for each negotiation as an interaction between a negotiator and his party and within his party between the constituencies present before, and during, the other main negotiation that occurs between the different negotiators put against each other. This process is a characteristic of all multi-party/multi-constituency negotiations – for example, the Geneva disarmaments talks, negotiations between the European Economic Community as represented by the Commission and the Japanese government on the trade imbalances which exist. The frequent recourse to adjournments by one or both parties may indicate the negotiators' need to re-establish contact with his party or a particular constituency as the negotiation proceeds to new issues or when they suspect that they are close to their margin of freedom.

The practical consequences of the structure of the negotiations as they relate to the parties and their relationship will be examined in Chapter 3, as they affect the selection of a strategy.

SECTION II – ANALYSIS OF THE ENVIRONMENT

The second element which structures a negotiation is the environment within which it is taking place. In any negotiating situation, there is a part which is static and one which is dynamic. There are some elements which are given, about which the parties have no control, and some elements which they can alter, change or manoeuvre to their advantage. Therefore, at first, a major distinction should be made between what is the context/environment of the negotiation, and what it is that the parties are going to do to take advantage of it. A second distinction can be made conceptually within the environment, which may be divided into two parts: the part which remains fixed in the short or even medium term, and the part which is readily changeable.

Clearly the environment present some features which it is not in the power of the parties to modify or to alter in the short run. For instance, to illustrate the point very simply, in a commercial negotiation, when a specific item is concerned, the market may be a seller's or a buyer's market. In a labour bargaining situation the type of skills of the employees represented in the bargaining unit may be scarce, or easy to find. Unemployment may be high or low. Conversely, some other parts of the environment are readily modifiable. For instance, a buyer can look up other sellers in a given geographic area or it may be technically feasible that he easily change slightly the specifications of the product he is looking for.

The domain of the readily changeable parts of the environment and of action of the parties to modify it as well as to take advantage of the permanent features belongs to the domain of the strategies and tactics. Much of the rest of this book will be devoted to the strategies, the tactics and their implementation. Presently we wish to concern ourselves with the structure, therefore with the context, and the permanent, or at least the long term or medium term, elements of the environment.

For the purpose to better perceive and analyse the environment and to allow a person placed in a negotiating situation to understand what is important or not, relevant or not to his situation, in any given negotiating context, we will present below a grid of analysis of the environment.[4]

In order to introduce this method of analysis we shall take as examples two labour negotiations which took place some years ago in the USA. They are the cases of the New York City transit dispute of April 1980 and the US airline controllers' dispute of July 1982. In the first case, after a week of conflict, the unions got away with about anything they demanded at the outset. In the second case, 12 500 employees were dismissed and not rehired, work resumed on the same conditions as before the conflict and the union was destroyed. Of course those two negotiating situations present some similarities and some differences. However, they can be usefully compared because both concern labour relations and involve a similar type of conflictual situation and negotiations. Both also concern the transportation industry, and both involve a public employer. Nevertheless there are limits to the comparison, for they have different scopes, city-wide and country-wide and end up with thoroughly different results. One is a major victory for labour, the other a major victory for management.

Recalling here their main features will help us establish successively the elements of our grid.

(a) The Parties Concerned

First, who are the parties concerned? The response seems immediately obvious: management and labour are the ones which are fighting over wages and conditions. But are they the only interested parties? Are they the only ones who are going to influence the outcome of the dispute? Certainly not. One of the most interested parties, and also the one whose attitude, be it support or disapproval, can swing the issue of the negotiations one way or another, is the public, deprived of transportation, and unable to conduct its daily business during the conflict but likely to face later increases in fares to cover eventual wage increases included in a settlement. At this point it should be remarked that in the two cases the public concerned is not the same. In the transit strike case, it concerns everyone in the area who has to travel. In the case of the air controllers' strike it involves only a select number of people in a larger area: those who travel by aeroplane countrywide. It is likely that the reaction, the expectations, the choices of the two populations are going to be very different. Therefore the exact nature of the constituencies constituting the parties concerned, for the purpose of an accurate analysis, should be clearly identified and described.

Of course other interested parties can be listed, beyond the public: management, which is, respectively, New York Transit Authority, and the Federal Aviation Authority. Nevertheless, management being a public entity, elected office holders are closely interested in the outcome of negotiations; in one case, this means, at the minimum, the Mayor of New York City, and the Governor of the State of New York, and their staffs; in the other case, the President's cabinet and the President himself are concerned. It is also likely that other unions of public employees are closely watching the dispute, ready to put in a claim of their own if the labour side achieves significant gains in the running negotiations. The list of interested parties can almost be further lengthened at will. Nevertheless, in order to keep it useful and manageable for a party involved directly in a dispute and a negotiation and bent upon analysing the context and the environment of that negotiation, it cannot be too long. Therefore this list should be limited, but the limit cannot be drawn arbitrarily. It consists of the relevance of the parties in regard to the outcome of the negotiation. For instance, in both disputes the public is certainly a relevant party and its potentially likely reaction should be further analysed. The extent to which political elected figures are or are not relevant parties may depend on a variety of factors such as the importance of the dispute for the local or national economy or closeness of upcoming political elections. This analysis should be run for all parties listed to determine how relevant they are to the negotiation process. There is probably no limit to the number of parties interested more or less remotely in a labour conflict. However, the key to a significant analysis of the interested parties is to limit the study to the parties likely to have a major impact on the negotiation process or its outcome. In other words, the parties which should be considered relevant are the ones likely to be concerned and to receive from and/or produce on the direct negotiators a major impact in a kind of feedback loop. The feedback effect is the practical tool to gauge the degree of relevance.

(b) Stakes

Second, what are the stakes of the parties to the dispute? Clearly this is going to be extremely important in influencing their behaviour. In other words, how important is the result of the negotiation going to be for them? This of course includes the analysis of what they have to gain and what they have to lose but it goes beyond a simple computation of potential gains and losses in material terms. Other non-material stakes are important such as: what have the parties invested into that negotiation and how much do they need to bring back a certain result? As was demonstrated in the case of the airline controllers' dispute, wages and conditions were not the only issue; credibility was at stake for one party – management; and for the union its very existence – which it lost – was at stake.

(c) Resources and Constraints

Then, once the relevant parties and their stakes are described, the analysis of the environment should be conducted in terms of constraints and resources. If we take the example of a card game for a brief moment, the parties, given the present condition of the environment itself, even before the beginning of the game (the negotiations), have been dealt a more or less strong hand, more or less rich in points, or picture cards, or trumps. Before they decide on a strategy they must take into account what may work in their favour and what may work against them. The environment in which the negotiation will take place structures it. It contains constraints of which the parties have to acknowledge the existence and which they can ignore only at their own risk and peril, as well as resources which may help them reach their objectives, if they are able to discover, mobilise and use them.

For instance, in both our cases of labour disputes the fact that the labour side controls a near monopoly on transportation within their respective scopes (city area and long distance travel) is a very strong resource.

The need for transportation by the public puts pressure on management to settle; it is a constraint for it. On the other hand the fact that airline communications affect strongly the economy limits the resources for the airline controllers whom may see not only public resentment appear against them but also other parties getting involved such as chamber of commerce, business organisations, and others. The prospect of a steep rise in fares could have a similar effect in the case of New York City transit. In the same line of analysis the fact that they are sworn employees not allowed to strike is a strong constraint for the airline controllers. If they, purposedly, ignore it, as they did in fact, they take a risk. Constraints for the Transit District workers come, for instance, from the existence of other means of transportation; private bus companies and the availability of private cars. Of course constraints and resources are not static. As the negotiation proceeds, as the strategies of the parties come into play, each one is going to try to manipulate his own, and the other party's constraints and resources. Some of the events which alter them are beyond the reach of the parties. For instance, the very hot weather is a resource for the striking transit workers because it makes commuting more difficult, a bridge breaking down would be an additional one. On both they have no control and it is in that sense that they structure the negotiation. In the same way in the case of the airline controllers, one can imagine that an airline accident would have been a major resource for influencing towards a quick settlement of the negotiation.

Other resources which the parties can create belong to the domain of the process of negotiation to be discussed below: for instance, strikers can try to build a new resource by making traffic more difficult for motorists and private buses by setting obstacles, blocking streets or breaking traffic lights. It is also to that domain that belong the actions which aim to alter the parts of the environment susceptible to short-term change or to take advantage of existing resources and avoiding the pitfalls of present constraints: the parties will purposely increase their resources and decrease their constraints and increase the constraints and decrease the resources of their opponent. Examples in our cases have consisted, for instance, of management having a $1 million fine imposed by the judiciary on the transit workers' union, of the president increasing the constraints on the union by successfully firing more than 10 000 striking controllers, of the controllers' union trying to enlist support from foreign colleagues to block out international flights. The actual manipulating of constraints and resources efficiently for oneself and the other party is the role of tactics within the framework of a strategy, to which we shall devote complete chapters later on. Their adequate use implies that the analysis of the environment in terms of resources and constraints is carefully carried out and revised continually because once the negotiations have started the environment remains dynamic and is likely to change to a more or less marked degree.

Finally, it is clear that the same event which constitutes a resource for one party is often a constraint for the other and vice versa, but it does not always need to be, and most importantly, the magnitude that the same event recovers for one party as a constraint is not equal to the one it represents for the other party as a resource.

These last two factors make attempts to quantify the resources and constraints, in order to compare them summarily between parties in terms of added figures, quite risky. However, this has been tried under a somewhat different form and terminology, interestingly but perhaps not totally convincingly.[5] We believe for ourselves that the following grid, without getting bogged down in a morass of complex and sometimes misleading quantitative methodology, is a sophisticated enough tool of analysis of the environment:

	Stakes	Objectives	Resources	Constraints
Party 1				
Party 2				

FIGURE 1   *Grid for the analysis of the environment*

(d) Objectives

From the definition of who are the parties and what are their stakes,
resources and constraints, a first broad and rough outline of what are
tentatively the objectives of the parties can be arrived at, or guessed
at, for not only are they likely to be hidden at first but also they may
be far from clear and evident, as pointed out above, and they are
shrouded by the bonds on each party's rationality. This is a point to
consider both when thinking of a party establishing its own objectives
but also at the level of our own bonds in considering the other's
objectives.

A later section will be devoted to clarifying the process of the
establishment of objectives.

(e) Changes in Time

Of course the grid must be continuously revised within the dynamic
process of negotiation to monitor changes in the structure of the
negotiations as well as the impact of the process. Changes may occur
in resources and constraints and even in the list of the relevant parties
concerned (coalitions, alliances). These changes come mostly from
the effects of the strategies and tactics of all parties involved and of
the behaviour of the negotiators, although they may also, in some
cases, issue from the fact that the environment is slowly changing,
either through its own dynamic, or under outside pressure.

An example of variation in time of structural elements can be taken
from the stakes of the parties. The negotiators can raise the stakes.
For instance, an illustration can be given by the example of a beggar
trying to get a coin out of a passer-by, in exchange for leaving him
alone or satisfying his urge for charity. It constitutes a negotiation. At
first, the beggar may seem powerless, having almost no way to coerce
any amount of money from the passer-by. As will be clear from our
discussion below,[6] very few are the situations where one individual
has no power whatsoever. If the beggar needs the money badly
enough, if his stake is high, he may begin pestering the passer-by
strongly enough, which constitutes his power, so that the latter shall
hand him out some change, in order to be left alone, for his own stake
is very low and a few coins represent little or nothing to him.
Nevertheless, if he feels that he is being pestered too much, he may
react violently, and not withdraw from a street scene, which was the
behaviour that the panhandler expected from him. He may even

begin to look for a policeman to teach a lesson to the beggar.[7] The stakes are no longer a small sum of money, but are now affective or emotional.

For another typical example let us assume that negotiations on wages at a railway yard have come to an impasse and that a strike is on. The strikers may begin picketing the yard, management may call upon non-union engineers who shall cross, peacefully or otherwise, the picket line. A fistfight may occur. Violence may increase. Strikers may then lie on the rails in front of the trains, management may have the riot police carry them away, then the strikers may start a hunger strike in front of the yard, and so on.

This example may seem far-fetched for a wage issue. Nevertheless examples of that nature do exist in fact, although mostly around employment issues. What the labour side has done in this negotiation is, at each turn, to move the stakes one notch up. It has successively raised them from wage demands, to work stoppage, to violence on the picket lines, to political issues, to human life. Thus, in negotiations, the parties may vary the stakes and therefore change completely the framework of negotiations involving new parties, new resources and constraints, and so on.[8] All elements of the structure of a negotiation may change given enough time, albeit at a very different pace. Such changes must be monitored.

SECTION III – BARGAINING POWER

The third element of the structure of a negotiation is bargaining power.

The analysis of the environment as carried out above is of primary importance for it is from the environment that bargaining power is issued and that, at the same time, bargaining power can be used to attempt to modify the environment. For instance, the capacity to mobilise resources towards one's own objectives, to overcome one's own constraints, to overturn the other parties' resources and create constraints for them can be expressed as one major facet of bargaining power. At the same time, resources and constraints are issued from the environment and they determine bargaining power.

Analysts of power cover a broad range, from those who assert that there is no such thing as power, because everything is predetermined in advance by whatever superhuman forces may be at play (such as the Will of God or the class struggle, for instance) down to those who see power everywhere. An analysis of the various theories of power in society would be tedious and useless to our purposes. Nevertheless we believe bargaining power to be at the heart of the bargaining process, to constitute its essential feature. Therefore we need to address the problem. However, the notion of power is elusive and we want to track it down in very practical and operational terms, therefore the following developments will move from theoretical definitions to applied concepts.

(a) Definitions of Bargaining Power

In general terms, a classic definition of power is the capacity to exert influence.[9] From it we can infer that power is characterised as the ability of a person or a group to cause a degree of controlled change, in the direction wanted, in another person or group. With an identical effect, but in different terms, the definition of power almost always includes the capacity 'to overcome resistance in achieving a desired objective or result'.[10] Weber has already defined it as the probability that one actor within a social relationship will be in a position to carry his own will despite resistance.[11]

Implemented in a negotiating relationship, power becomes bargaining power and can be expressed in more specific terms. The bargaining power of a party will rest in its capacity to influence the outcomes of the negotiation towards its own goals. Crozier[12] adopts and adapts slightly a definition given by Dahl[13] and defines the power of A over B as the capacity of A in a negotiation with B to obtain favourable terms of exchange. Or it can also be expressed as the capacity of A to obtain from B what B would not have given or done without A's pressure. Chamberlain has focused on the process of bargaining and has produced an even more operational definition of bargaining power.[14] It is the ability to secure another party's agreement on one's own terms. It depends on the cost for that party of disagreeing on the terms offered as compared to the cost of agreeing on them. For instance, in a collective bargaining relationship, the union's bargaining power depends on management's willingness to agree to the demands of the union. In turn, this is a function of the cost incurred by management in a settlement as compared to costs of a strike. The reverse analysis gives management's bargaining power.

These definitions of power are convergent. They are useful not only because they allow us to better grasp the concept we are discussing, but also and foremost, because they have very practical implications and pragmatic consequences, particularly when we put them in the framework of bounded rationality, which we now outline.

(b) Bargaining Power is the Essence of the Negotiation

Let us note that if one party has no power over the other, we are no longer in the framework of a bargaining relationship, but in a situation entirely different, in another type of case where, for instance, only hierarchical power counts. For example the employer/employees link is a typical bargaining relationship because each party has power over the other: management has the power to withdraw wages and terminate employment, labour has the power to withdraw work or goodwill. Elements of bargaining are lacking in a situation when one party has total control over the other one. For instance, master–slave or lord–serf relationships are no longer bargaining relationships, at least if we assume for a moment that the slave or serf is totally devoid of power over the lord or master. This assumption itself may be questionable and was discussed above. In the same way, in commercial negotiating, both parties have power over each other. They have something to exchange. Buyer and seller keep over one another the power not to buy or not to sell, to pay or to keep their money. A commercial negotiation could not take place if a party had no interest whatsoever, however playful or academic in buying or selling.

Therefore bargaining power is the essence of negotiation.

(c) Characteristics of Bargaining Power

1 – Bargaining power is relative
As Chamberlain[15] first and then Crozier and Friedberg[16] point out, bargaining power is not an 'attribute', that is, it does not exist by itself. It is not a quantity that an individual can own, hoard or stockpile for future use in any situation, against any other party. Bargaining power does not exist alone. It appears only within a relationship. It does not exist in itself. It is always relative to the environment and to whomever may be the other party.

A. Bargaining power is relative to environment

In following with our analysis of resources and constraints for both parties, it is obvious that bargaining power is a function of the environment where it finds its sources. It is the environment which predetermines the resources and the constraints of the parties. It is of course foremost the more or less permanent features of the environment, unchangeable in the short term, which are of importance. For instance, in a commercial negotiating relationship, the condition of the market, prevalent prices in the area, the state of competition are factors which issue from the environment and are imposed by it. If one wants to buy a house, factors such as the rate of inflation, the rate of interest on mortgages, the availability of housing in the area, the condition and quality of the dwelling offered are all facts dictated by the environment for both parties. This under no circumstances should be understood as meaning that the parties see those facts under an identical light or agree on them. First, the environment may appear to be of a different scope for each party (for instance, the buyer is looking at several different areas to buy a house but the seller considers only one area, the one where his house is located). Second, the environment is almost always understood differently by the parties, even if it happens to be geographically the same for both, as we shall illustrate later. Third, each party acts within the bonds of its own limited rationality. But the relevant point is that, however it is understood differently by the parties, the condition of the environment is a given, that is, it cannot be changed by their efforts in the short term.

B. Bargaining power is relative to the parties involved

This implies, in practical terms, that among similar relationships it varies according to whoever is involved. It is in fact an economic oversimplification to speak of a buyers' market or a sellers' market, because the bargaining power of a seller or a buyer, though of course strongly influenced by the condition of the market, also is specific to this specific buyer, this specific seller and the specific characteristics of the relationship between them whatever the general trend of the market be.

An example can usefully clarify this point. Let us assume that a plumber and a customer negotiate the price of work to be done in the latter's kitchen. The market for plumber's services has generally the reputation of being a sellers' market. In fact if the plumber is the only one in town he can pretty much demand whatever price he wants. But if there are other plumbers, or if the customer can hire out of town, the plumber's bargaining power is sharply decreased. Nevertheless the customer's sink may be leaking, his kitchen flooded by water and overflowing into his neighbour's flat, in which case it does him little good if other plumbers are available tomorrow, or next week (or next month more likely). On the other hand the area's plumbers may have decided on price-fixing and common rates, or not to take work on which one of them has already given an estimate. But even in that case the customer may also be a prominent magistrate able to influence bargaining by a threat of an enquiry into illegal price overcharging or restraint of trade, or he also could be the owner or manager of several blocks of flats and the plumber could be influenced to give a good deal because he wants that additional business. On the other hand, the plumber may be a lay judge within a commercial court and fear little from an enquiry into prices, or he may already have too much work. This brief example could go on and on. But in a very simple way it clearly illustrates the fact that bargaining power is relative to a specific relationship between given individuals. It would be different if different individuals were to be involved even with the same object of negotiation and in similar roles.

C. Bargaining power is relative to the stakes of the parties

If the stakes of the parties vary enormously, for instance, when the object of the negotiation is a life or death matter for one party while it represents a trivial amount for the other party, it is going to affect the bargaining relationship, the power of each party and the relative power of the two parties.

2 – Bargaining power is independently set
Each party's bargaining power is set independently from the other one. That is, a high bargaining power for one party does not imply that the other one has himself either a low, or high bargaining power. In other words, knowing one party's bargaining power, within the relationship with the other party, tells us nothing about the other party's power. For example, in Chamberlain's terms, within labour negotiations, knowing the union's bargaining power, which is rooted in the high cost of a long strike for the company, tells us nothing about management's bargaining power, which in that case may be rooted in the workers' unwillingness to go all out for a long strike. The fact that the bargaining powers of the parties are independently set implies that even in the framework of a negotiation analysed in

terms of power relative to the other party and to the situation, estimating one's own bargaining power is not enough. It should also be compared to one's estimate of the other party's power.

It is the balance of the bargaining power of the parties that should additionally be considered.

3 – Bargaining power is subjective

This balance will be an estimate. and only an estimate, never a certainty. For bargaining power is not only relative to the environment, the parties and the stakes, as demonstrated in the cases described above, but it is also subjective. It can be said, in the terms used by a researcher on negotiation, that it has a cognitive nature[17] in the sense that it actually only really exists to the extent that it is perceived as existing. The situation, the environment, the context, as it stands, may contain abundant resources and formidable opportunities to build up the bargaining power of one or both of the parties. Nevertheless if the party(ies) are not aware of these opportunities or neglect them, their bargaining power does not come into existence,[18] or at least not to the full extent to which it could be built if the factors which are ignored were taken into consideration. It is also partly another consequence of the fact that bargaining power is not an attribute that it exists only in a relationship and does not exist by itself alone, independently of a situation and of the relevant parties, as it was explained above. Even when located in a given situation, a given environment, it exists only inasmuch as it is perceived and recognised as issuing from the configuration of that specific environment. More generally, of course, it is a result of bounded rationality.

In practical terms the subjective nature of bargaining power carries two consequences.

A. Perceptions of the environment differ between parties

As was pointed out above, the same facts are often perceived in very different ways by different people. And even if perceived as being roughly the same, the same facts are then subject to very different interpretations. This explains why the belief that bringing figures into bargaining should stop all arguing and settle the negotiation is often so misplaced. Figures may come from various sources and are subject to very different interpretations. Each party may just as well bring its own set of home-made statistics at the bargaining table. Even agreement on the accuracy of statistical data does not carry agreement about what use to put it to, or what consequences to draw from it.

This can be clarified by an example. Let's assume that a used car price is being negotiated.[19] The table below illustrates the way the 'facts' of the situation are seen by the parties.

This example illustrates the idea that the same facts are perceived and understood very differently by different people, especially when

Facts	Seller's understanding of fact	Buyer's understanding of fact
The Blue Book's price for that year's model.	That same model has sometimes sold for more than the blue book figure.	I know people who have paid less than the book value for that type of car.
Car bodywork looks in good condition.	It is still in very good condition considering.	It is just a plain model with nothing out of the ordinary.
8000 miles/year average mileage.	This is just below average driving usage.	Altogether for this number of years, that is a lot of miles.
The engine shows no apparent problems and has been checked by a mechanic.	There is no reason why it should break down now any more than it did before.	You never know what might happen after I bought it. How do I know he maintained it well?
The car features a radio and tape deck.	That should bring me extra money for it cost me a lot to get installed.	He cannot take it off anyway for there is already one in his new car. It should be free.
Whitewall and snow tires come with the car.	That should bring me extra money for they cost me extra.	I hate whitewall tires and I never see snow where I live. Besides, I hate skiing.
Rate of inflation.	With other costs going up I cannot afford not to get a decent price for that car.	With other costs going up I cannot afford to pay too much for that car.
Rate of interest on financing.	It is now lower than past year, so if he cannot pay cash why doesn't he finance it.	Consumer credit is an unbelievable 20%.
The car is a rather powerful model.	It is roomy comfortable and moves fast.	It is a gas guzzler.
Buyer is younger than seller.	Nowadays young people make incredible amounts of money. It is the middle age group like me who get pressured.	Young people like me cannot afford to spend too much.
The demand on that model is about average compared to other models.	This car sells very well.	That model is often left car unsold.
A price tag is on the car.	Why doesn't he make me an offer.	Isn't he going to lower his asking price.

FIGURE 2   *How two opposed negotiators see the same facts*

they are at the opposite end of a negotiating relationship. The same identical facts are subject to very different interpretations. Two reseachers have gathered quantitative evidence which supports this point by measuring the differences in reactions between union and management negotiators in collective bargaining situations.[20] Although the study is restricted to the problem solving process in labour negotiation, its results are perfectly applicable to other aspects of negotiation. Besides, it should be recalled here that psychology teaches us that different individuals perceive and retain different facts from the same situation according to various characteristics and their different cognitive maps.[21]

It should be added that it is almost always the case that nobody has knowledge of all relevant facts and one of the parties may put emphasis and base its positions on facts not known to the other one. Also, facts, which exist in the environment and which are known, can be voluntarily ignored, disbelieved or not acknowledged by one party. When we take these additional factors into account together with the point that the same facts are perceived differently by different persons, it is clear that bargaining power should be understood not only as a function of the environment, but of the vision of the environment as it is perceived by the parties involved.

B. Bargaining power issues from the opponent's perception

Bargaining power is subjective in still another sense – if we analyse more fully our own definition of it. We stated above that in a negotiation, one party's bargaining power is *his* opponent's perception of the cost of agreeing versus the costs of disagreeing with his position, offer, proposals or demands. Therefore our bargaining power is not really a function of the way that the environment is perceived more or less accurately by us, it is foremost a function of the way the environment is perceived *by our opponent, not by ourselves*. A party may see facts which provide him with a high degree of power in the relationship. If the opponent ignores them or does not perceive them it is just as if they did not exist. For instance, a party who believes that non-existent potential strong resources are present in the environment in favour of his opponent gives him power. Conversely a party who does not know that he is powerless, that his opponent has at his disposal all the means necessary to make him yield, withdraws the power of his opponent, maybe temporarily and only until he is proven wrong, but effectively during that time. This illustrates to some extent the relative power of ignorance. In that sense, inexperience may sometimes be a very powerful weapon. An inexperienced negotiator may avoid, in a bargaining situation, all traps and factors playing against him, just by not realising that they exist. Of course one cannot consciously count on it and it cannot be faked. For this to happen it is necessary that both parties should not be aware of it. Conversely ninety-nine times out of a hundred, experience is a totally positive asset in negotiating. We simply want to point out that it may just happen that total inexperience may be from time to time a totally wild winning card. But one cannot consciously plan on it, for, by definition it has to be an unknown factor for the party for which it is an asset.

The important point which should be remembered here is that it is what the opponent believes about us which gives us our bargaining power, and not what we believe, or believe we know about ourselves. Therefore already we can understand that parties aiming at increasing their own bargaining power will have to affect the opponent's perception of the situation and not only the situation itself. If one believes that the other party is powerful it is of little importance whether it is powerful or not, at least at the first stage of negotiations, because one will behave as if the opponent were powerful, even if he is really very weak. It is the perceptions which are important and the perceptions of the other party as much as our own. Of course they will change with time and the dynamics of the negotiating process.

SECTION IV – THE SOURCE AND MECHANICS OF BARGAINING POWER

We have already arrived at a satisfactory definition of bargaining power to the extent that we know its nature, but it leaves unanswered the question of where it takes its roots, of its general determinants. In other words, we know what it is but not yet how it works. Given that for each party it rests on his opponent's perception of the situation, the questions we now address are: what are the common factors in all situations which alter bargaining power? And what, in very practical terms, are the elements on which we can play to increase our own or decrease the other party's bargaining power?

(a) Sources

A relatively large number of theorists have researched into the source of bargaining power. We shall limit ourselves to recalling the most famous: French and Raven[22] in a classic discussion identify legitimate, referent, expert, coercive and reward power. Mechanic[23] points out three elements: control of access to information, of access to persons, of access to the persons' instrumentalities. He points to the great amount of power held by the lower ranking members of an organisation. This view is related to that of Simon[24] who, following Barnard,[25] finds the source of power no longer in the means at the disposal of the superior but in the willingness of the subordinate to follow instructions or orders which fall within his 'zone of acceptance' (or zone of indifference according to Barnard). Schelling[26] has underlined the importance of commitment. Crozier and Friedberg find the sole source of power in uncertainty.[27] Bacharach and Lawler, who offer a thorough study and criticism of some past theories, find its only source in dependence,[28] following the path opened by Blau.[29]

In our point of view, all of those approaches have value and point to remarkably interesting and fruitful converging insights. The only two problems are the following. On the one hand, some of the above quoted authors privilege one source as the only source of bargaining power. For instance, Crozier and Friedberg account for Schelling's theory of bargaining power through commitment within their framework but understand it in a given single way as it relates to uncertainty. For us, as we shall explain below, commitment finds its place more among the tactics used to manipulate bargaining power than as its source. For instance, it can be used to raise the stakes, as discussed earlier. On this latest point we adopt the same attitude with regard to French and Raven's or Mechanic's analysis.

(b) Mechanism

This drives us to our second point. To remain on operational terms we need to distinguish between the theories which attempt to establish or list the sources of power and the ones which attempt to analyse the mechanism of power, that is to say, how, from whatever source power comes, it is effectively put into action. In our eyes, the first theories find their place in the tactics, that is, the manipulation of the environment, to influence it so that it provides resources and constraints, and it is there that French and Raven's Mechanic's and similar theories belong. The second category theories are those relevant for discussion at this point.

Therefore we need to address the two main conceptualisations of the mechanism of bargaining power which have been proposed in theory and our contention is that both of them have explanatory value, that they are both justified to some extent and that they should coexist. Neither one alone is fully explanatory, but both provide a complete picture and useful insights.

1 – Conflict and co-operation: dependence

We started at the outset, in the first section of the first chapter, by outlining the prevalence of conflict in all aspects of life and by establishing the facts that negotiating is fundamentally a way to solve conflict and that it is also at least partly involved in alternative ways to do so. But now we must also point out that in negotiating there is also a built-in element of necessary co-operation. Negotiators do not really seek to destroy each other, although they may in some cases resort to that extreme. Nevertheless it is not their main objective.[30] What they are looking for is to obtain something from the other party that he can provide for them. They would not enter into negotiations if they could obtain it in any other easier way.

In other words, and according to the characteristics of negotiation retained in our attempt to define it, it is unavoidable that there would be automatically a degree of conflict in a negotiating relationship because the parties are divided about an issue; both parties want at first to settle the issue on the terms which are most favourable to their own position. This is because, if they could do so in any other way, there would be no need to negotiate. But there is also a built-in degree of co-operation because both parties need to reach a settlement in order to get something that they want and which they can get from the other party. To go back in very simple terms to the example of the sale of the used car, buyer and seller disagree on the price of the car. Both would like to gain a 'good' price and it is in opposite directions for each of them, but the seller wants cash which the buyer has, and the buyer wants a car, which the seller has. In any other case, they would not bother to meet, and there would not be any negotiating. Therefore they have a degree of common interest in making a settlement. Thus bargaining contains mixed incentives to compete and to co-operate, in amounts depending on the strength with which each party feels the incentives in each direction. Negotiating therefore implies to some extent an amount of mutual dependence.[31]

As a result, and this has fundamental consequences in practice, a party's bargaining power is based on the other party's dependence on him. A party will stay in a negotiating relationship and give what the other party expects of him and settle on the other's terms, if he wants badly enough what the other party has to offer him. The more he depends on the other party for getting what he wants to get from him, the more he will be inclined to settle and give in.

In turn, what is dependence based on? It includes two elements:

First, it is based on the degree to which a party can get what it needs from alternative sources: our buyer can find other cars in the classified ads of his newspaper. But the ease with which he can do so depends on the model of the car which the seller has to offer. Some types of cars are more or less popular, and the supply for some popular year or models often in the short run is largely below demand. Some collector's models, for lovers of old sports cars, appear seldom, if ever, on the market. The seller has a higher bargaining power if he wants to sell a model very much in favour, produced in small quantities and not advertised by anybody else in the classified ads for a long time, because the buyer looking for that model has few alternative sources for what he wants. On the contrary, selling a cheap, mass-produced, not very successful model provides the buyer with many alternative sources.

Second, it is based on the degree to which a party wants, needs and values what it is that he is looking for: namely, the object for which he has entered into the negotiating relationship – in other words, the value he attaches to the result of the negotiation. If we turn again to our used car example, for the same type of car that he is selling, the bargaining power of the seller will depend on what the buyer is looking for exactly in that specific car, and therefore in how much he wants to obtain it: does he want a reasonably cheap means of transportation, easily available under several forms on the market, or does he want a fancy sports model sold almost as soon as it gets on the used-car market, or is he a manic collector desperately in search of that specific year's model of that specific sports car of which only a few have not been wrecked in accidents, and which, additionally, is the only one missing in his collection?

Conversely the buyer is 'selling' cash. His bargaining power depends on the alternative number of potential buyers and on how desperately and how soon the seller needs that cash.

This is well in agreement with one major element of our definitions of the relativity of bargaining power in a negotiating relationship: the bargaining power of a party will depend on his *opponent's perception* of his own dependence on the party in terms of the existence of other sources to obtain what he needs from that party and in terms of how much he values the result of the negotiation. But let us point out that both the opponent's perception and the party's own perception are shaped by the different bounds on the rationality of each of them.

Already we can see that, although tactics and strategies fall into several categories and types, they will be related to bargaining power. They will tend to influence the dependence of an opponent on us, in terms of his actual dependence or simply of perception of his dependence, or they will tend to influence (decrease) our dependence on our opponent (in terms of actual dependence or in terms of perception of our dependence). In both cases we shall tend to increase the number of our own perceived alternatives and decrease the value we put into the outcome as well as decrease our opponent's number of alternatives and increase the value he puts into the outcome.

2 – Uncertainty
Besides dependence, a second type of mechanism of bargaining power has been put in evidence.[32] It works out of uncertainty. It starts from the same postulate as dependence theory. That is to say, it is assumed that two parties are not in conflict for the sake of it, that they have stakes, which may include a playful or ludic element,[33] but which nevertheless are real and serious stakes to the obtainment of which they are more less committed. In the same terms as we developed in the previous case a party engages in a bargaining relationship in order to obtain something from the other party, his opponent. The party wants to obtain from his opponent an object, a behaviour, a concession or something else. This 'something' is important for the party's own capacity to pursue his own objectives. Thus by his behaviour it is the opponent who to some extent controls the possibility for the party to reach his objectives.

The degree to which an opponent can keep his future behaviour uncertain for the other party controls how much he still can extract from this party in exchange for granting him what it is that he wishes, that is, the object of the negotiation. Therefore the bargaining power of a party is a function of the degree of freedom available to his opponent, of the zones of uncertainty which he controls and which are relevant for the other party's objectives. Once a party has lost the capacity to leave his opponent uncertain on his future behaviour in their negotiating relationship, the bargaining power of the party opposed to him is greatly increased. The opponent knows precisely how much he can exact in exchange for the behaviour wished for by the other party and is therefore the master of the outcome.

Again, a very simple example relating to a used car deal can be outlined in order to clarify this point. Let us assume that a seller is asking £5000 for a car generally valued at between £4000 and £5500, but is ready to settle for £3000 because he is short of cash, the down payment on the new car that he ordered amounts exactly to that sum and it is due immediately. As long as the buyer does not know those facts and is uncertain about the real needs of the seller, the seller may expect to get somewhere between £3000 and £5000. Maybe not the full £5000 but certainly more than his reservation price of £3000. As soon as, through some betrayal of confidence, for instance, or any other means, the buyer becomes aware of the real conditions of the situation, as soon as his uncertainty ends and is no longer controlled by the seller, he will get the car at the lower price, and the seller has no longer any bargaining power left.

According to what was mentioned above, one apparent exception to that state of things seems to be the tactic of commitment, by which a party lets its future behaviour be perfectly certain in the case that his opponent would not settle on his terms. That tactic will be discussed in detail below, but it really does not consist only of making one's behaviour totally predictable. It consists merely of 'raising the stakes' and adding a new dimension, new stakes and new zones of uncertainty to a given situation.

Therefore the two theories on the mechanism of bargaining power are quite compatible. Both assume bargaining power to be relative and subjective, both base it on the dependence on the other party in the relationship. The only difference is that they insist on different aspects of dependence. In one case, dependence is spelled in terms of the existence or not of perceived other alternatives for the outcome that one wishes to accomplish in the negotiation and the degree to which the outcome is valued and needed. In the other case, it rests upon the control of uncertainty over the acceptable terms of settlement by the party. Both illustrate different aspects of the negotiating relationship and both will give rise to different tactics and strategies, but both are present in any negotiating situation.

Part II
The Process of Negotiation

The preceding two chapters were concerned with the way the environment structures a negotiation and sets some of its most important features; and with the understanding of this environment within the limits of bounded rationality, particularly to the extent that it shapes bargaining power. We now move on to the second stage of our representation of negotiation: the process. Within the structure outlined above, a process takes place. It pits against each other two or several parties, who are going to prepare to act and act towards each other. They will outline strategies and prepare and use tactics. Strategies and tactics are the substance of this second part. The latter will be later implemented through the actual moves of 'live' negotiators, as distinct from the conceptual parties. This will be the object of Part III.

3 Determinants of the Choice of a Negotiating Strategy

This chapter assembles a series of elements which are going to be the building blocks out of which strategy can be erected and tactics selected.

In order to decide on a strategy, a party will have to consider the weight of a set of elements. Some of these elements are issued from the structure of the negotiation, flow directly from the considerations of the precedent chapter and need only to be elaborated upon; some others belong to the level of the process as defined earlier and should be examined more in depth now. Together, the two categories of elements which must be reviewed by a party before deciding on the choice of a strategy include the level and balance of bargaining power, the consequences of the relationship between the parties, the objectives of the party and the nature of the items to be negotiated.

SECTION I – THE ESTIMATE OF THE BALANCE OF BARGAINING POWER

The essence of the negotiating relationship, as it was discussed above, is bargaining power. The orientation of a party towards one of the several strategic options which will be defined below will depend largely on bargaining power as defined above. This is not to say that the other elements that we will consider are unimportant, but bargaining power is likely to be considered first when deciding on strategy.

We must recall that bargaining is independently set, relative and subjective. Therefore a party should not limit itself to considering what he believes to be his bargaining power. Because it is independently set he should analyse separately his own and his opponent's bargaining power and the resulting balance of the two. Because it is relative he should use the grid of analysis presented above in order

63

to, through the evaluation of relevant parties, stakes, resources and constraints, establish the bargaining power of his opponent(s). Because bargaining power is subjective he should try to estimate his own bargaining power, that is to say, how much power the opponent believes that he has, and not what he thinks that he has himself. In doing so, he can use the grid, from the position of the opponent tentatively using it to analyse the bounds on his rationality.

In other words, he must estimate how dependent, in terms of alternative sources and need for his objective, as well as how uncertain on his own objectives and bargaining power the opponent believes that he is. He must also establish how dependent on him and uncertain, in the same terms, the opponent is. After that the balance of the two is to be considered.

In a rather straightforward manner it can be assumed that a balance of bargaining strongly in favour of one party will orient it towards a conflictual strategy, for it will be under the impression of being in a position of little dependence as well as having the means to obtain his objective. It is generally assumed to be the case. Rubin and Brown, for instance, even though working from very different premises than we do, consider that 'a party with high power tends to behave exploitatively'.[1] They also consider that equal power among bargainers tends to result in more effective bargaining than unequal power and that the less powerful party tends to behave submissively.

On those two latter points we tend to have a somewhat different opinion. However, it should be recalled that Rubin and Brown's conclusions are based on the evidence of experimental results, mostly individual negotiations, and that they consider efficiency in co-operative bargaining. When we deal with collective negotiations, consider conflictual negotiations also to be potentially effective in certain cases, and take into account the analysis of the observation of case studies, their results may be qualified with possible exceptions. For instance, practically, we tend to believe that in most situations the balance of the relative bargaining power of the parties will very seldom be considered equally distributed. One generally will seem to have more power than the other, for, either he can draw upon more resources issuing from the environment and the mutual relationship or he has fewer constraints. Intuitively, we may believe that, if this is not the case, chances of deadlock may be higher, for no party has a strong incentive to settle. Therefore power differences, in considering situations which may be co-operative or conflictual, may in some cases tend to bring a faster settlement. Equal power situations may drag on for longer periods, even into deadlock, each party retaining a fixed position. This view is confirmed by Magenau and Pruitt,[2] who quote research which supports the point that, when the power discrepancy between bargainers is low, they will be out of phase in their expectations and are likely to enter a conflict spiral leading to no agreement.

Also another issue should be taken into consideration. One should never underestimate the willingness of a party visibly weak and holding an unfavourable balance of bargaining power to go for conflict instead of settlement. He often has less to lose in absolute terms, even though this may not appear so in relative terms and it may also appear to him a good way to get even with the apparently stronger party, even though he has fewer resources at this disposal, because he resents its obvious display of power. For instance, going on a short strike may sometimes appear to employees a good way to get even with management, whatever the costs or potential gains of the case. In the same way saying no to a rich or powerful person may seem a good way to affirm one's identity for an ordinary man. This point clearly exemplifies the play of bounded rationality and the subjectivity of bargaining power. In the individual's rationality the cost of a strike may be estimated weak then, and its benefits high, because of the great weight he places into non-quantifiable issues.

SECTION II – ACCOUNTING FOR THE RELATIONSHIP BETWEEN THE PARTIES

(a) Consequences of the Degree of Permanence of the Relationship

First, if a relationship between negotiating parties has some degree of permanence, the relationship itself will have value for the parties, independently of the items to be negotiated. Its maintenance itself can also become a subject of negotiation. It can be an incentive towards co-operation for one or both parties.

A second consequence of a more or less permanent relationship is that it actually becomes easier to negotiate because some degree of trust between the parties may already have been built up. The trust may be reinforced by the ability to 'read signals' better among the negotiators – if they are regularly the same ones representing the parties – that is, the ability to gain the knowledge of what is meant rather than what is actually said literally. In many instances, this trust within the relationship will serve to limit the range of items being discussed – both parties have experienced an ongoing learning process. Therefore, here again, strategy is influenced towards co-operation. This impact of permanence on the attitudes is fragile however. This can be illustrated in the strains which develop when the relationship is soon to be discontinued. For example, in a case of international capital project negotiations, the refining complex is built, the plant is commissioned and in operation. Now the client and the contractor are locked in a bitter dispute over design changes and delivery delay. Both parties are aware that the trust generated earlier does not appear to carry over into these additional negotiations. The dangers of negotiating in bad faith should be underlined in such a case.

Third, because the relationship between the parties will continue after the negotiation, tactics and strategies used during the negotiation will influence its future, whatever the factual results of the negotiation. The use of a very conflictual strategy characterised by violent or scare tactics may create a climate made of various elements of hostility, lack of trust, bitter feelings and incentive to conflict for later, as well as a will to exact revenge in the ongoing relationship.

Fourth, it must be recognised that the results of one set of negotiations have long-term effects. Experienced negotiators are keen to avoid very sharp swings of the pendulum from one negotiation to the next. A 'victory' in industrial relations negotiations by management, that is, over wages per hour, may subsequently have to be corrected by larger increases in following years because of the need to retain labour. In the same way, in purchasing steel tubes for the oil industry a multinational corporation will be sensitive to the need to maintain sufficient manufacturing capacity to ensure price competition among suppliers, in particular as the manufacturers often have close links with their own government who may require local procurement in return for rights to explore and produce.

In summary, it is clear that the choice of a strategy, as well as the way the negotiations will proceed, and the tactics used are influenced by and are partially a result of the existing relationship. But obviously not everything can be sacrificed to the relationship. Altogether the items under negotiation have to remain the main focus. Also in a permanent relationship it should be remembered that the result of the present negotiation will compulsorily be the starting point and the basis for a next round of bargaining at some time in the future.

(b) Consequences of the Attitudes of the Parties

These are rather straightforward. A negative attitude, in principle, of a party towards its opponent, for whatever reason, either linked, but mainly not linked, to the issues under negotiation, whether ideological, born out of prejudice, or having some other cause, will lead to a conflictual strategic orientation and will be an obstacle to the introduction of any co-operative aspect.

However, the effect is also likely to be negative for the party holding this attitude. It can almost always be said that as soon as one lets ideology or personal prejudices enter the negotiating room, everything else goes out. The sanction is immediate and swift. The party who commits that mistake will almost certainly get a much worse deal than it would have got otherwise.

Conversely it should also be clear that a negotiator must accept having to face a very high degree of localised hostility over some specific items, important to both parties. This localised hostility may also be increased and complicated by conflicting attitudes over interpretation of the issues, undertanding data, different styles of different individuals.

(c) Consequences of Collective Negotiations

1 – Intra-organisational negotiations
The first consequence of the collective nature of negotiations is the existence of intra-organisational bargaining as defined above. As a result of this process of internal bargaining, within each party, whether formally or informally, a common platform of more or less explicitly argued upon goals and positions will exist. A broad type of understanding, more or less nebulous, will be arrived at for each side, before any formal negotiation between the parties' representatives takes place. The decision-making capacity, the capacity of the negotiators effectively to bind their own side, themselves and their constituents, by agreement, is only the capacity which has been vested in them by the various constituencies within their own organisations. Therefore one primary duty of the negotiators before committing themselves is to make sure that the necessary minimum of understanding exists within their own organisations about what is acceptable as an outcome of the negotiation. The first order of priority should be to get a negotiating brief from their constituents.

In practice, before negotiations can commence, as far as possible, a broad understanding should be reached explicitly on goals and priorities. Without it the negotiations would be reduced to a snail's pace or could not reach an enforceable agreement. A negotiator who would fail to obtain a clear brief in terms of objectives and what is acceptable as an outcome may quickly be discredited. However, for tactical purposes, this brief will be kept secret of course. In some cases, for the same tactical reasons, it may sometimes appear that the negotiators for one party are not in total agreement and have not sorted out their priorities. In some licence negotiations between Western companies and Chinese organisations the deliberate creation of two strictly segregated agendas, technical and commercial, negotiated by different Chinese representatives, has sometimes been able to obtain large concessions from an unaware Western company.

Conversely negotiators may have some leeway, within that brief, to arbitrate between their constituents' multiple demands and issues and to decide which ones they want to drop or to push, which ones they believe they have a better chance to negotiate, or which ones are likely to cater to special interests or will realise a common acceptance ground within their own organisation.

2 – The distinction party–negotiator and its consequences
The duality between party/constituencies and negotiators has several major consequences. It issues from the same factors which make it so that there are divergent interests represented within each party and that only the negotiators deal with each other.

A. Expression of collective rationalities

The logic and the rationalities expressed by the negotiators will be the expression of collective rationalities combining goals which were initially divergent or different and reached after an internal unilateral process of negotiation within each party between the different constituencies. We already have found out above that rationality is far from absolute even when dealing with a relationship between two individuals. Bounded rationality makes it such that it is initially chancy to make assumptions based on the rationality of the opposite negotiator. But here in a collective negotiation we deal with an even more complex situation. The 'other side's' rationality will be a collective one which is a lot more complex to out-guess or penetrate than a single individual's bounded rationality because it is already the result of having combined several or multiple individuals' bounded rationalities within each party. Within each party, arbitrations will have taken place before between what were at first incompatible objectives. Priorities will have been set among contradictory needs. Therefore each negotiator or team of negotiators will represent intrinsically different value systems put together and combined rationalities and on each side the negotiator will decide according to a compromise of different value systems as seen through his own bounded rationality. Facing the expression of a compromise and a collective rationality can produce some unforeseeable or unpredictable results at the bargaining table such as discontinuities and apparent incoherence. Some decisions may appear completely sudden and irrational to the opposite negotiator whilst remaining internally perfectly consistent within the party's collective rationality. For instance, two concessions with a similar cost for one party may have a widely different value for the other, if something specific has been promised beforehand to the other party's constituents. In the same way, a settlement of a labour dispute may not occur even when management backs down, over several weeks, from a 7 to a 9.9 per cent increase, but can suddenly take place in a day, at 10.1 per cent, if the union had promised 'to beat the two digit inflation' ahead of the negotiations. Collectively bounded rationality takes into account the 'objective' aspects of issues even less than an individual's bounded rationality.

B. Relationship between parties and relationship between negotiators

The distinction parties – negotiators means also that, as we mentioned above, the relationship between the negotiators must be distinguished from the relationship between the parties. Also the behaviour of the negotiator will be influenced by his relationship with his party. McGrath[3] carried out experiments based on the premisses that the behaviour of a negotiator is subject to forces towards three positions: the opposing party, the broader organisation in which all parties participate, and the party that the negotiator represents. The latter forces (R forces) are of two types: the role obligation of the negotiator to represent the group, and his attitudinal identification with a position of the group. Morley and Stephenson,[4] who review McGrath's premisses together with additional research, add that R forces may affect the negotiator either directly or indirectly, via his perception of his party's position. In any case this will affect the relationship which will exist between the negotiators during their interaction, and which could also separately be analysed in terms of their reciprocal attitudes, and permanence. Pruitt[5] considers that, in the absence of contrary indications, negotiators tend to view their constituents as desiring a tough non-conciliatory approach. He concludes that a negotiator for a party facing an individual negotiating for himself should achieve the larger outcome, even though he notes that there is no experimental evidence to support this point.[6]

Rubin and Brown[7] review the influence of audiences on negotiators. Audiences may be physically present or absent from the bargaining site, more or less dependent on the negotiator (up to be a constituency), more or less salient, and so on. They note that the simple presence of an audience, even without any particular salience or dependence, motivates bargainers to seek that audience's positive and avoid its negative evaluation, the more so of course if any such salience or dependence is present. Various other factors must be taken into account, such as accountability, loyalty, commitment and advocacy by the negotiators to the audiences,[8] but also status and trust granted by the audiences or parties to the negotiators.[9]

Clearly those various factors impinging on the relationship negotiator – party will apply additional bounds on the negotiators' own rationality as individuals, beyond the limits already issuing from being representatives of a collective bounded rationality.

SECTION III – OBJECTIVES

(a) Range of Contract

Both individuals within the limits of bounded rationality and negotiators for parties with multiple constituencies within the limits of collective rationality will formulate and establish objectives. For the subsequent analysis we will start with a highly oversimplified industrial relations situation in which only one item is being negotiated, the hourly wage rate, which could be likened to the price of an item in a commercial negotiation. Subsequently we will add a degree of complexity by examining a simple buy-sell situation. It is assumed now that each side, through the process we described above, has a rough estimate of an idea, at the outset, of where it wants to go and within which limits it can agree to concessions towards the other party.

Two possible solutions must be distinguished[10] and can be illustrated as follows:

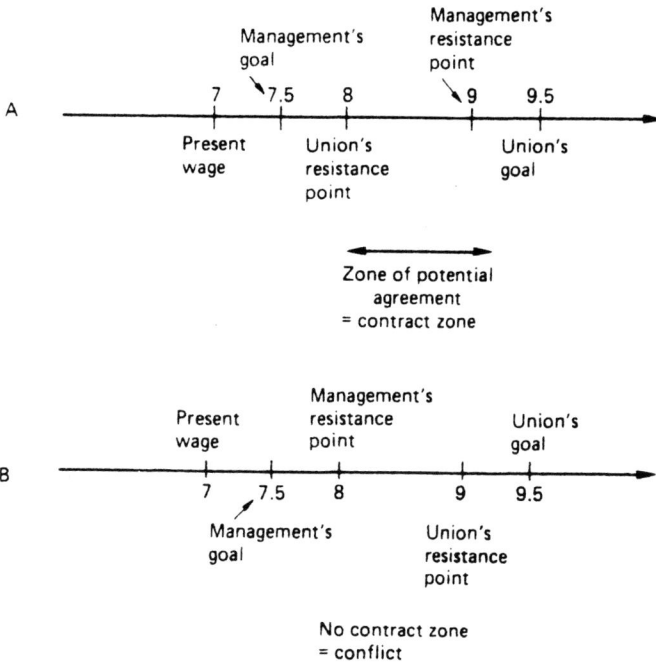

FIGURE 3 *The two possible cases for the initial contract range*

The current wage rate is $7 per hour. Both parties, management and the union, have a goal and resistance point. The resistance point identifies the absolute minimum acceptable. The union has to achieve an increase if only to justify its continued existence and the benefits of membership. The management has a maximum for its labour costs beyond which it perceives it cannot go and continue operating. Each 'goal' identifies what the union will aim for and would like to get and what management would clearly like to settle for. In situation B above, conflict seems unavoidable if neither party move its goal and/or its resistance point. In the other case, situation A, there exists a contact zone or an overlapping bargaining range within which at the start of the negotiating process one may expect the final settlement will fall. From this example we see that management would rather face conflict than concede more than $9 per hour and that the union would resort to conflict or walk out rather than accept less than $8 per hour. There is room for a settlement between $8 and $9.

However, this does not compulsorily mean that there will be a settlement even if a contract zone exists at the outset. The potentiality of conflict is not totally excluded even in situation A because each team of negotiators has a subjective utility owing to their bounded rationality which may be different for each figure. Besides, a party may misread the situation and 'overload' its demands, pushing them too far. Also issues of prestige, of principle, may take precedence over substance and draw the negotiators into a conflictual spiral. Finally, while running the negotiating process the goals and resistance points will be revised by each party and may shift downwards but also upwards. There often exists a period at the start of the negotiations which is particularly aimed at persuading the other party to shift their goals and resistance points or to demonstrate a major investment, financially, organisationally, psychologically, in the principle of satisfying one's own goals and resistance points, which of course remain hidden in actual terms.

In the same way, it should be pointed out the non-existence of a contract zone does not compulsorily mean that there will be a conflict. In a similar, but opposite, process a party may revise its objectives and resistance points downwards. However, intuitively, it may seem that it is probably less likely that an agreement be reached when starting out from a position with no contract zone than a conflict arise out of a starting-point with a contract zone.

Finally, it must be underlined that, in theory and practice, the existence of a contract zone, or its non-existence, is not known to the negotiators at the outset because each party keeps its objectives secret. This is almost always the case unless the parties have deliberately made a decision to avoid secrecy because of time pressures or to go out publicly because of a tactic of commitment. This seldom happens but examples of such cases do exist. For instance, in a labour dispute the government may threaten to intervene if, after a short delay, the parties have not reached agreement. Other instances could be found in some of the wage negotiations in the UK in the 1970s under the statutory wage and income policies.

(b) Limits

The goals and resistance points of both parties take into account both absolute limits and real limits. They are determined by the objective of each party. They can be considered as the upper and lower limit of a given bracket in order to simplify further. The absolute lower limits of the contract zone identifies a settlement point at which one or the other party would prefer to break off the relationship rather than accept the settlement. In labour relations terms this would be the rate at which workers would rather go to work elsewhere than stay and work in this given plant for so little money. Conversely the absolute upper limit of the contract zone is constituted by the wage rate at which management would rather close the plant and move somewhere else than continue to operate at that rate. They are, respectively, a function of the labour market and of the production function and product market for the firm. In commercial negotiations, they are very simply the price at which each party would rather go to the extreme step, beyond looking for another buyer or supplier, of changing its business or closing operations.

Nevertheless, in the case of formal negotiations, within these absolute limits a more accurate estimation of the objectives can be carried out. According to Walton and McKersie[11] the actual objectives are arrived at by the parties in weighing a subjective balance of the costs of possible conflict against the costs of concessions and/or advantages to be gained and the respective probabilities of gaining/ losing these advantages/costs. In other words, they are arrived at by estimating the amount asked for, weighted by the chance to obtain what is asked. We should note here that demands are almost always to some extent related to a scale deemed 'reasonable' for each party. Demands outside a particular range communicate a wish either to impose a settlement without real negotiations or to choose conflict rather than to negotiate. A management demand in the case of our above example of a wage reduction to $5 per hour or a union demand for $20 an hour is tantamount to saying 'I want conflict, I do not wish to negotiate'.

(c) Goal and Resistance Point

Conceptually and practically, objectives can be conceptualised as a range between two salient points which constitute its limits: a goal and a resistance point. In order to derive these limits we are going to follow again a procedure borrowed from the one described by Walton and McKersie[12] to better analyse how objectives are reached by the parties and how goals and resistance points are established. We again start from a present wage set by hypothesis at $7 per hour. Each negotiator will take into account the network of constraints described above and issuing from the fact that he negotiates for a group. Thus for the union each point gained above $7 will have a different subjective utility in weighting gains and risks of conflict whose costs are described below. We can assume that the utility of moving from $7 to $7.5 is very high because the union has to prove it is able to bring back something. 7.5 may constitute its resistance point. Depending on the rate of inflation, the profitability of the company, the condition of the labour market, and so on, further increases will still have high utilities, but probably with a decreasing rate of increase. These utilities are of course also influenced by the company's bargaining power, fixed by the perception of it by the union, within its bounded rationality according to our definition, which comes into play through the estimation of the likelihood of a potential conflict and its costs.

After one given figure is attained, say, for instance, US $9, we have reached the maximum of the objective of the union: its goal. Figures above that will have negative utilities compared with the potential maximum. Should the union secure an increase of between $9 and $9.5 per hour it may create major problems for itself. The utilities are subsequently not as attractive as may appear at first. Too high a settlement in these negotiations may require accepting a low settlement in the subsequent round. A high settlement may bring about a demand for similar settlements in other plants which the union may not be able to achieve without considerable costs. High expectations may be created among the members and become a source of potential breakdown in further negotiations or can result in forcing major concessions which can also destabilise the process. Finally, the union may even secretly recognise that too high a cost of labour may drive employment down by inviting the employer to mechanise equipment.

The same reasoning can illustrate the process followed by the employer's bargaining team in fixing the objectives in terms of goal and resistance point. He also weights his gains with the likelihood and costs of a conflict associated with each given objective through the lens of his own bounded rationality. He also acts within the network of constraints which constitute collective rationality. Finally, his choice is influenced by the same environmental factors, however differently perceived, relating to type and characteristics of industry, markets, bargaining power of the union, and so on. It can be assumed that the employer's side sees no positive value in cutting the present wage of $7 per hour. It is assumed that he feels that he must do something to maintain wages at the level of the market and/or inflation. Most employers see a gain and a positive value in keeping their present work-force, if only because on each shop floor conditions of work, of production, are specific to that given shop and probably different from the next shop doing the same type of work in the same company, not to mention other companies producing the same type of output. Because of the history of succession of plant and equipment and its modifications, because of the social custom of the work-place, each shop is a specific place.[13] Therefore it will take some time for a new worker to reach productive capacity, for, outside of the mastery of his technical skills, which may be total, he also needs to become familiar with the specific equipment and customs of the new place. Thus it is economically sensible to grant wage increases to keep the present work-force and avoid the cost of replacing people who may leave if the wage is too low. These costs will include not only working at under-capacity for some time but also the other usual costs of turnover in terms of replacement, hiring and eventual training. Further, some employers may decide consciously to pay slightly above the market in order to keep a quality, or hard to train or to find, work-force.

In commercial negotiations, this element towards a co-operative attitude can be assimilated to the weight given to the comfort of dealing with somebody trusted, used to one's own habits, specifications or idiosyncrasies. Nevertheless at one given point the utility for the employer of a wage increase, or for the supplier of a discount, becomes negative because it raises production costs far too high or decreases revenue far too much. Then it is likely that higher wage figures or a higher discount will have a sharply decreasing utility.

It is to be noted that, in experimental work, Yukl[14] has found relationships between goals and resistance points (called limit and level of aspiration in his model). Notably he found that they were positively correlated, increasingly so with time elapsed, and that the resistance point (limit) tended to remain constant whereas goal (aspiration) tended to decline towards the resistance point (limit).

(d) Costs of Conflict

In establishing their objectives in formal negotiations both parties will take into account the risk of conflict and the potential costs which would have to be offset against what might be gained if insistence on a particular objective results in conflict. For example, the question

A. *Case of a consumer product manufacturer*

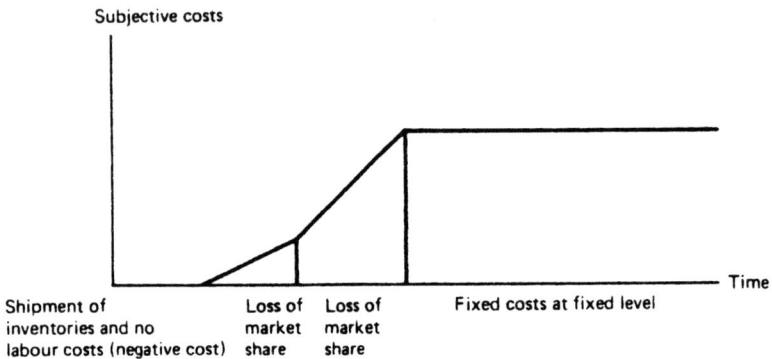

Subjective costs

Shipment of inventories and no labour costs (negative cost)   Loss of market share   Loss of market share   Fixed costs at fixed level   Time

B. *Case of a continuous process industry*
(Plate glass or aluminium)

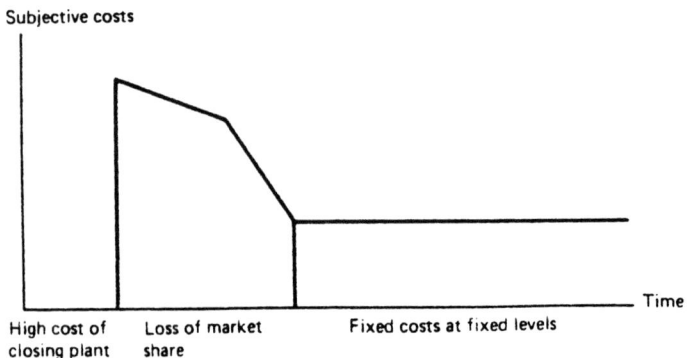

Subjective costs

High cost of closing plant   Loss of market share   Fixed costs at fixed levels   Time

FIGURE 4a   *Cost of a strike to management*

(Cost to be taken into account by the union in deciding on objectives)

Possible Case A

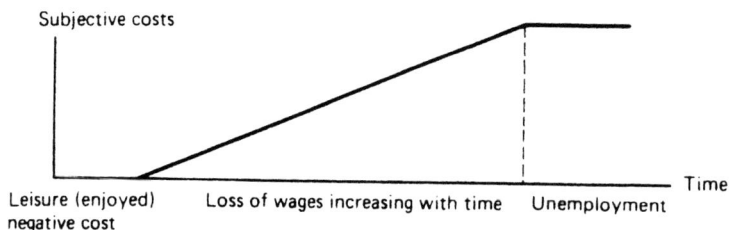

Subjective costs

Time

Leisure (enjoyed)   Loss of wages increasing with time   Unemployment
negative cost

Possible Case B

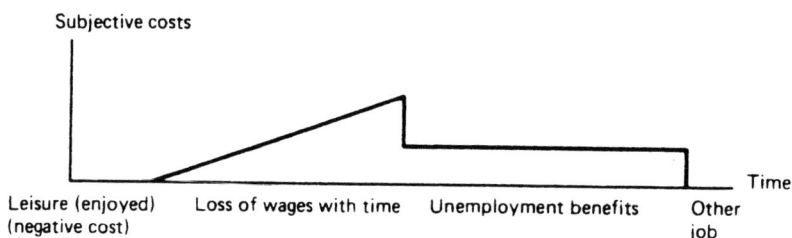

Subjective costs

Time

Leisure (enjoyed)   Loss of wages with time   Unemployment benefits   Other
(negative cost)   job

FIGURE 4b   *Cost of a strike to employees*

will be raised as to whether a strike of several weeks is not too costly
for an increase of 5 cents per hour (always in the framework of our
simplified example where no other stakes than wage are considered).
In a less simple example these costs can be allocated to three distinct
categories as Chamberlain does with the costs of concession:[15] direct
costs, indirect costs and non-market costs. The costs also have been
listed by Walton and McKersie.[16] The direct costs of conflict include
lost wages by employees or members, strike pay to members for the
union and lost profit contribution and eventual loss of market share
for the company. Indirect costs for the union include the risk of losing
members and influence, for management the risk of losing status and
potential damage to their careers or the acquisition of a reputation as
negotiators who 'rock the boat'. Non-market costs for both parties

are the reduction of mutual goodwill and respect, a decrease of trust and the acquisition of a bad image in the eyes of the public. Depending on economic, market and technological conditions within the industry, the costs curves will take very different slopes for union and management in each specific instance. Examples are given below inspired by Walton and McKersie.

(e) Objectives in Practice

Our discussion in this section until now has mostly focused on labour negotiations, but it can easily be carried forward into the field of commercial negotiations. When individuals negotiate on behalf of organisations exactly the same processes take place for all types of negotiations. It may be conscious and rationalised in the case of formal negotiations, sometimes unconscious for informal negotiations, but it should be kept in mind that it is always submitted to the limits of bounded rationality.

Commercial objectives are set with a goal and a resistance point and it is clear that not reaching a deal after it was seriously contemplated by both seller and buyer has costs for both. Only the benefits, costs and utilities are to be expressed in terms of commercial relations instead of labour relations.

We must also underline that our purpose above was to get a better understanding of how objectives are formed and not to present a guide on how to quantify objectives (which would be impractical because every situation is actually a different one). Therefore we have simplified a real situation. Nevertheless the method that we developed is valid in itself and can be used in practice to establish a checklist, which is extremely useful and not as constraining as a guide to quantification, if it takes into account the fact that real situations are more complex and therefore present more features.

In particular, to that end, there are two points which should be recognised. First, gains or losses and utilities are not strictly measurable or quantifiable because they are subjective and to a great extent unknown or hidden from the oppponent. In most instances they are not even precisely defined by the negotiators for themselves because of their own bounded rationality and also because they are likely to shift over time during the negotiations. The success or failure in reaching one's objectives depends to a considerable extent on the amount of information available – both about one's own position and that of the other party.

Information is never complete, it is always partial and a large part of a negotiator's work is to evaluate and refine the relation between subjective utility and possible costs of his approach on each point negotiated relatively to all the other points subject to agreement. At an elementary level negotiating can be construed as gathering a maximum of information from, and about, the other party in order to determine when it is appropriate to say 'Yes' of 'No'.

A second point which must be recognised is that negotiations seldom focus on a single item, they consist of several points. In commercial negotiations not only is price at stake but also such related issues as quantity, quality, specifications, terms of delivery, financing, and so on. This point should never be ignored and can be put to fruitful use, for example, in oil trading it is possible to spend a considerable amount of time negotiating over a 5 or 10 cents differential per barrel, which certainly can amount to a large sum for the total quantity to be delivered, but the contract which backs the agreement may also have opportunities for one or other party to gain or lose up to thousands of US $ on administration, for example, when and how payment is to be made. It is more visible in labour negotiations where wages, vacations, conditions of work, pensions, union security, and other benefits are discussed at the same time.

(f) The Aspiration Effect and Its Limits

A note should be added regarding the setting of objectives by the negotiators themselves. Taking into account the discussion just completed, it is clear that one party's objective, even arrived at through the most formalised process, will have no exact fixed value, whether it concerns the target or resistance point. There will be some amount of leeway around it, therefore a major question is whether the negotiator should correct it to upwards or downwards?

Several studies have demonstrated the efficiency of the 'aspiration effect'. A review of experimental work by Rubin and Brown[17] ends with the conclusion that 'Bargainers attain higher and more satisfactory outcomes when they begin their interaction with extreme rather than moderate demands.' This can also be felt intuitively. It is obvious that, in a negotiating situation, the opponent is seldom, if ever, going to grant on his own something which has not been demanded by the other party.

Therefore the aspiration effect can be summed up as 'aim high, settle high; aim low, settle low'. In other words, the higher the objective is set, the better is the result likely to be. To some extent we get from a negotiation what we are expecting to get before entering it.

Nevertheless there are limits. We have already noticed that an initial demand from a party which is unrealistic and totally unrelated to the situation in fact equals a statement to the effect of 'I do not want to negotiate'. In other words, 'unnegotiable demands' cannot be the object of a negotiation. Demands without that 'fantasy' characteristic, but nevertheless very high in regard to the situation and the possibilities of the parties, have also a negative effect. Experience shows that if a negotiator sets such a very high or tough objective and commits himself to obtaining it, this will have a number of side-effects upon the negotiations. First, the negotiator will appear more committed to his own opening position; he may become a mean concession-maker, adopt a very competitive strategy and be prepared to risk a high degree of conflict before yielding on any particular point. Within the context of imperfect information, the other party cannot know whether the position adopted is because of the negotiator's personal aspiration or emanates from instructions laid down by the constituencies he represents. Second, clearly excessive aspirations can undermine the credibility of the negotiator by forcing him later to make large concessions to get into the contract zone or 'realistic space'. At that point one large concession may not be enough – the other party may suspect that another large concession can still be obtained if sufficient pressure is applied. Third, it can also lead to deadlock for the other party is then obliged to hold fast to its own position for fear of being dragged too high if it makes a single concession. Finally, it will raise questions about the viability of the final settlement. Can a party who cannot be trusted for a relatively realistic appraisal of the situation be trusted to stick to a deal established much lower than his initial demands? Warr[18] warns against pushing to the limit the common sense idea that a huge claim will achieve more than a moderate claim and considers that there is much evidence against it. He represents the aspiration effect under the shape of a curve at first steeply rising, then rising at a decreasing rate and then decreasing.

Negotiators, and particularly inexperienced negotiators, may sometimes suffer from what can be called 'aspirational rigidity'. Even in the chance encounter or one-shot negotiations they can apply hastily-arrived-at decision rules or translate norms which act as an influence in that direction. This is particularly the case in cultures which put strong value on a 'tough' attitude and where rigidity and lack of flexibility are, mistakenly, considered by the general public as attributes of 'good' negotiators who 'play hard ball'. However, too high an objective is clearly counterproductive.

Therefore the aspiration effect exists but has limits. A question which requires an answer is how big should the aspiration effect be? Of course the answer largely depends on the precision of the relevant market considered. How exact can we be when we say 'the going rate' or 'the market price' for such and such an object? In a low precision market like housing or the art market there is quite a lot of room for the aspiration effect, whilst in a high precision market like that for currencies or gold, where information is total and almost instantaneous, there is very little room for it. Thus the correct way to answer this question is to ask oneself how much room there is for aspiration effect within one's business, be it within the framework of labour or commercial negotiations. Once this first question is tentatively answered, a good way to manage one's aspiration level is to set one's objective in terms of realistic number plus 'a nibble'. Within reasonable limits, and in general terms, one should not be afraid to up one's aspiration level. In the precise market, saturated with information, it may be a minute amount or even non-existent. In an imprecise market it may be quite high.

(g) Objectives and Opening Statements

It should be underlined that a major point was implicit during our discussion of objectives: it should be made obvious now. However, it is of such importance that it will need to be reiterated and elaborated upon a little further. It is clear that, except for the aspiration effect, most of the processes that we described concern only, and strictly only, the way one party arrives at its own objectives. It does not mean in any way that once decided upon these objectives are compulsorily communicated immediately to the other party. They are objectives not opening statements: they are what one negotiator and the party that he represents hope to achieve.

One last development concerns the elaboration of both the objectives and demands that will be communicated to the opponent at some point during the negotiation and in particular the opening statement. However, the two concepts must be distinguished first. The objectives are what one party wants to obtain from the negotiation. According to our earlier discussion of bounded rationality, in some cases, they may not even be clearly and consciously decided by a party. Nevertheless, in following with the logic of the same concept of bounded rationality, a party in a negotiation, formal or informal, will always have objectives, formulated to itself or not, conscious or not. In order to reach these objectives the party will at some point in the negotiation translate them into demands communicated to the opponent. These demands may take the form of an opening statement or a later concrete proposal or statement of position. These are tactical moves which will be discussed later. However, as already discussed, very seldom will one party make its objectives known to his opponent even when they are consciously and clearly formulated. The process we just described therefore concerns the formulation of objectives by one party for itself and itself only. However, the last paragraph, which concerns the aspiration effect, is applicable to both the objectives as set for oneself by the negotiating party and the demands, communicated to the opponent. Here the aspiration effect plays at full strength. Clearly outsized or excessively low demands will also have the effects on the opponent described above for the demands that are the translation of the objectives. The objectives, however, latent or manifest, generally remain hidden at the outset.

(ii) Classification of Objectives

Finally, a last point must be made about the objectives. In most real-life negotiations they are likely to be multiple. Besides, for each given objective several different levels of satisfaction may be identified. In formal negotiations, when they are relatively clearly and consciously spelled out and where one thinks that the other party has its objectives also clearly and consciously spelled out, it is useful to classify them into categories. A convenient process to apply to both objectives and demands and designed to ease their formulation will be described below when dealing with concessions.

SECTION IV – NEGOTIATING ITEMS

In the previous section we pointed out that it would be an oversimplification to consider that a negotiation takes place around a single item. In most cases, several items are at stake between the parties. Besides, new items may be generated during the process itself, often as apparently unforeseen consequences. A clear example of this effect can be easily illustrated: a trade union request for recognition or negotiating rights will tend to generate a list of new items from pay to safety. In a negotiation over the cost of spare parts for cars a retailer may want to avoid the issue of his failure to pay suppliers promptly. If, for instance, the agreement was for payment in 30 days, his average may have been 55 days. Were the retailer to press for a lower price he must count the danger of being asked to pay promptly in the future or face penalties.

Since we assume that a negotiation most often contains several items, it can be very useful in practical terms to try to outline the different categories in which these items may fall and to evaluate the consequences of this categorisation.

Walton and McKersie[19] have suggested drawing a distinction between issues and problems. Issues would cover conflictual aspects and problems might or should evoke a co-operative mode of negotiating. Whilst this distinction has obvious attractions, it also has problems and we do not adopt it here. In practice it may be possible for an issue to become a problem and a problem to become an issue. This dynamic will arise as a result of the interaction between the parties, the operation of an imperfect information system and collective bounded rationality comprised together. An experienced negotiator described the dilemma neatly: 'One man's problem is another man's opportunity and one man's issue is another man's non-issue.' Whether we speak of items, issues, problems or points, we are describing what is at stake during the negotiating. That is what the parties are bargaining about. It has value which can be financial, organisational or psychological. The key factor is that it is real and meaningful ultimately to both parties, although of course not compulsorily to the same extent.

However, this is not to say that the items cannot be divided into categories in order to ease later the elaboration of a strategy and the use of tactics.

(a) Categories of Items

An American writer[20] on industrial relations, with exceptional first-hand experience of the arbitration and mediation process, analysed items as being 'real' and 'not real' and identified three categories among the real ones: those items which focus on the institutionalisation of past practices; pie in the sky; and finally the 'laundry list' of in-between items around which the real issues are located. This analysis could be applied equally well to commercial negotiations mostly but not only when dealing with established, long-term relationships. The institutionalisation of past practice aims to legitimise and give the status of a must to customs more or less silently agreed upon within the past relationship. For instance, a food manufacturer may have, over the previous six months, provided merchandising support to a major national retailer in London. Now the retailer wants this support formalised. Items such as packaging, schedule of delivery, and so on, which were not initially the object of the negotiations and were unilaterally decided by one party and not protested against by the other party, when in fact confronted with it, also fall into that category.

'Pie in the sky' items should not be confused with excessive or unrealistic demands. They aim to prepare the ground for further demands and advances. For instance, in industrial relations, retirement at the age of 60 has for a very long time figured among the list of national trade unions' demands, only to be almost immediately brushed away when the negotiations started, by common agreement between the parties. However, there is no doubt that this use of it as a 'pie in the sky' item for a long time has prepared the ground for its present acceptance as a real negotiable item when economic circumstances have changed. Therefore 'pie in the sky' items should be capable of being conceded by the other party as a result of changed circumstances. Such would be the case for a seller whom a buyer uses to provide himself with one product for a segment of his geographical market. The seller who, over a long period, mentions, during negotiations for successive contract renewal, that the buyer should consider all the line of products and the global, geographical (eventually world-wide) market, may at first have this demand considered as a 'pie in the sky' item and rejected out of hand. However, if circumstances and the bargaining power relationship change over time, it may ultimately have the effect of making it more easily acceptable to the buyer. The concept of 'pie in the sky' negotiating items is aptly summarised by Bismark's words: 'a long-standing ambition becomes an acquired right'. However, 'pie in the sky' items clearly can be distinguished from the translation in demand terms of unrealistic objectives: they should not only be possible to concede for the other party on the one hand, but they also should not be insisted upon as demands on the other hand. To insist on 'pie in the sky' is probably one of the clearest indicators of unrealistic aspirations or a naïve and inexperienced negotiator.

Finally, the 'laundry list' of items concept can be of considerable value in practice, beyond the fact that it indicates the limits of a potential contract zone for one party, because it opens up the possibility of a wide range of potential settlements and may serve also to hide one's own objectives whilst waiting to discover the other party's position.

Another useful distinction has been suggested by Adam and Reynaud,[21] also in the field of labour negotiations. They draw a distinction between conflict on the rules and conflict on issues within the rules, drawing the attention to the fact that bargaining may centre around items recurrent in a permanent type of relationship between the parties but may also take place around the relationship itself. It thus constitutes conflict on the rules. Attempts to change the relationship, to break a pattern, fall in that category. Other examples can be found in items such as the frequency and location of meetings, the level of negotiations, whether items are subject to negotiation or what are acceptable sanctions and so on. In labour relations terms, this may be illustrated by attempts to change the bargaining unit, to move from regional to national agreements or from plant to industry bargaining, for instance; or on how many people can be present at wage negotiations and whether they should be paid by the employer whilst engaged in them. In the commercial situation a public sector purchasing agency may wish to insist that, in addition to competitive bidding, it requires the suppliers to accept post cost investigations by auditors to determine that they did not make an 'unfair' profit. Attempts to break a monopoly from each side or to move from sealed offer bids to another process would be other good examples. Here negotiating does not centre so much upon the substantive items as upon the process by which these items are decided upon. Conflicts on issues then would involve the substantive items; the discussion of wages and working conditions or the price of spare parts or the duration of warranties provided by the manufacturer.

In multi-item negotiations other categorisations of items can be used profitably in order to set objectives. They can include:

- Monetary versus non-monetary items. A buyer may insist that his supplier print a special wording on a food product stating, 'made with care for Jones Brothers' or demand that the product be sold under its own label. In industrial relations job titles may become an important issue – semi-skilled plant operators become 'process technicians', unskilled labourers are called 'plant assistants' and janitors 'surface operators'. However, union security provisions also fall into this category.

- Short-term versus long-term, that is, the length of the contract or the use of escalation formula and price review clauses on capital projects which may take years to complete, or the cost of living increases in salary negotiations.

- Contingent versus matters of principle, with examples of the latter being management's right to manage in industrial relations or the trade union's exclusive right to represent all staff irrespective of whether they belong to the trade union or not. Contingent items arise simply out of the matters of principle, that is, the frequency of unions' management meetings, the shop steward's notice board. Commercial matters of principle would involve international arbitration or the selection of a jurisdiction in advance in case of disagreement.

- High versus low cost items – a distinction too obvious to require amplification.

- Items with foreseeable results versus those with unforeseeable results, that is, a given amount of increase in price or cost plus contracts versus price indexation.

Rubin and Brown[22] draw our attention to another distinction which has its importance, and whose full impact will be better understood when we deal with tactics. It is close, but not similar, to the distinction that we made above between contingent versus matter of principle items. Earlier in their work those authors quote research to the effect that, 'there are strong culturally defined pressures on individuals in our society towards projecting an image of competency, strength and effectiveness to others regardless of the particular context in which social interaction occurs'; conversely, situations of deficiency and ineptitude are to be avoided or repaired.[23] When placed in a negotiating context, this means that, besides concrete or tangible issues, there will be intangible issues dealing with honour, public image, face, status, appearance of strength or weakness and self-esteem. The presence of audiences may amplify them but they are present between the negotiators, even without audiences or parties.

All of these categories of issues may and do coexist within the same negotiation, they often overlap to a large extent, and all items are interrelated to one another.

(b) Distributive and Integrative Items

This review of negotiating items will be concluded with an assessment of a distinction made by Walton and McKersie in their original study and which has been reproduced in virtually every book written about negotiation. They suggest that it is possible to distinguish between distributive and integrative items and that the former lend themselves better to a conflictual mode from the parties whilst the latter may give rise to a more co-operative mode.

In Walton and McKersie's own words, items 'can be differentiated in terms of two dimensions of the underlying structure of payoffs: the total value available to both parties and the shares of the total available to each party. Distributive bargaining is the process by which each party attempts to maximize his own share in the context of fixed sum pay-offs. Integrative bargaining is the process by which the parties attempt to increase the size of the joint gains without respect for the division of the pay off'.[24] The authors go on to describe mixed bargaining which combines both processes but to which they later devote less attention. We want now clearly to distinguish items from bargaining style, for we believe that the two concepts are confused in Walton and McKersie's terms, but we want to keep and make use of their initial framework, which has proved particularly useful and relevant.

1 – Conceptual differences
The point should be made within that clarification that some issues are distributive whatever the tactics used and the style the negotiators adopt to deal with them. This means that what one party gets, the other loses. The gains of one are the loss of the other. In game theory terms they are fixed sum or zero sum games and can be illustrated as follows.

If, for instance, the parties start bargaining from a position illustrated by point A and move to a position illustrated by point B, it is clear that party (M) suffers a net loss from point M1 down to point M2, while party (U) gains from point U1 to point U2. Examples can be found, for instance, in capital project negotiations in which the contractor is required to submit a fixed price which includes his own judgements about inflation of price of raw materials, the pattern of wage advances to staff, and currency movements. In industrial relations the inclusion or exclusion of a specific provision, for

Gains for party M

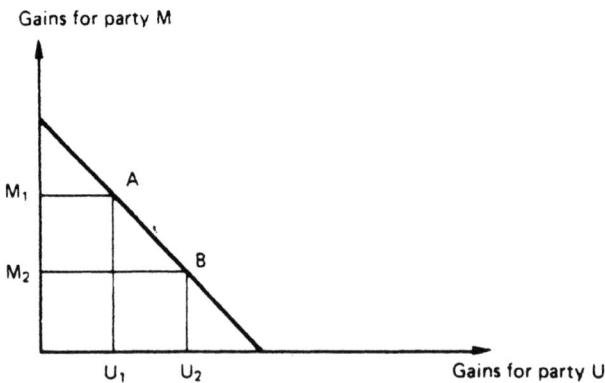

FIGURE 5   *Distributive issue or zero-sum game*

example, union security, may be described as a distributive item. Most 'Yes or No' items are good examples. If they do not reach agreement, the parties incur the costs of not getting what it is that they want from the other, but they do not forfeit potential additional gains. It appears obvious that these distributive issues are likely to be perceived by the parties and their representatives as being subject to the most competitive form of negotiating. Earlier we suggested that the negotiating relationship is characterised by a mixture of conflict/ competition and co-coperation. Distributive issues will incite the parties to adopt competitive/conflictual strategies which seem the more obvious answers to the situation in that case.

Conversely, other items are perceived in a different way by the parties. The opposition between their interests and positions may not be absolute. For example, a buyer for a department store may need some items because he is short of stock whilst the seller may have a large inventory and need the order. Obviously, if they reach an agreement, they may both win, if they do not reach agreement, both lose more than the cost of not getting their objectives fulfilled. These types of item are 'integrative' items or variable sum items in game theory language. Failure to reach agreement not only has its costs but also means forfeiting significative potential gains. Reaching agreement means increased satisfaction for both parties. In a pure form, the more the parties agree, the more they have to gain. Obviously, here again, these items are more likely to be treated at the co-operative end of the negotiating conflict/co-operation relationship; again without prejudicing of the actual behaviour that the parties are going to adopt. Game theorists illustrates those items as follows:

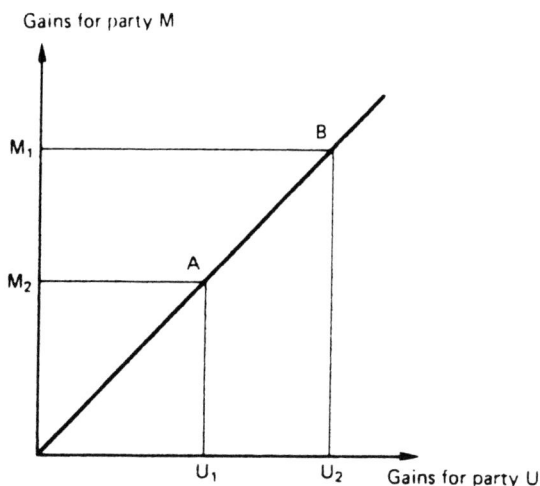

FIGURE 6   *Purely integrative issue or variable-sum game*

From the point O, of no agreement, where either both parties have no gains or can incur a loss at negative solutions, the more the parties co-operate, and agree, the more both stand to gain moving along both axes.

Such integrative items of course are quite different from distributive items and demand a very different type of strategy, tactics and behaviour. In industrial relations one can identify institutional arrangements which embody integrative items; for example, the US steel industry had for a long time a continuing negotiating board. In the same country workers in the automobile industry saw complex agreements in which lower wage increases were accepted in return for maintenance of employment. The British attempts to link pay and productivity in the late 1960s and early 1970s and the present 'single union agreements', are another example of attempts to formalise the concept of integrative items as is the present French pattern of decreasing actual working time linked with a shift pattern allowing 24 hours operations and a 'modulated' work-week.

Yet the same industrial relations systems we referred to show the limitations of that concept. For instance, subsequent attempts to introduce a time delay of six months before payment of increases based on productivity failed to overcome union suspicions in the UK. The same integrative item in one industry did become distributive in another. The distinction between a distributive and integrative item is certainly conceptually very useful, for it helps to distinguish two very separate aspects in bargaining. Nevertheless it might not be of considerable pragmatic use. Many negotiation theorists, following Walton and McKersie's framework, decided to favour integrative bargaining as style, regardless of the nature of the items at stake, as it appeared to offer a more peaceful, less overtly conflictual, approach to the resolution of conflicts of interest with less emphasis on the use of power. Besides, this approach was philosophically and emotionally in tune with prevailing cultural values of the times and the place where it was proposed, of which it embodied most of the specific features. But, for instance, cross-cultural commercial negotiations do not so easily lend themselves to that style. In our view the actual nature of the items around which the negotiations occur has too often been conveniently forgotten but yet it remains a central issue.

Therefore the operational value of the distinction between distributive and integrative items itself is not always totally convincing. Prior to negotiations starting, one party may perceive item x as integrative. Will he, on the basis of imperfect information and bounded rationality both at the individual and collective level, have been 'correct'? Will the other party treat item x as integrative within his own perceptions? If not, may not that item at least be perceived as 'mixed' with significant implications drawn from his ongoing appraisal of the other party's resistance? 'But I thought item x was integrative' is of little satisfaction if, at the conclusion, either no settlement is achieved or the negotiator is forced to accept the other party's goal because of their effective use of power. Conversely, there are also situations in which both parties may agree to transfer items from the 'distributive' category to the integrative one in order to find a mutually acceptable settlement because the costs of a conflictual approach are then seen as too high for both sides.

2 – Most items are mixed
We believe that most items are actually mixed items, not purely distributive or purely integrative. To illustrate this point, first, most

integrative issues may be considered as taking approximately one of
the following shapes:

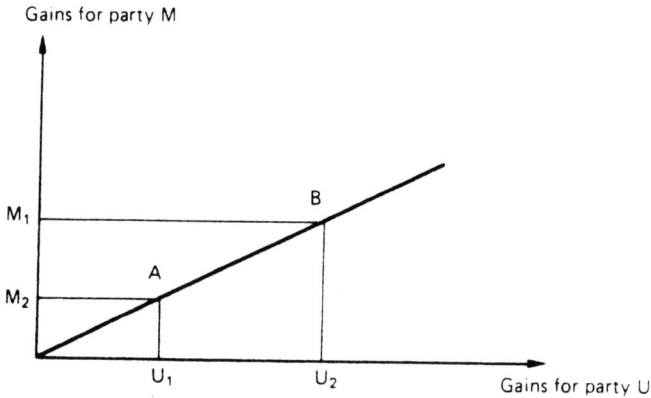

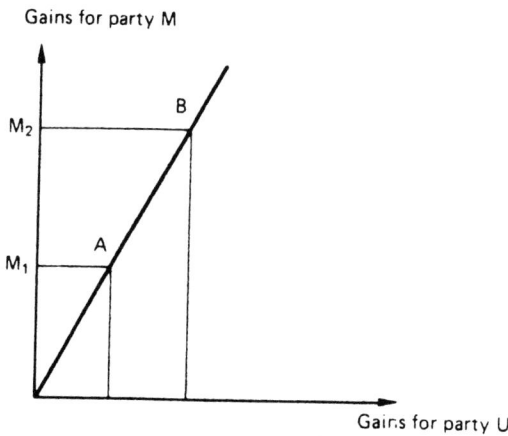

FIGURE 7   *Mixed integrative item; one party gains more than the other*

This means that, even if both parties gain if they co-operate in the
process and reach an agreement, one stands to gain much more than
the other. A commercial example illustrates this clearly. Distribution

costs savings can be made by a manufacturer through supplying his
large retail customers to their depots rather than their stores, who
may in turn benefit from lower prices. But how will these savings be
divided and to what extent will they be passed in price cuts? How
much of a share will the retailer obtain of the indirect savings caused
by more efficient route planning and scheduling? Bargaining with
ignorance towards the other party's utilities cannot be described as a
method of identifying integrative issues. Besides, there is no reason
to believe that the power changes in the relationship caused by the
move to an integrative negotiating mode, are worth a smaller gain
relative to the larger one to its opponent for a party.

Secondly, we believe that, in many cases, issues are actually mixed,
with some potential for co-operation and some potential for conflict.

To illustrate, the issues may remain integrative and subject to a
co-operative solution, the inequality of gains for both parties
notwithstanding, until point (A) is reached. There, for one, or both,

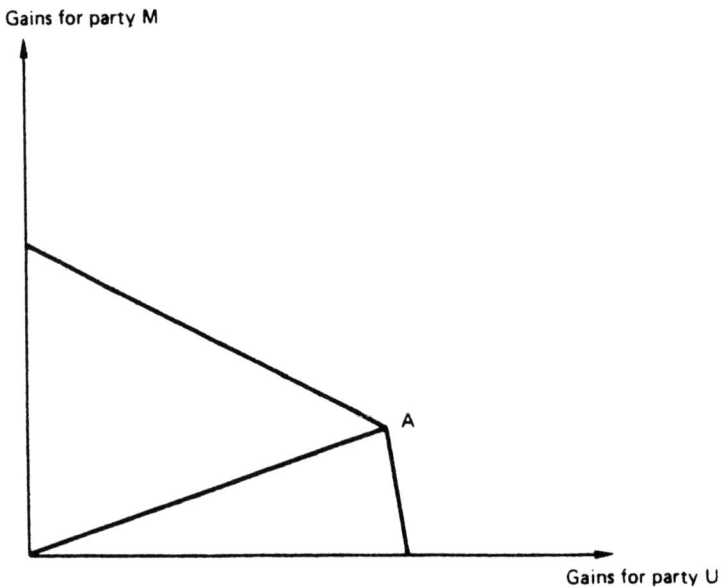

Gains for party M

A

Gains for party U

FIGURE 8   *Mixed integrative item: after a point the item becomes distributive*

parties it becomes distributive again, because a point of no return has been reached in concessions. Negotiators often refer to 'crunch issues' in that light.

In concluding this analysis it is useful to identify what may happen in those negotiations in which several or even a significant number of items are either distributive or mixed items heavily weighted towards the distributive side, but where room is made for a degree of co-operation. The parties may manage to complete their search for an agreement by the process of give and take or log-rolling. For instance, they may exchange a concession on one 0-sum item against a gain of another 0-sum item. From a set of distributive items, by trading one against the other, the parties have constructed one, or several, integrative issues.

Examples in commercial negotiating may be that a seller gives a rebate on the price but the buyer pays for insurance and transportation costs. In labour negotiations management may be liberal on fringe benefits and the union may not pursue the wage claims stridently. This now identifies a second essential and practical characteristic of the process of negotiating. As we pointed out earlier there is an ever-present lack of information. The first feature of an experienced negotiator is to be able to continuously gather and to analyse information. The second feature put in evidence now is his ability to identify and close the deal, that is, to transform several potential distributive items into one or several mixed items subject to possible integrative treatment.

Also it should be noted that the fact that most issues should be considered as mixed issues will have important consequences on the treatment of tactics later on. However, a consequence of the bounded rationality of each negotiator should be underlined now: There is no reason to believe that two negotiators will consider a same given item as belonging to the same category. Also, as Warr points out, each party is very likely to attach a different importance to an item, and, just the same, on the same side, a party and the negotiator representing it may attach a different importance to the same item.[25]

Finally, as for the consequences, it is clear that items weighted towards the distributive side, or the presence of a majority of such items on the 'laundry list', will orient a party towards conflict. The same result will occur from the introduction or questioning of 'intangible' items, as defined above.

4 The Selection of a Strategy

The formulation of a negotiating strategy is in practice an important task and it is necessary that a party be aware of its role and process and undertake it prior to entering the third stage of negotiation, marked by the interaction of the individual negotiators for each party, who then will enter into contact with each other. It belongs therefore to the second step, the process. In this chapter we will examine the elements to be considered to complete the choice of a strategy among several options, resulting from the combination of the determinants discussed above.

A few words are called for to clarify what we mean by strategy. Volumes have been written about the difference between strategy and tactics, where the first one ends and the second one begins, and what are their reciprocal roles and contributions to the search for an agreement. We do not wish to enter this particular debate but we need to clarify our own concept of strategy. We shall define it as the organising scheme behind the actions, attitudes and behaviours within the process of negotiating. The negotiator is faced with a bewildering range of choices, many specific actions are open to him prior to the start of the process. Once the negotiations start, the choices include additional issues, such as personal styles or team deployment. If these choices are exercised at random and without regard to an overall schema there is a great risk of this being counterproductive. Strategy is the unifying concept which guides the selection of the relevant solutions to the various decisions we have to make during the negotiations. Our strategy describes orientations towards the other party or parties. Tactics, styles and behaviours are the specific moves selected in order to implement strategy.

SECTION I – THE ROLE OF STRATEGY

Obviously the environment in which the negotiation takes place will influence the selection of a negotiating strategy. The correct reading and deciphering of that environment in terms of resources, constraints, stakes and relevant parties remains the required first step, the prerequisite to any negotiation if any hope of a successful outcome is to be entertained. It is clear also that strategy will be influenced by and will influence the objectives.

Bargaining power with its relative and subjective characteristics finds its source in the environment. One party's bargaining power rests with the other party's analysis of the situation, within the bonds of its rationality, setting the structure of the negotiation.

Nevertheless it is also clear, and it should be underlined now, that the environment and the structure do not imply by themselves that any given outcome to a negotiation is to happen automatically. They set the stakes, resources and constraints, influence the objectives of the parties and are the foundation of bargaining power, but are only a starting point. It should be kept in mind, and this is easily evidenced.

First, very different outcomes from negotiations have occurred while starting out from very similar environments. For instance, whatever the effort at pattern-setting from a national union or employers' association, some very different union local collective agreements exist in the same industry. In a similar way, commercial negotiations may result in a widely varied combination of results in terms of price and quality, although started from the same environment in terms of market, product, competition and so on, between similar parties. For instance, individual dealers facing individual suppliers within a relatively atomised market for a commodity will pass significantly different agreements.

Second, the environment itself changes as the negotiation takes place; it is a dynamic process. Environmental changes over the period of the negotiations will cause the parties to revise their perception of the resources and constraints that they themselves and their opponent have at their disposal, thus building new opportunities or destroying existing ones. New items for discussion will become salient and, most important of all, the parties will revise their perceptions of the other party's bargaining power. For instance, in commercial negotiations between a pharmaceutical manufacturer and an importer from a developing economy the dynamic environment may have the following effect. Initially the manufacturer is concerned with improving the profitability of his overseas sales. A developing debt crisis and discussions by the host government with the International Monetary Fund cause him to shift to a policy of building and retaining market share, possibly through agreeing to export of bulk product and local packaging, eventually to lead to licensed production. As a further step the exporting company may accept counter trade in crude oil from a recently developed offshore field. The shift of process is in part in response to environmental factors and in part from the continued wish to retain a flexible approach to markets. It is all the result of a strategy.

Then, after the analysis of environment, the assignment of the opponent's bargaining power, the estimate of one's own bargaining power as one expects it to be seen by the opponent, and the setting of objectives, a strategy to reach these objectives has to be mapped out. Without an adequate strategy, even in a very favourable environment, a negotiator can find himself at the bad end of a bargain. Conversely, an adequate strategy can, if not completely, turn around the effects of an unfavourable environment, or at least mitigate its effects.

One consequence of the formulation of a strategy is that the negotiator provides himself with a criterion whereby to judge his negotiating behaviour both within the negotiations themselves and also within the final agreement. The formulation and communication of the strategy among the interested constituencies prior to the start of the negotiations may also act as a form of organisational cement at its most simple and in some instances create for the negotiator the freedom of action and opportunity which he requires to achieve the desired outcome. A negotiator working in Eastern Europe alone seeking to secure sales of petroleum products for his parent company, a multinational oil corporation, can only do this effectively if the strategy which he is implementing is known to all other relevant departments of his company, including his headquarters. The person involved might put it this way, 'Out of sight, out of mind with a strategy, knowing that I am not tearing myself apart trying to serve too many masters – just one strategy.' But, foremost, the role of strategy is to act as a guide and as a framework for consistency in the later selection of tactics, style, behaviour and modes of management of the meeting among the potentialities described below.

SECTION II – THE DETERMINANTS OF CHOICE

Negotiating is a method of solving conflict. We have established that conflict is a built-in element in any negotiation because the negotiator seeks to satisfy his own concerns; his stake in the results is important for him. But we have also pointed out that negotiating has certain built-in co-operative elements. We negotiate because we want something, but we want it from the other party which has some degree of control over it, who can provide us with it. Therefore we want to satisfy the other party to the extent necessary to obtain what we want from it. In the absence of both incentives, to conflict and to co-operate, there would be no negotiation. What will determine the choice of a strategy is the balance between the two upon which we are going to settle. The other party will follow a similar process. The point at which we are going to settle on the balance between conflict and co-operation in turn will depend upon the stand taken on each of the basic elements of a negotiating strategy that we have just described.

(a) The Balance of Bargaining Power

It is of course of foremost importance. As discussed in detail in the preceding chapter, its effect is quite straighforward and there is no need to come back to the points discussed. A balance of power strongly in favour of a party will generally drive it towards a conflictual attitude, with the qualifications discussed above.

(b) The Relationship and Attitudes between the Parties

The relationship between the parties should be considered next. If one party feels that he is within a relationship which has a high degree of permanence, when he holds no prejudice or ideological bias against the other party, which has existed for a long time with a past history of agreements easily reached, he will of course be influenced towards a more co-operative orientation. Besides, because he sees the relationship in a positive light, he will have concern toward the other party's own concerns. Conversely, finding himself in what is felt to be a one-shot relationship, or involved in ideological disagreements, or facing prejudice or hostility towards himself as a person, or following in the line of a series of repeated bad past experiences, he tends not to push towards a co-operative attitude, as well as showing no interest for the other party's concerns.

As we pointed out above, the relationship itself may have value for the parties independently of the items to be negotiated. At one extreme, one party may put such a high value on the relationship that what he has at stake in the specific forthcoming negotiation is vastly outweighed by the importance of the maintenance of the relationship itself. He may be willing to go to almost any length to protect it. Such would be the case of a subcontractor doing 90 per cent of his business with the same customer for instance. Conversely, a party can put very little weight on the relationship, consider it of little or no value in itself, and pay no attention to it. This can be the case either because it really has little importance and the other party can easily be replaced by another one, or because it is felt the relationship is mainly of advantage to the other party, or because it is not expected to last, or because it is experienced negatively. This does not push towards a co-operative attitude. A state-owned public utility providing essential services to an individual customer would be in this position. It is unlikely to alter its set-up standards for price and conditions whilst 'negotiating' a renewal of the contract for the services it provides. It would also be the case in a sale after which the parties have little chance of seeing each other again. Neither of them would be inclined to co-operative moves in order to establish a relationship that they both know is unlikely to develop and produce later resources.

If the negotiations are collective, the relationship between the negotiators, to be distinguished from that between the parties, as outlined above, will be superimposed on it and may either reinforce or mediate its characteristics. This point has been illustrated in Chapter 3.

(c) The Pressure of the Objectives

Second, another determinant of choice rests in the weight of the stakes. In other words, it rests in the importance of reaching their own objectives for each of the negotiating parties. Partly it rests with the commitment of the negotiator to a given level of his objectives, and partly relates to his concern with the internal issues in the negotiations. This concept allows us to treat the effect of the intensity of commitment to objectives, within either a collective or an individual negotiation, on the direction towards conflict or co-operation, in the same way. In that light, the concept of issues of the negotiation really has two aspects. The simpler one is concerned with the idea of how important it is for the negotiator(s) to reach his own objectives, that are his stakes. It is set according to the process we outlined earlier: a strong emphasis means that coming as close as possible to the objectives is all important and a lower emphasis that some leeway is allowed.

A second aspect appears also as soon as negotiation becomes collective. This then carries the consequence, in the sense outlined above, that the negotiators will represent sets of constituencies. It involves the role of audiences, as defined, and how much the negotiators are committed themselves to reaching some objectives in the eyes of their constituents and how important success in reaching them is in maintaining cohesion and satisfaction with their own sides both at the negotiating table and in the process of ratifying the agreement. In other words, what are the constraints on the negotiators issuing from intra-organisational strategy and collective bounded rationality?

There is one point however that we need to clarify before continuing. It is obvious that the need to satisfy one's own objectives is a major factor in the choice of a strategy. It translates as the importance of the stake and/or the high importance of internal issues in collective negotiations. Clearly, the higher the importance of the stake, that is, the greater the need to satisfy one's own objectives, or the higher the importance of internal issues, the more the trend is for the strategy of the party to be conflictual and the less it will be to be co-operative because it is pushed ahead by the pressure to fulfil the objective. However, given that this is the case, other things being equal, the importance we attach to the relationship with the other party is an influence towards co-operation. Therefore, with a given state of the relationship, the stronger the need to satisfy our needs the more conflictual will be the strategy.

But at the same time we should remember here the earlier discussion of bargaining power. It implies that the more we need to satisfy our own needs the higher is our dependence on the other party and therefore the greater is the bargaining power of the other party, other things being equal, (that is, given his degree of uncertainty about our strategy and attitude and given the existence or not of potential sources other than him to obtain what we need).

Should not then his high bargaining power, contrary to what we have just discussed, make us tend towards a co-operative rather than conflictual attitude because we know that our adversary is powerful?

The same factor here may seem to appear to play in opposite ways: Because we need strongly to satisfy our objective our strategy will tend to be oriented towards conflict, but at the same time because that very same factor increases our dependence on the other party and therefore its bargaining power it should influence our strategy towards co-operation!

We want to emphasise that the contradiction is only apparent, for two reasons:

On the one hand, there would be an actual contradictory effect only if everything else remained equal; however, other factors come into play to determine both our strategy (importance of the relationship, for instance) and the other party's bargaining power (uncertainty about our attitude, range of other sources for what we need open to us).

On the other hand, and foremost, we should recall that bargaining power is independently set. Our high need to satisfy our goal effectively does certainly tend 'ceteris paribus', to increase the other party's bargaining power, but it says nothing about our own bargaining power which may be high or low and which depends on his dependence on us and his uncertainty about our moves and strategy.

Therefore our need to satisfy our goal may or may not drive us to a conflictual attitude. It is a factor which can play both ways depending on other factors and foremost among these factors depending on the balance of bargaining power: his power as we know it versus our estimate of what he may consider our power to amount to.

In other words, our high need for fulfilling our goals and reaching our objectives correlated with a balance of bargaining power that we estimate in our favour will drive us strongly towards a conflictual strategy, whereas the same high need correlated with a balance of power strongly in favour of the other party will drive us towards a much more co-operative strategy. Then, as described below, other factors such as the importance of the relationship or the nature of the items come into play to finally determine our strategy.

(d) The Nature of the Items

Third, negotiating items of course will strongly influence the orientation of a strategy towards conflict or co-operation. Purely distributive items will draw towards conflict, purely integrative ones will draw towards co-operation; we should recall that most items are mixed items and can be treated either as distributive or co-operative. We must recall here that all negotiations have conflictual built-in aspects. Co-operative elements have to be consciously introduced by one or both negotiator(s) without running the risk of opening their position to an opponent's possibly highly conflictual strategy. It should also be noted, on the subject of items, that if, obviously, monetary items tend to represent a high stake for each party, it is nevertheless probably negotiation on matters of principle which pushes towards the most conflictual strategy. The role of the presence of intangible items, which has been dealt with in the preceding chapter, must also be recalled here. Conversely, the importance of negotiation of the rules is not always fully perceived in all its potential consequences by a party for the reason that it often entails no immediate potential monetary costs.

SECTION III – THE FIELD OF CHOICE AND THE FIRST STRATEGIC CHOICE

The orientation towards a strategy directed mainly towards conflict or co-operation will be determined by the balance resulting from the relative sum of the effects of the preceding factors. At one extreme is the case of a negotiator who believes his party's bargaining power to be high, the balance of bargaining power to be in his favour, entering a one-shot relationship with an opponent distrusted and disliked in principle, for whom he has low concern, meeting their representative whom he distrusts and despises personally, committed individually to the objectives of his party which are very high and must be fulfilled, and facing a set of issues heavily weighted towards the distributive side and including intangible ones. There is no doubt that the strategy will be extremely and totally conflictual. On the contrary, a negotiator, estimating his party's bargaining power to be low, the balance of power to be not in its favour, engaged in a long-term relationship of importance and high concern to it, with an opponent looked upon favourably, and meeting their representative whom he trusts and likes, with a low personal commitment to his party, very moderate objectives on items strong on the integrative potentialities, with no intangible underpinnings, will be oriented towards a very co-operative strategy.

Each of the dimensions on which we positioned the two extreme cases just described may be conceived as being a continuum: bargaining power estimated from high to low, balance of power from favourable to unfavourable, length of the relationship, concern for the other party and attitude towards it, quality of the relationship between the individual negotiators and their reciprocal attitude towards each other, distributive to integrative weight of the items, with the absence or presence of underpinnings of intangible issues.

Each continuum ranges from conflict to co-operation, with the qualifications discussed just above and in the preceding chapter. When we combine the various possibilities that they offer and put them together we are faced with a range of possible options for each party.

The diagram[1] below attempts to summarise and illustrate the range of options for the selection of a strategy. Specific points have been singled out because they indicate prevalent directions for choice.

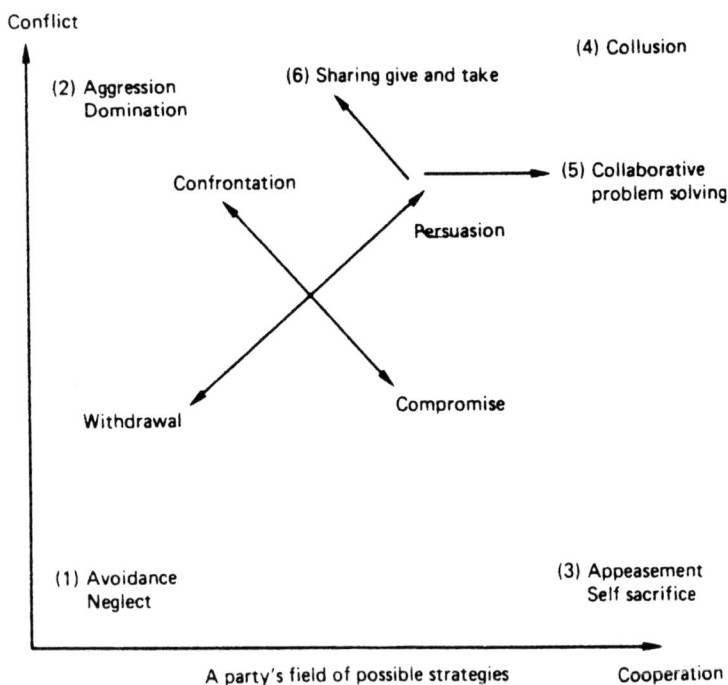

Conflict

(4) Collusion

(2) Aggression
Domination

(6) Sharing give and take

Confrontation

(5) Collaborative
problem solving

Persuasion

Compromise

Withdrawal

(1) Avoidance
Neglect

(3) Appeasement
Self sacrifice

A party's field of possible strategies   Cooperation

FIGURE 9   *A Party's Field of Possible Strategies*

At point (1) with a low incentive towards both conflict and co-operation, a party's strategy will consist in avoiding the negotiating relationship, not to respond to stimulus. If already engaged in a negotiation he will break off at the earliest opportunity. He will be ready to withdraw given any chance. He will eventually have to be persuaded to negotiate, or his perception will have to be changed. He has little to lose and thinks that he has little to gain.

At point (2) a party will adopt a strategy of maximum and open conflict. He will use all possible means of confrontation mobilising all the sources of power he has at his disposal. This strategy is characterised by an extremely competitive attitude where initial demands are hardly negotiable, pressure tactics are predominant and the opponent is considered as an enemy to be dominated. Many examples can be found in the commercial negotiating field when dealing with 'one-shot' types of deal when the outcome is important for one party and the balance of power in his favour. He has little regard for the relationship, to which he attaches little value, does not care for the other party's concerns and sees the items as sharply distributive, and/or he decides to treat them in that way. It is well illustrated by the conflictual end on all the continua described just above.

In our view the value judgements implicit in the language of conflict and co-operation should not be allowed to distract our attention away from the practical issues towards almost philosophical ones. A strategy of conflict, or co-operation, must be judged by its results within the relationship between the parties. A highly conflictual strategy may be unavoidable if the concern with one's own internal issues and outcomes imposes it. It should not be automatically discarded. Nevertheless its use is subject to critical conditions. There should be no continuing relationship, for it opens the door to reprisals. There should be no guilt from the party using it when the negotiations are concluded, for the practical effects of guilt can be as damaging as those of open conflict. The other party must remain unaware of the strategy used against him as far and as long as possible. Finally, it should not last too long: one should remember one of Machiavelli's principles, 'When doing good, do it little by little, when doing evil, do it all at once.'

At point (3) the need a party has for co-operation, and his incentive to co-operate, is extremely high and the incentive to conflict is very low. He will probably adopt a very conciliatory and co-operative attitude and be ready to give in as much as necessary. This is illustrated by the other co-operative end of the continua described just above.

There are cases when this strategy is unavoidable, for instance, when the permanence and weight of the relationship is all-important, the internal issues and the constituencies' pressures as well as the need to satisfy one's goal relatively weak and the balance of power seems all in favour of the other party. For example, a subcontractor doing almost all of his business with a single, very large customer known to be able to move quickly towards multiple sourcing, and negotiating delivery schedules and terms of payment accessory to the main contract which is in the process of being renewed, would be in such a situation. This strategy presents, however, strong dangers and is unlikely to be selected if other choices are possible. For it is an open door to disaster, even with integrative issues, if the opponent adopts a strategy of conflict around point (2).

Point (4) is a position of collusion. Both parties have high incentives to co-operate because they have much to gain from the other in the outcome of the negotiation, but they also have a lot at stake and a high incentive towards conflict. Nevertheless they can both shift their reciprocal costs of agreement onto a third party: examples of such third parties are consumers at the expense of whom trade unions and management can agree to pass on the higher costs resulting from wage increases. A commercial example may be found in cost plus contracts which characterise some arrangements in the defence procurement area.

Points (5) and (6) are both characterised by high incentives towards conflict and high incentives toward co-operation. However, they may differ in terms of strategic emphasis. Point (5) puts the emphasis on the co-operative aspect and point (6) on the competitive aspect. This dual possibility arises from one earlier point we made that most issues in a negotiation are by nature mixed. But here all elements are of importance: the weight of the relationship is high, the need to satisfy the goals, and importance of internal issues are high, power is estimated high on both sides and the balance of power is felt to its advantage or at least in equilibrium by each party. Point (5) would be ideally suited to more integrative items, point (6) for more distributive issues. Actually, real issues being generally mixed, the strategic emphasis will most often vary between these two points. In some cases its location may depend on the attitude of the individual negotiators towards each other or of the presence or absence of the play of intangible issues. Point (6) may involve compromise, give and take, log-rolling; point (5) more innovative and creative outcomes: it can be defined as problem-solving.

In practical terms, all six points should be understood more as strategic trends, strategic directions, than actual positions exactly and precisely defined. When the assessment of conditions clearly drives the strategy toward a direction, a second strategic decision will entail consciously deciding how far in that direction the negotiator wants to go. The first strategic choice entails deciding in which direction to go.

Also, and in practical terms, there will be few cases where all incentives drive towards points (1), (2), (3), (4). Besides, point (4) is most often unethical or illegal, and all-out conflict, co-operation, or almost total lack of the two are seldom encountered although it may be kept in mind that such situations do exist and happen. Therefore most cases in practice will tend to be found around or in-between points (5) and (6).

SECTION IV – THE SECOND STRATEGIC CHOICE – THE POSITION

Sharing and Give and Take, as well as Collaborative Problem Solving are not single points. They each can be represented by a continuum going from a very high level to a moderate level of either conflict or co-operation. The second strategic choice involves locating the strategy on this continuum.

Each continuum may be conceptualised as two directions away from a central position. The central positions being respectively a clear, firm strategy of confrontation and give and take and a clear, firm strategy of collaborative problem-solving.

Around each central position a direction goes toward increasing confrontation and the opposite one towards increasing compromise. It is not necessary to refine too much the number of positions on each continuum for, as will be discussed below, this would hamper rather than help the negotiator. Nevertheless it is extremely useful for the choice of relevant tactics (to be described in the following chapter) to be able to decide roughly where one stands on the continuum, whether the first strategic choice involved sharing and give and take or problem-solving.

Therefore, for each of the two cases, around the central position, two additional positions have been established below, together with the effect of their consequences on the choice of tactics. This gives three positions for sharing and give and take and three positions for collaborative problem-solving:

– Give and take very high/public, strongly loaded towards confrontation: a communicated willingness to risk a breakdown of the negotiation and/or a move towards open conflict: in industrial relations terms, a willingness to face a strike with the relevant preparatory moves by management in terms of building for stocks, customer relations and so on. In commercial negotiating terms, a 'fixed price' attitude, together with an explicit willingness to enter negotiations.

– The central position of give and take clear/firm: an acceptance of protracted negotiations in which threats would be made and the costs of a failure to reach an agreement for the other party would be clearly spelt out. The emphasis is on communicating one's own strength and the costs to the opponent. In commercial negotiations an example would be the announcement of a possible decision to move from single sourcing to dual or multiple sourcing.

– Give and take low/cautious, tempered with a degree of willingness to compromise: a recognition that the risk of not reaching some form of acceptable agreement might be very high and that only necessary counter-demands should be made in order not to provoke open conflict. A willingness to enter lengthy negotiations with a relatively low opening demand or a clear response to the opponent's claim which indicates that, over time, a settlement can be reached. In some instances with the help of third parties' intervention who reassure the other party that an agreement is not seen as unlikely.

Problem-solving low/cautious, marked with a potential for confrontation: a willingness to table a relatively long agenda of items for negotiation and potentially to risk a more expensive initial settlement which may only yield a benefit at a later stage. A reluctance to disclose large amounts of information because of uncertainty as to their use and interpretation by the other party.

– A central position of problem-solving clear/firm: the identification of major areas of joint gain to both parties and the quantification and presentation of the potential benefits to both parties.

– Problem-solving very high/public, loaded towards co-operation: the establishment of working parties to identify areas of potential benefit to both sides. A willingness to release information well in advance of the negotiations themselves at all levels in the organisation – 'an open book policy' building on the assumption that both parties recognise certain constraints and see the opportunity to develop their relationship through this negotiating opportunity.

In practice it is both relatively easy and essential that prior to the negotiations the negotiator, be he alone or part of a specially-organised team, should discuss with his constituents and/or fellow team members what the three stages on either of the continua mean for them, notably in terms of tactics permissible or to be avoided. To seek to do this during enforced adjournment will only risk bringing a condition of disorganisation.

No more than three points/stages should be identified in order to avoid confusion. If the stages are not clearly differentiated in the minds of the negotiators they will not subsequently be able to communicate them effectively in the negotiations themselves. The foreseeable consequences and action plans can be clearly spelt out for each stage in terms of resources, costs and benefits, which are associated with each one. Also it should be underlined that the choice of a given strategy should not be conceived as a straitjacket. The level of commitment to give and take or problem-solving for instance, changes over time, during the negotiation process. During the various stages of the process each party will continuously revise its strategy according to revised expectations and objectives, acquired information, attitude and behaviour of the other party, changes in resources and constraints in the environment and estimates of bargaining power. Typically these revisions are formalised for the parties themselves during adjournments between meetings.

Two operational consequences also follow from an earlier analysis. First, the identification of the initial position is critical. Should too extreme a position be adopted, movement backwards becomes very difficult. Negotiators become entrapped in their own commitment and often fail either to communicate effectively or to listen to the other party. They become prisoners of their own rhetoric. Besides, a move away from an extreme position may undermine credibility.

Even if we want to be co-operative we do not want to look as if we shy away from conflict, which would convey an attitude of weakness and appeasement and mistakenly be construed by the opponent as around point (3). On the other hand, hesitantly moving away from a commitment to a high degree of conflict may also convey a message of weakness. Consistency is important.

Second, one should move slowly along the continuum between confrontation and compromise, not by large shifts but very gradually, if one wishes to avoid the 'flavour of the month' syndrome. Credibility is also affected by sudden moves – 'blowing hot and cold on issues'. Although our strategy should remain flexible we must recognise that the early decision-making process tends to generate a momentum and commitment of its own.

5 Negotiating Tactics

In this chapter our aim is to understand what tactics are and how they are used. This is necessary from the standpoint of a party using a tactic, but also from the other side of the table: from the standpoint of the party towards which a tactic is directed. It can be suggested that a tactic understood is, in practice, much less of a problem to a negotiator.

Why do we use tactics? To alter the other party's perception of our bargaining power and his estimate of his own bargaining power as well as his estimate of the balance of the two. We aim also, with the use of tactics, to manipulate the resources and constraints in the environment, through the elements of it which might be changed in the short run and by improving our information in order better to mobilise or avoid them. Therefore we try to manipulate dependence and uncertainty in order to change the mechanics of power. Of course all tactics cannot be used indiscriminately. Tactics are the actions through which strategy is implemented and therefore must work towards its implementation.

Before we embark upon a more detailed discussion we need to recall the theoretical premises which we have established – the concept of bounded rationality and the specificity of the sets of goals of each negotiator. To a considerable extent each negotiating situation is unique and we cannot set out to formulate a general set of rules which will apply to all situations and will be effective under every condition. We can nevertheless proceed to a description and evaluation of negotiating tactics but therefore keep in mind that they are to be used within the limits imposed by the analysis of the environment and the strategy selected. A review of the literature and discussion with negotiators in many different contexts allows the identification of topologies or categories which can be related back to our analysis of strategy. The product of this review of tactics will be a much clearer indication of whether or not a specific tactic is appropriate, given a particular strategy, and whether it will be effective in the circumstances.

The first step in our analysis of negotiating tactics[1] is to recognise a distinction between certain general principles, rules of procedures which are worth observing in a majority of negotiations and moves and ploys and gambits which are sensitive by nature, whose application tends to be specific and whose use depends to a considerable extent on situation specific factors.

SECTION I – PROCEDURAL RULES

The key characterisic of this category of tactics is that they are dealing with the interaction of the negotiators and the process itself. They are rules of form rather than specific actions which aim to alter the balance of power. Their application should facilitate the realisation of strategies aiming at sharing or problem-solving. Two notes of caution, however, are necessary at the outset. First, we must be aware that the opponent may respond quite differently. In the context of highly conflictual and highly co-operative strategies they need to be constantly reviewed and modified.

Second, we have characterised them with the name of principles and opposed them as being rules of form against specific moves or ploys to be described below. As such they may seem to have a more general applicability than substantive tactics, but the above warning should be recalled; they also have exceptions and their use should not be systematic but carefully weighted in advance within the framework of the strategy selected.

Four broad clusters of procedural tactics can be identified: the control rules, the information rules, the concession rules, and the linkage principle. As it will be obvious later they can be accompanied and/or implemented with moves and ploys described later.

(a) Control Rules

In most cases negotiators consider it a definite advantage to control the process of the negotiations. They will try to establish their position by taking control and keep control over the various phases of the negotiation. Nevertheless, if the opponent balks, they are not going to relinquish the control to him, but will share the control if it becomes necessary and make attempts to regain it or exercise it jointly.

The most usual ways to establish and keep control are the following:

Calling or initiating the meetings may establish control at first. Then one party will have its own prepared agenda and attempt to have it followed. Control of the agenda insures control over what will be discussed in which order, and also quite importantly, control of what will not be discussed.[2] The best way to avoid argument and concession around an item about which our bargaining position is felt to be weak is not to have it discussed. This of course depends not only on us but also on the opponent.

Control may also be established by staging a mini-presentation about the situation, on several items, thus giving the other party a task to accomplish: looking at a diagram, a series of pictures, for instance. The party seeking control will use checklists and insist on every point of it. He will ask clarifying questions from time to time and summarise the situation, and of course summarise it as he sees it, all the while trying to obtain the opponent's agreement. He will also initiate adjournments in the meetings, keep a record of what is said and eventually decided, with the hope that this will become the minutes of the meeting. Obviously one is much better off in case of later disagreement with one's own notes as the minutes. In the same way, the negotiator seeking control will attempt to draft the agreement as the negotiation draws to its close. Also negotiators attempting control of the process will often use formal titles and language to emphasise their legitimacy in doing so.

Finally, control may come from managing the geography of the conference room. Negotiators may make quite deliberate attempts to either display and enhance their status to the other party by wishing to hold the meeting in an environment that indicates wealth, power and prestige or alternatively they may seek physically and psychologically to disadvantage the other party, for example, by providing crowded seating.

The European or North American manager who negotiates in Japan is often disconcerted by the use of conference rooms/meeting areas which do not provide any clues to the status and decision-making power of the other party. 'If you negotiate with the Chief Executive Officer on his turf you know which league you are battling in' was an observation made by an experienced oil company negotiator.

The long debate over the shape of the conference table which was a feature of the Vietnam peace talks in Paris in the early 1970s was a very clear example of the need of both parties to seek to establish their control. Commercial negotiators in an established relationship may deal with this problem by the simple convention of using third party premises or having meetings alternating between the offices of both parties.

(b) Information Rules

As was outlined above, information is always an essential factor in a negotiation. The better-informed negotiator almost invariably gets the best from the negotiations. When we remember that bargaining power is based upon dependence and uncertainty, information about how dependent an opponent is and the certainty of his reactions to our attitude will make his moves predictable. It drastically affects bargaining power. With enough information we understand the bonds on his rationality and therefore we can predict him and his behaviour better.

The basic attitude of the negotiator regarding information will therefore be to try to gain as much of it as he can about his opponent and provide as little as he can about himself and his position. Nevertheless the exchange of information is unavoidable if the negotiating process is to proceed. This is why most negotiators follow two very simple rules. The 'exchange rate' which spells out the concept that, on the one hand, one does not disclose more information than is obvious and that, on the other hand, exchange is based on reciprocity. The amount of information volunteered should be roughly equivalent to the amount obtained. A single review of our own experience will show that we feel most comfortable where there is incremental disclosure. However, when involved in a highly conflictual negotiating strategy, one may be compelled to break the exchange rate rule.

The second, very simple rule followed by experienced negotiators concerns the timing of information. In the initial phase only outline information should be presented. As the negotiations proceed details are filled in. In the final phase no important new information should in principle be given for it may open the risk of allegations of a lack of integrity, for instance, it may provoke the following remark: 'Had you said this earlier I would not have agreed to. . . .'

(c) Concession Rules

Negotiators must also follow rules relative to handling concessions. Concessions are often difficult to make for untrained negotiators, but they should be seen as part of the negotiating process, even in highly conflictual situations. Nevertheless they should not be made indiscriminately. Stevens[3] points out that concessions represent a basic dilemma for negotiators, for, if they are necessary in order to reach agreement, they are likely to be seen as indicators of weakness which invite exploitation. Pruitt[4] underlies that concessions incur both position loss (in abandoning a desirable outcome which cannot be regained) and image loss, in the eyes of opponents, constituents and self (in appearing ready to make a larger concession). However, not to make them corners a party into an untenable situation.

Experienced negotiators start by giving themselves room to negotiate – if they have not got real concessions to give they may start by creating some – the withdrawal of a demand is a concession just as might be the agreement to examine one item in detail rather than another. Linked to this is a simple point – substantive concessions should not be given unless the negotiators are authorised to do so. The negotiator who returns to his head office after a long and exhausting overseas sales trip will not be warmly received if he broke established policies and guidelines to secure his agreements.

From the outset it is critical to value the concessions both in one's own terms and the opponent's, for, because of bounded rationality, it is likely that a different value may be attached by the two parties to the same concession. This can also lead to the same concession being valued differently at different stages of the negotiations. A particular concession may close the deal or simply be swallowed up with nothing obtained in return if it is not clearly valued at an appropriate time.

Timing of concessions is also all-important. Starting from the simple premiss 'give little, give late', the negotiator can have the greatest impact upon the expectations of the other party. By not being the first to make a big concession he avoids the danger of raising the other party's expectations and aspirations. A major concession made early on almost certainly will prompt pressures in an attempt to extract further concessions. A negotiator who, being aware of the time deadline, will try successfully to hold out and avoid giving concessions too fast, may be able to avoid giving as many as he would have otherwise, in particular if each concession is linked to a counter-demand. The simple maxim, 'If you give, get', can also be used very effectively. Pruitt[5] introduces the idea of the parties matching their initial demands in a 'concession rate' out of which he derives a theoretical demand/concesssion model.

In practice, first one may ask for more than one gives, second the giving can be made conditional on a whole range of points and thereafter the offer can be withdrawn if not accepted in total and within a specific time limit. In oil trading, characterised by the use of telephone and telex negotiations, offers are often made 'fixed and firm for 15 minutes'; once that time limit has elapsed the whole offer is withdrawn.

In practice, also, a concession should be preceded by the conditions which are attached to it or the circumstances in which it is valid. Failure to do so results in the concession being taken up and the conditions being ignored. Emphasis should be put on the fact that the concession is conditional both on the final agreement and the conditions and that it can be withdrawn. We are all used to sale prices ending on a Saturday and 'normal' ticket prices returning on Monday when the department stores re-open.

There are some instances in which a negotiator may decide that, if he obtains a concession, he will not necessarily give one in return, as it does not always follow that 'if you get – give.' It may be important to signal to the other party that they are not in what you perceive as 'realistic space'; they must radically revise their goals towards your goals and resistance point. Unlike most people, who avoid it, experienced negotiators are prepared to say 'No'. But this is often followed by the question 'Why?' from the other party. The experienced negotiator will be prepared to face this challenge and provide the other party with the information which may cause him to withdraw the demand.

Except, again, in highly co-operative situations, goodwill concessions, with the only purpose of maintaining or improving the 'climate' of the relationship, should be avoided. Often they are seen by the opponent as a sign of weakness and he may become tougher and revise his objectives upwards. An experienced negotiator made two observations about goodwill concessions both of which are direct: 'What can you buy with goodwill except a warm feeling?' and 'If you negotiate with a shark do not feed him, all that happens is that you end up with more sharks.' In that light it should be emphasised that some negotiators, very competitive or conflict-oriented, are adept in manipulating concessions on 'intangible' issues[6] and exchanging them against substantive concessions.

(d) The Linkage Principle

The fourth and final procedural tactic is both simple and clear: 'Nothing is finally accepted until everything is settled.' The negotiator must not allow himself to deal in parts, or he will fall victim to the salami tactic described below. As the negotiations proceed both sides may exchange concessions (conditionally, of course). For instance, in complex multi-item negotiations the shape of the final package begins to emerge near the end. A range of concessions have been made, both parties have made trade-offs but it must be remembered that it is the final agreement which is both the objective and what counts. Giving partial agreement and granting definitive concessions on the way allow the opponent to 'eat you slice by slice'. Thus, as pointed out, concessions should almost always be tentative pending final agreement, and a party should retain the possibility of withdrawing them and not be bound by one-sided concessions. In the same way, in multi-item negotiations the parties may start by agreeing on the simplest and easiest (in terms of conflict potential) items. Such partial settlements should also be kept tentative. Tactical exceptions, of course, do exist, but even in the case of very co-operative strategies these should be carefully considered.

SECTION II – USE OF THE PROCEDURAL RULES

The procedural tactics or principles which we have described have a relatively large range of application; however, their use is best demonstrated by showing how they can be utilised in three basic negotiating problems which are encountered relatively often.

(a) Being under Pressure, Feeling One is Losing Control

At some point in a negotiation one may experience both objectively and subjectively the feeling that nothing appears to be working as planned. The initial conditions of calm and good humour which characterised the start of the negotiations have given way to panic and frustration. However, some options are available.

All of the control rules can be used. One can try to adjourn the meeting – without realising it one may be creating pressures on the other party, his constituents may want to talk to him, or all the phone calls that he ignored are waiting to be answered. One can summarise the position of both parties; when 'played back' it seems much less worrying. One can ask questions, in particular, the ones which seek to clarify the points that the other party raised; the subsequent explanation takes the edge off the pressure. In particular, when alone it may be worth taking notes, often slowly. The most effective use of this approach is if one is having to negotiate alone against a large team from the other side. It may be important to confirm points with each individual present. As the negotiations develop the agenda tends to fade. It may be appropriate to return to the starting-point and select the next topic or another topic about which one hopefully feels more comfortable. We should not also forget the very simple advice, 'speech is silver, silence is gold'. There are many negotiating situations where the effective use of silence can be quite decisive. How will the other party interpret it? Have they made a tactical mistake which has been identified? It may start to shift the anxiety.

The linkage principle may also be applied. Items can be linked logically and tactically. For instance, being under pressure when discussing the price of crude oil can be dealt with by reference to delivery dates or loading. A tactical link can be used. In this case the type of crude oil under discussion may have different value in different refineries – a link beween residual refinery values and price may therefore be made and used tactically to justify rejecting a particular price.

In dealing with pressure voluntarily applied by the opponent we would also wish to reiterate a point made previously: concessions should not be made to get out of pressure. The reverse may, however, be of great value. The last thing the opponent will expect is a coherently argued and well-presented counter-demand.

(b) The Negotiations are Stuck

There are two forms of deadlock and the negotiator must seek to identify which type he is seeking to resolve. The first one is found where there is no overlap in the minimum positions or resistance points of either party. Some experienced negotiators are prepared to recognise the situationally determined aspects and quit at this point. Unless the representatives of one or both parties can be persuaded to reappraise their limits then no deal is possible. The observer of the 1984–85 strike in the British coal mining industry could probably see that no deal was possible between the position of the National Coal Board, bolstered by government support, and the National Union of Mineworkers. After a strike of virtually one year's duration the return to work without an agreement was heralded by some as a victory, by others as an avoidance of defeat. In some sense this is an example of the peculiarity of industrial relations negotiating in cases where the employer cannot in practical terms hire an alternative labour force. In commercial negotiations most buyers will seek alternative sellers and most sellers will identify alternative buyers. But bilateral monopolies may evoke similar outcomes.

If the negotiators feel that the negotiations are simply 'stuck', but that they are within the range of contract and can be 'dragged back on course', there are a range of procedural tactics that can be utilised to move back towards reaching an agreement. They can choose from among the following alternatives:

- To restate the issue or point in dispute. It could at its simplest be a communication failure, in particular, in cross-cultural negotiations this could be the case because of the issue of 'face'.
- To watch for signals. For example, if the other party says, 'I cannot agree to this', does he mean that his superior or other members on his team will take the same position or not?
- To send signals. For example, we might say, 'We are not prepared to accept delivery in 40 ft containers because of the demands that this might generate from the trade union.' We may hope the other party will recognise that we did not mention that a 20 ft container would cause the same problem.

Both sending and the receiving of signals could be rewarded/ reinforced with conditional concessions provided the key word 'if' precedes the proposal and outlines the linkage.

- To use an accurate summary may contribute in a number of ways: by showing the progress that has been made and therefore putting a limit to the deadlock in perspective; by outlining the demands and concessions of both parties with the clear implication, 'Why stop here?'; by linking the accurate summary to a mental description of the costs to both parties of a failure to agree.
- To change the people and the place. For example, in some negotiations a deadlock may result from 'poor chemistry' and soured personal relationships. In cross-cultural negotiations Europeans and North American negotiators often underestimate the link, both perceived and actual, between age, seniority and authority. For instance, a 32 regional marketing manager in his early 30s may not be considered senior enough to really commit a major company to a licence agreement with Japan's leading brewer?
- To relocate a negotiation may have a major beneficial effect because, without necessarily recognising the impact of our physical environment, we respond to changes by becoming more alert.

Adjournments and meal breaks, by restructuring the mode of communications to a less adversarial one, may have the same consequence. The new location may also formulate or create the opportunity for informal contacts. We have all heard reference to 'corridor deals'.

– To use third party help might ensure the passage of new information or suggest the examination of new alternatives or proposals which neither party wish to initiate but might wish it could respond to positively. It constitutes a well-known answer to the concession dilemma. It might also be possible to suggest and organise the formation of a working party or subcommittee, which could propose ideas, and that the principal negotiators would not want to be seen to have initiated, because of pressures from their constituencies and intra-organisational bargaining constraint.

– To move towards other items on the agenda, leaving the contentious item aside for later reconsideration.

It should be remembered that with time circumstances change even if people do not.

(c) The Close of the Deal

There are some situations in which the negotiators on one or even both sides feel that something is needed to 'close the deal'. A range of alternative procedural tactics can often be used either alone or in some combination:

– To start by being positive. Without realising it one can become prisoner of one's own negative expectations. The negative self-fulfilling prophecy may have taken over. The experienced negotiator does not give up with the first 'no'.

– To try to proceed to a summary close – an accurate summary in which the negotiator highlights the concessions he has made and identifies the benefits that both parties have created in their search for an agreement.

– To resort to the concession close, which may be worded as follows – 'If it will secure agreement on the whole deal we are prepared to. . . .' In making this announcement it is critical to start with the ever present conditional 'if' and this might also be linked to a counter-demand. Concessions should be offered only where the other party has the authority to close the deal. In industrial relations negotiation it might be dangerous to use this tactic if the opponent trade union negotiator has clearly indicated that he must return to his members to put the agreement to their vote.

  – To offer the soft and nice close which might be worded as follows – 'I see your problem but our company policy on overriding discounts is well-known in the industry.' The negotiator is seeking to communicate that he is aware of the other party's demand and that in other circumstances he might wish to find a way out but that he is bound by existing constraints, custom and past practice. There is a discrete indication of commitment to a position which the other party should be aware of and therefore be brought to revise his expectations.

  – To propose a temporary solution. For instance, 'We could try this for three months and see how how it works.' The negotiator hopes to reduce the level of commitment required from the other party and at the same time hopes that administrative, bureaucratic inertia may subsequently take over.

  – To offer alternatively a limited solution. For example, 'Why do we not see how this works on the first batch and make any revisions in the light of the results, which gives both of us more data to work on.' The negotiator is seeking to limit the risk to both parties and create a mechanism for further agreement.

  – To remove the immediate time pressures and therefore take the risk of postponing the matter under discussion in the hope that a changing context may make the proposed agreement more acceptable. For example: 'We could delay the preparatory site work until the spring and this will also allow us to ensure that when we start there will be no delays because of equipment being held up by the customs authority'.

  Other closing tactics also exist but they are of a different nature: the either/or proposition, the 'or else' one, as well as others, belong to the more situation-specific tactics discussed below.

SECTION III – SPECIFIC TACTICS

Besides procedural tactics, a second category consists of the specific situational ones. They can be defined as actual moves and ploys no longer geared towards the process of negotiation but towards altering the perception of bargaining power and consequently of influencing the opponent's strategy towards compromise or confrontation. The importance of some of these moves, ploys or gambits is often overestimated in the literature on negotiating; they are of course of importance but they must be selected carefully and used sparingly. In the hands of the inexperienced negotiator they may dominate the process with negative consequences both on the quality of the agreement and on the relationship. In some instances an over-reliance on them may even be associated with deadlocks and bringing overt conflict – they are likely to lead to mutually assured failure to reach agreement.

Bargaining power being relative to a given situation, these moves and ploys can be used to increase one's bargaining power, that is, the other party's belief in his dependence on the negotiator and his belief in the negotiator's independence of him, as well as his perception of the uncertainty of the negotiator's attitude. Alternatively one can seek to decrease the other party's bargaining power by increasing one's own certitude of the opponent's dependence on one, one's lack of dependence on him, and one's perception of the predictability and certainty of his attitude.

We should remember that bargaining power is also subjective, therefore one can aim to alter the actual dependence and certainty or simply the perception of dependence and certainty.

There is a very wide array of these tactics available. All negotiators would like to be able to refer to a simple but powerful taxonomy of substantive negotiating tactics – those that work and those that fail. It would be a handy classification but unfortunately it does not help us in those situations where a tactic, having worked in one situation, does not prove effective in a second one! Again bargaining power is both subjective and relative and we operate within the bounds of rationality: ours, in our estimation of the effects of the tactics that we select; and our opponent's in that we do not know how his own will affect his perceptions of these same tactics. Therefore there is no 'sure fire' tactic. However, a detailed taxonomy may help us select the ones appropriate to a given situation within the framework of the strategy that we have selected according to the procedure outlined above. Four categories of situational tactics may be delineated: pace, information, people, and pressure, which can be relatively clearly identified and we will now examine each of these in more detail. It should be understood that this classification is built for the purposes of selection of tactics and that it has no scientific basis. Some tactics which we have fitted into a category might very well be placed into another by another observer and some are borderline cases. However, the following presentation is convenient for the exposition.

(a) Pace Tactics

Pace tactics are those concerned with the rate of progress which is
made or not made during a specific meeting. Some of the most
common examples follow, but we could all add more to this list.

  1. The repetition of detailed and lengthy statements – 'bore them
to tears'.
  2. Delaying discussion of an issue until circumstances have
changed – 'letting the problem mature'.
  3. Speeding the pace of negotiating in order to avoid discussion of
a complex issue on which the negotiator feels vulnerable – 'skating on
a point, or avoiding opening a can of worms'.
  4. Brief discussion of an issue which might otherwise endanger the
search for an agreement and the relationship – 'skating on thin ice'.
  5. Constantly bringing up an issue or demand which initially was
outrageous but because of its frequent repetition now becomes 'well
worn' – drum it and drum again until it almost becomes familiar and
no longer unrealistic.
  6. The long sitting – dragging the negotiations out in the hope of
securing a concession.
  7. The collapsed timetable – reducing the time for discussion to
force the other party to make all of their concessions in a short period
and lose sight of their values in perspective.
  8. The effort to capitalise on the time already invested in the deal
by a party. Without any firm commitment on his part, the negotiator
will multiply meetings, drag the negotiations out over an extended
period of time, in the hope that, after having spent so much time in
trying to convince him, the other party will settle on terms close to
his, rather than go over the same process again with a new person.
  9. Replacing the negotiators or team and requiring the other party
to repeat the previous meeting.
  10. Replacing the negotiator with a person of less authority.
  11. Using a negotiator who has no authority to make decisions and
must report all concessions/offers for review by his constituents.
  12. Using interpreters or staff with limited fluency in the language
of the other party.
  13. Shifting deadlines. The idea that a negotiation will start at a set
time, last for a given duration of time, and end abruptly at an
agreed-upon deadline is often false and even more often misleading.
Except in very specific cases, when it is imposed by an external factor

or agency, a deadline can be considered as just another item, that is, negotiable also.

14. Dragging out negotiations until the deadline is near. Then pressing for settlement and beginning only at this point to really negotiate. This, in the hope that the other party, already committed to other activities, will give in, in order to proceed and go on with his plans.

15. Ignoring the deadline, when one is set.

Some fairly general advice can be given to the negotiator who encounters the pace tactics being used against himself. He must recognise that flexibility in time management is essential. We can directly build or reduce our power through the management of time. The old adages, 'It all comes to him who waits' and 'He who sits by the river will see it carry the body of his enemy', contain a strong element of negotiating experience within them. However, it is also just as true that 'the early bird gets the worm' and he should not shy away from seizing opportunities suddenly revealed. Here also all situations should be considered as specific and warrant exceptions to all apparently specific rules. It is the joint application of the grid of analysis of the environment together with the strategy selected which must direct the use of specific tactics in each situation. For instance, the negotiator must manage his relations with his own constituencies to prevent them making him the prisoner of the other party's pace tactics.

We should also recognise that the negotiations do not start at a given point when the parties actually meet in an office or conference room. They actually start as soon as the parties know they are to enter a negotiating relationship. Pace tactics may be used before the formal meetings start: the telex, fax and the telephone are the most obvious mediums used, often with considerable effect.

16. Pace tactics may also be more geared towards influencing the strategy of the opponent towards compromise; they include use of check-lists to prevent partial and incomplete agreements. In particular, when negotiating on the telephone it may be felt that it is important that both parties should avoid concluding agreements that are incomplete. A major source of subsequent conflict and administrative effort can be saved. For example, in an oil trading company the introduction of an `A' to `M' check-list had two effects: deals negotiated were easier to execute and relations with other traders

were improved. There were no 'come backs'. Having spent a considerable amount of emotional energy in securing the agreement there is often an absence of attention to detail: for example, the omission of the other party's correct title and address without which payment documents would be delayed.

17. Having prepared questions and asking them. We have already made the point that negotiators operate with incomplete information and are often unaware of the constraints upon the other party. Simple advice is try to find out. Think through what is needed – frame the questions and start presenting them. The majority of us answer questions easily and naturally and regard as more sensitive and considerate the person who asks them. Clearly the corollary is also true. If you not want to answer a specific question, you can indicate this directly or indirectly. However, a failure to answer still provides the other party with information.

When negotiating with a team one way negotiators develop and control their less experienced colleagues is by giving them the task of asking the questions.

18. Using summaries. As the negotiations proceed and the number of issues raised increases there's a danger that progress will be impeded unless one party provides a summary – both of items discussed, the outline agreement that has been achieved or the scale of the disagreement which remains outstanding. Summaries serve several purposes – they act as an antidote to our short-term memory and our lack of attention and concentration over time. In particular, when negotiating with a person who is not using his first language, a summary may enable the other party to confirm the situation and thus reduce what would be a mounting level of anxiety or frustration.

Earlier we identified summaries also as a useful tool in control rules. We should be aware that there are several forms of summary: one which is accurate and two which are inaccurate. The former is self-explanatory. There are, however, situations in which the two inaccurate forms may be found. The first is the progressive inaccurate summary in which the negotiator seeks to include items which have allegedly been agreed upon when this is not the case. The second is the regressive inaccurate summary in which one or the other party seeks to withdraw or back out of a concession previously made. The more suitable forms of progressive and regressive summaries appear by use of language to alter the qualitative nature of the meeting. These may be signalled by such phrases as 'I feel that we are making a lot of progress' or 'Clearly we have a long way to go as we appear to be very far apart.'

19. Adjournments. In many meetings the use of adjournments may facilitate both the process of reaching an agreement and improve the quality of that agreement. We are all aware of the danger of being caught up in a tide of events which causes us to lose our sense of perspective. Equally we have experienced the negative impact of fatigue on the quality of judgements we have made and on our effectiveness, both when alone and when acting together within a team. Adjournments offer many opportunities and benefits. Some can be organised around the natural timetable of the day or the week – meal breaks, weekends, and so on. Others may be much more spontaneous – the time to break off the meeting for only a few minutes whilst a point is communicated to a colleague or an offer or demand is renewed. In many instances an adjournment should be regarded as an opportunity afforded to the other party to consult with one or more of his constituencies not represented directly in the meeting and it should be used for the same purpose by the negotiator. Information presented either immediately before adjournment or directly after the meeting is resumed may have both greater perceived value and impact.

It should be recognised that, when bringing new ideas and/or facts or ideas which do not compulsorily belong to the bounded rationality of the other party, or may even seem contradictory to reason within its framework, time is of primordial importance. We need time to accept new ideas or facts: time to identify that they exist, that we can adjust to them, that they may influence us. Therefore, when bringing out one's own position, one should be careful to outline it slowly, element after element, while allowing sufficient time for each element for exposition of the ideas and for the other party to ponder them. Simply to realise that a point is new, then, is of importance and to be considered seriously already demands time.

(b) Information Tactics

Information tactics deal with the use of data during the negotiating process. As we have already noted, information forms a crucial element in the process. Handling it well can increase one's bargaining power. The effective management of information can cause the other party to review his own position, the cost of moves, and, foremost, alter his bargaining power through the manipulation and reduction of uncertainty. According to the same principles a party well informed about the other's strategy and objective will get the most out of the negotiation by controlling its uncertainties. Conversely, the handling of information is a powerful means of increasing one's bargaining power, the dependence of the other party upon oneself, the other party's uncertainty about one's own moves, the consequences, and the costs he incurs.

Information tactics can be subdivided into two broad subsets. The first one is concerned with its collection, interpretation and evaluation and the second with its communication or handling both before and during the meeting.

1 - Collection
A consequence of bounded rationality and of the dynamic character of the negotiating process is that information about the environment and the other party is always incomplete. Therefore to acquire, permanently improve, and keep up to date information is a primary prerequisite of negotiation. Questions about the other party's objectives and resistance points can only at best be partially answered. For instance, what do the demands represent? Goals to which the party is committed? 'Testing' the waters, or a wild shot or desperate gamble to achieve a normally impossible result? Under how much pressure is the negotiator to settle? It is often surprising how negotiators fail to utilise all the sources within their own organisation. Answers to this set of simple questions from colleagues could prove very valuable: 'Who knows their negotiator?' 'How does he react?' 'What happened in previous contacts? Do we have any contact with their negotiator outside this face-to-face encounter? What do we know about his party, its organisation, its turnover, assets, and so on? Are there reports about their negotiations with other companies in the same industry including our competitors?' Without difficulty the negotiator can and should, alone and with others, build his information bank. The growing interest in competitor intelligence systems by companies in many areas of high technology and the capital intensive process industries should reinforce the point. Efficient marketing, the implementation edge of competitive strategy, will be hampered without an

effective intelligence-gathering system. No military commander would wish to involve himself in a major operation without his sources of accurate and up-to-date information. Why should the negotiator ignore this accumulated learning?

There is never enough information about the opponent's situation and position and how it evolves. A remark should be made here. According to the discussed pace/time tactics, one can probably get more information before the formal negotiation starts but when one already knows that a negotiating relationship will develop. The opponent tends to be less guarded then and anyway it is useful to do one's homework in advance.

2 – Management

Information tactics include not only the acquisition of information but also its management during the meetings (that is, communication and retention) in addition to the simple rule of the exchange rate already discussed. On the one hand, a party will want to prevent the opponent from gaining useful information detrimental to one's own position, but on the other hand one wants to communicate information useful to reaching agreement. How much, who, when, why? – the answers to the questions should take into account the procedural tactics mentioned earlier – both with regard to control and the process of information management (the exchange rate and the timing rules). Our discussion here will focus on the substantive issues:

1. Give an absolute minimum. 'What they do not know will not concern them.' It is an often heard response in industrial relations when managers feel that the detailed level of the order-book, the backlog, should not be disclosed. However, the other party may have this information already from other channels or may be able to ignore its absence in the meeting itself. A reply to the denial of information could take the following form: 'If management won't tell us, that is their problem – we simply want our members' claims for an increase in line with changes in the cost of living met today.'

2. Give too much information – often unstructured, 'doing a snow job'. For example: 'If they want the test results they can have them, and the calculations and the print-outs, let us give them the whole lot – and let them sort it out?' In other words, either the relevant information is drowned in meaningless data or not enough time is available to the opponent to process raw 'data' into information.

3. One person insisting on giving an overly detailed response. The expert witness who will usually come armed with data and self-justification should be asked to summarise his key points.

4. Taking one point in a presentation, discovering an error in a table of statistics or a typographical mistake, focusing attention on it and using this to disregard all the data in support of a case. The reasoning is along the following lines: 'I have found one error, how many more will I find if I start to dig deeply? . . . Please do not try passing shoddy results off on me.' One should then admit the error but not withdraw the case.

5. Being the out-of-context optimist. 'One good result confirms the case!'

It should be noted that, except for a conscious and well-weighted decision to resort to disinformation, it is often generally inadvisable to provide incorrect or false information, even in extreme conflictual situations. Apart from purely ethical or moral problems, if discovered it totally destroys any kind of credibility for any other tactics and opens the door as well to measures of retaliation. The modulation of information, correct in itself but over- or under-stated, is less dangerous but always difficult to manipulate and can also create problems of credibility. The old 'cry wolf' saying fully applies here. This of course does not means that all the information one has available should be candidly offered to the opponent. Information detrimental to one's position should be selectively withheld and favourable information suitably emphasised. In a similar way, information communicated by one's opponent can be ignored if detrimental, built upon if useful, or opposed by counter information from your own source.

The use of experts in negotiations to sustain one's position has about the same convincing value as the use of statistics, already discussed above, in the theory of negotiation. If the opponent produces an expert, one can generally bring one's own. Someone can always be found who is the author of three books, five monographs and ten articles in learned journals to sustain an opinion contrary to that of the other party's expert, who has merely written three books, five articles and no monographs at all.

Finally, a last set of information tactics deals with the manipulation of communication channels.

In the use of the situational information tactics it is a major area of discretion that the negotiator has. He can, for instance, in some cases have access and resort to the media; newspapers, radio and TV have strong impact. Regular communication mechanisms are easier to use – for example, the Annual Report, quarterly statements and reports of results. Sales and promotional literature can be made more or less explicit on a particular point. For example, a company manufacturing uninterrupted power supply systems and static inverters may show their equipment being air freighted or placed in earthquake-resistant cabinets – with the implication that it is part of a standard financial package or an extra paid for by the client. During wage negotiations present actual wages may be published by management.

The printed word often has the power of legitimacy. Somehow if it is written it is true! We appear to be unwilling to argue with a price tag at Harrods in London but feel no doubts on being entitled to do so on holiday in a street market in Morocco.

As a general rule, it is almost always necessary to keep open a channel of communication and/or the possibility of reopening the negotiations with the opponent, even after a deadlock when negotiators have separated. The position of one or both parties may evolve and, if no communication is possible, the negotiation will nevertheless abort, because one party has no way of knowing that the other party's position has changed, and by how much it has changed. Thus it is very often useful at the end of an unsuccessful meeting to think of fixing a date deadline for exploring the possibility of a new meeting, or to agree to call each other to check positions, or to keep messages running between the two parties.

As it has been pointed out that this is the case for all general rules, this one also sustains exceptions. A given information tactic consists precisely, in front of a deadline and an offer, of breaking off communications, in order to leave the other party with the responsibility of open conflict, by making an offer and denying the other the possibility of making a counter offer or any other tactical move. Such a tactic was followed during a labour conflict involving the French airline controllers. Their opponent was the French Government, and the union had set a strike deadline for the Monday. On the Thursday the Minister of Transport made a wage and conditions offer to the union, and until Monday morning the Minister, his assistants, all persons able to modify it, were away and unable to be reached. However, although dealing with the manipulation of communications, this tactic is strongly linked with the pressure tactics to be examined later.

One of the main barriers to communication is the other party's bounded rationality as well as one's own. Your rationality may not make sense for him. All the information communicated to him may be disregarded, or considered irrelevant to his case, or simply not heard because it does not fit with his understanding of the facts. Therefore several points should be kept in mind. First, as was emphasised above, logic will be of little help. One's logic, based on one's understanding of the environment and one's own bounded rationality, will have little or no effect on the opponent even if it reinforces one's own conviction of the rightfulness of one's case. Secondly, the pace tactics here are of major impact and should be linked with the information tactics. New information demands a long time to be communicated, evaluated and thoroughly assimilated. Thirdly, abstract information and reasoning is of little use. One is seldom persuaded by abstract reasoning but rather only by very concrete facts that one can compare readily with one's own situation.

Also, often as negotiations proceed, the decision about who should communicate the information becomes sometimes almost as important as what is actually said. If the two senior negotiators are locked into an apparently adversarial relationship lower status team members may be used. 'He will take it from you but not from me' illustrates this situation.

In many commercial negotiations and in cross-cultural negotiations it may become important to manage the location of communication. What is said apparently informally over dinner in a 'getting to know you' situation will have a very different impact in the more formal structure of the conference room. Many negotiators actively seek prior informal contact for two reasons: first, to 'get a feel' for how the other party reacts to a wide range of ideas and points; and second, to check whether there are any barriers to communication. For example, if negotiating with a French importer who previously had only considered importing German cars into France and whose English is 'rusty', the English negotiator, instead of making a greater effort to use his schoolboy French, may hire a French-speaking colleague or use an interpreter.

(c) People Tactics

These refer to any attempt to make a distinction between the negotiator in his role, for example, as a representative of a party, and the role occupant himself.

We should, for example, recognise that negotiators can be said to operate at several levels of authority. One may find oneself negotiating with (a) the boss (the chief executive officer) who will be prepared to make a decision; (b) a member of the organisation decision-making team – a member of the board who may decide to refer back to his colleagues a particular proposal, although he may technically have full authority on the subject – this negotiator is often aware that his willingness to discuss issues with his colleagues develops trust and may protect him in those situations where he needs to make a decision without their direct involvement; (c) the delegated representative who has complete freedom of manoeuvre with a clearly drawn brief or remit. For instance, a negotiator who has been instructed, 'You can pay up to $27 for Brut delivered 1st July, Rotterdam, FOB', clearly can settle the deal at $26.90 but not at $27.10. Many trade union officials, when negotiating, find themselves in this position but with the additional anxiety of not knowing how a particular management offer will be received by their membership. This often prompts the ploy of a request for a sweetener or small improvement which is of value to a particularly vociferous constituency. For instance, 'If you add another $25 to the annual shift differential then I think I can sell it' falls into that category. Or one may negotiate with (d) the lowest authority level in negotiating, the spokesman. He may nevertheless have an important part to play in negotiations. His script may have been carefully prepared. His ability to make concessions may be virtually non-existent but he will be authorised to make his demands by whatever methods are considered appropriate. His particular role is to shield his organisation and its decision-making structure from the other party. His role may be illustrated most dramatically in negotiations involving political and criminal kidnaps and extortion demands.

The use of people tactics can also be seen in the deployment of negotiating teams against one or two representatives of the other party. For example, being confronted by six or seven strangers when the negotiator was expecting to meet only one or two people he already knew. The reason for the presence of the new team members is not made explicit – they may be a group of experts who will launch a series of problems and difficult questions? Or it may be a way to hide amongst the new team members a decision-maker of particular importance or a person with access to the highest councils.

In the negotiating of licence agreements and capital projects a people tactic that is often used is to deploy two different teams against the negotiator: one, for example, will only deal with technical issues, for instance, the specifications or the design of subunits, and the other team will deal only with commercial issues such as costs, payment terms, the financial package, currency issues, liquidated damage clauses, and so on. Each team will work in complete isolation from the other and may report to different parts of the organisation. A concession on the technical aspect does not compulsorily result in acceptance of a commercial counter-demand. Only at the level of the decision-making team will the two sets of results be integrated and a final decision reached. The single negotiator who has to deal with this situation is subjected to very considerable strains and is often forced into making concessions of which the cost in time is unknown.

In industrial relations negotiations management, negotiators often encounter a large trade union team which may contain a mixture of full-time trade union officials, elected local part-time officials (shop stewards, or staff representatives) and selected rank and file members. A team which already contains the different elements has a number of purposes: for instance, it may be in order to show 'solidarity' and cohesion or to prevent dissension by disaffected members by involving them as witnesses or allowing them to present their claims directly, or simply to put on pressure by numbers. Management negotiators are left with a range of problems. Should they seek to treat their bargaining partners as one and ignore potential internal divisions; or should they follow an irresistible tendency to seek to divide and rule at the conference table? This short-term advantage may be paid back with interest later. Should the management negotiator simply ignore the internal tensions and protect his relationship with either the senior full-time official or the senior locally-elected shop steward on the simple basis that they have to 'live with one another' and will have to get on after the negotiations.

Japanese negotiating teams of five or six, where it is relatively obvious that one or several members do not have a fluency in the language of the country in which they are negotiating, can be encountered. Team members sit politely and attentively, rarely commenting and never contradicting their colleagues. Perhaps one person only is used as main spokesman and asks questions. He may often read a prepared statement of full generalities and goodwill. Here the team represents the totality of the organisation, it is multi-functional and in the evenings will operate as a single group, reviewing what has been learnt, communicating, if need be, with different parts of the organisation. In later meetings issues will emerge gradually and will take into account the needs of each part of the organisation.

The discussion of people tactics can be concluded with a list of those which are frequently aimed at the negotiator as an individual:

1. Questions about personal integrity.
2. Issues about personal competence – for instance: 'How can you say that as an engineer?'; 'How long have you been working on stress dynamics?'
3. Remarks about alleged lack of authority – for instance: 'The organgrinder or the monkey'; 'We do not deal with messenger boys'.
4. Appeals to his common sense or willingness to be innovative, challenges to take a risk.
5. Attempts to divide the negotiator from his organisation or a particular department – for instance: 'We both realise that lawyers do not understand what happens on a construction site'.
6. Guilt by association – for instance: 'You would say that, after all that is the typical view of a multinational company that does not care about standards'.
7. Legitimacy assertions – for instance: 'What you have suggested is illegal, we cannot accept that we should deliberately flout exchange control negotiations'; 'This is standard practice in the oil industry, all companies in the area have a union shop'.
8. Attacks on an absent colleague: 'We could make some progress today as Herr Schmidt will not be able to delay us with his technical criteria'.
9. Identification tactics, when one will try to have an opponent identify individually with one's cause regardless of their respective constituents and issues. The party's cause can be anything from the future of the working class to the well-being of the national or international economy.
10. The comparison with predecessors: 'This was accepted by Mr X'; 'Mr Y did not have your background as an engineer – he was more of a "marketing man"'.
11. Emotional outbursts, dramatic gestures, tears and tempers, banging on tables, walking out, slamming of doors.
12. The use of precedents – for instance: 'You did it for them' (then you are committed to do it for us, or, why do you discriminate against us?)
13. The building of common ground, a relationship of trust between negotiators across the table, independently of the issues.
14. Defusing the issues of their potential personal aspects and attempts to deal with them ouside of value judgements.
15. Stressing the common interests.

Bacharach and Lawler[7] have identified what they call morality tactics. For example: (1) appeals to equality – 'Let us split it down the middle'; (2) appeals to equity – 'That request is not fair'; (3) appeals to responsibility – 'If we do not break even and show a good margin we may have to lay off 50 engineers'; (4) appeals to experience and knowledge, the 'Help me' tactic – 'I do not know anything about cars'; 'I am buying it for the family'; 'Can you show me what I need to look for'; 'I want to learn from your experience'.

A larger category of people tactics, which embodies these morality tactics, is what Pruitt,[8] drawing on Schelling,[9] calls mutually prominent alternatives, which a party can utilise, if they are to its advantage. Such an alternative must stand out for both parties because 'it embodies some standard of fairness and reasonableness or because it enjoys perceptual uniqueness, simplicity, precedent or some rationale that makes it qualitatively differentiable'. This includes equality of shares, but also of concessions or sacrifices, equity of contributions appreciated in terms of amount of effort, but also of skill, education, rank and responsibility, responsiveness to needs, which grants the greater outcome to the party with the bigger needs: it can be added, the opportunity norm which grants the larger share of the outcome to the party with the better opportunity to make a more profitable use of it. Finally, besides historical precedents already discussed, Mageneau and Pruitt[10] mention three occurrences of mutual prominence issuing from perceptual salience: a mediator suggestion, an option with a central position and perceptual boundaries (such as, for instance, one of each category alternatively, whatever the size or value of the categories). Mutually prominent alternatives may be several, or, when a single one exists, it may be of particular advantage to a party. The tactic consists in making use of its special characteristic for the party to which it is of advantage in order to gain the agreement of the opponent to settle on it.

The final category of people tactics is based on relationships. These tactics may consist in trying to build up an existing relationship into a highly personal one. For instance, the negotiator and his opposite number both have to administer the contract; they will have to negotiate together on another issue – 'It is tea this week and coffee next; you win some and you lose some'; both are victims who have only one another – 'They don't understand us, somehow they expect us to make it work'. They may also consist of changing the parties involved or altering the existing relationship. When negotiating in teams an often found tactic is the 'bad guy' 'good guy' alternation. A demanding and unpleasant negotiator is replaced by a sympathetic one who empathises with the other party, still with high demands, but with a much warmer attitude, and then, hopefully by reaction, obtains concessions out of sympathy, and out of spite for the other negotiator.

(d) Pressure Tactics or Power Tactics

The last tactic discussed was a borderline case. It brings us into power or pressure tactics. These are those which aim to persuade the other party of the costs associated with pursuing a particular aspect of their claim or resistance to a demand made or the benefits associated with agreeing to a specific demand. To the outside observer, pressure tactics and their use are synonymous with the negotiating process. In some instances they almost provoke a response of the type: 'Gentlemen do not negotiate – they solve problems'. Most experienced negotiators recognise that a larger range of more subtle tactics exist.

Pressure tactics are probably the best known and least understood by observers because they are apparent and obvious. Their use is fraught with danger because, although they are ideally suited to highly competitive strategies, they tend, because they may be perceived in an undifferentiated way, to move agenda items towards a distributive mode. It is also clear that, if one opens competitively and applies pressure immediately, one may not have the opportunity to close collaboratively, and may face a breakdown, after a conflictual spiral, even if one did not mean it to end in this way.

Despite the dangers present in using pressure tactics, it is necessary that negotiators fully understand that they exist, and what is involved in using and responding to them.

The first point that must be made is that they are not 'immoral'. Value judgements have a place in negotiating but this should not block our need to understand how to cope with pressure tactics when used by the other party against us. It is vital not to go naked into the conference room.

Foremost among the pressure tactics are the tactics of commitment analysed in depth by Schelling.[11]

The characteristic of commitment tactics is that the negotiator seeks to bind himself. He may manipulate his own position in such a way that he communicates to the other party in the clearest and most unambiguous terms his willingness to open or face an increase in conflict rather than move from his stated position. A very clear example of this was seen in the 1984–85 coal strike in the United Kingdom when the Government both at ministerial and prime ministerial level committed itself to the support of the National Coal Board when responding to the picketing tactics of the National Union of Mineworkers and their attempts to prevent individual miners from crossing picket lines and continuing or returning to work. At various times the government went further and broadened the issue from an industrial relations dispute over jobs security to one of the rule of law in a democratic society, using as a voluntary tactic the mechanism of the escalation in stakes described above. The words used reflected this commitment: 'scabs'; 'strike breaker'; 'common sense', 'loyal and decent'. The tactic of commitment thus consists of backing oneself voluntarily into a corner where the only issue acceptable is for the opponent to give in. Instead of remaining open to further possibilities of negotiations, a party states its irrevocable decision not to move any more. The range of outcomes of the negotiation is reduced to the level of party demands . . . or better. The party sets into a particular position in which the opponent has only one alternative to open conflict: to give in. It is often implied in the 'final offer first' or 'take it or leave it' position.

It is described by some as being the very negation of bargaining yet it can and does work in given circumstances. The key factor is that there is a clear willingness to explain the offer to the other party.

But the danger of this tactic is that subsequently to make concessions is to undermine totally one's credibility. Should a company resort to a 'final offer first' position, it must be prepared to communicate its decision before the negotiations start and not to move whatever happens. Another commercial version can be found in competitive bidding in which the client company clearly indicates that suppliers must submit their last and final offer and that at bid opening this will be the only criteria in deciding between the offers. Should two bids come in at the same level the process will be repeated. One can distinguish several types of commitment: the above examples can be described as commitment to the other party. A different form of commitment can come through a 'psychological contract'. That is, committing oneself to one's constituencies instead of one's opponents. The buyer may, in advance, tell his senior manager that he will not spend more than £10 000 on the air conditioning unit. A house seller may commit himself to a minimum price by agreeing to purchase another house and using that money as his down payment. A union representative may publicly commit himself to securing the reinstatement of a colleague dismissed for fighting on company premises. The directly concerned constituent provides one level of psychological commitment. Finally, the negotiator may commit himself to a third party: the buyer of a second-hand sports car may tell his friend that he will not pay more than £2000. The trade union official and the personnel manager may both, in interviews with the local radio or television station, state that their minimum demands are reasonable and non-negotiable.

Obviously commitments to third parties and to one's own organisation and constituents need to be known to the opponent to be efficient. It is here that the essential problem with the use of commitment tactics arises. Not only should they be known by the opponent, but they should also be credible. That credibility, of course, depends to a large extent on any past relationship, if there is one. The negotiator must, however, take into account the impact. A prime minister who publicly goes on record claiming that he 'will not be the man of a third devaluation' (within 18 months), and then goes on to devalue the national currency once more, is unlikely to be believed when he later claims that there will be no fourth devaluation, however hard he tries. Irrevocable commitments present the danger of leaving no place for backtracking without loss of face and loss of future credibility. The opponent either gives in or the conflict starts. Therefore correct timing in the use of commitment is essential.

Thus, in order to keep flexible, negotiators may adopt tactics other than commitment, but nonetheless geared to show firmness in one's demands. They constitute in some sense watered-down versions of commitment without the final inevitability of conflict. There are many such tactics; for instance, the one which consists of coming back repeatedly to one point, or refusing to leave it, emphasising the importance of a demand or its viability, identifying with a specific point. A less extreme type of commitment may be expressed in probabilistic terms, leaving room for not carrying out the consequences outlined; for instance, it may be expressed as 'there's a good chance that the engineering department could not design this at that price.' However the impact of the commitment is considerably weakened.

There are of course counter-tactics to commitment: they include ignoring the commitment, preventing the opponent from becoming committed, putting obstacles in the way of the realisation of commitment, should it happen, being committed first, raising the stakes (that is a counter commitment which makes the consequences of the first one appear negligible).

A second important type of pressure tactics is threats. They differ from commitment in the sense that they are more flexible, less irrevocable and have a wider scope. They have a wider scope because they can be of several types. They can be implicit or explicit. They can be automatically applied in the sense that they are the direct consequence of the breakdown of the negotiations and that they may be applied by the negotiator's own organisation: such is the case with loss of face and loss of the co-operative aspect of the relationship in the case of open conflict. They can also come from bringing in resources from outside into the negotiating relationship. Examples of the latter also come easily to mind: 'Not only will we not sign the contract but we shall sue you'; or 'If you do not lower your fee on this car insurance I shall cancel all my other policies with your company.' They are more flexible because they can be kept more equivocal: examples are, for instance, 'I may have to resort to . . .', or 'The boys out there at the plant may react strongly', or 'The company may have to shut the plant.' They can be made conditional also on one's own behaviour and not only on the other party's and they then do not have to have the final ring of a commitment.

Nevertheless they should be used sparingly as there also is a question of credibility if threats are made and then never put into practice. A party should at least be prepared to fulfil its threats if they are to be believed and efficient. The question of size is important; minor threats are easily ignored by the opponent, and threats which are too large are difficult to believe. An efficient way to establish credibility consists of making and fulfilling a minor threat within the negotiating process with the implication that a major threat would be implemented in the same way. An example of being prepared and showing a willingness to fulfil a threat can be seen in a classic case in American labour negotiations. A national negotiator for a union was involved in establishing his first collective agreement with a local employer just after union recognition and had threatened to strike in face of a management not yet used to negotiating in a loaded atmosphere. To back up his threat, he instructed the union treasurer to pay into the local bank, whose manager was on the company board, a very large sum of money, which could be used as an immediate strike fund, if needed.

Creating and fulfilling minor threats may be achieved by meeting postponements, adjournments or termination, whether in commercial or labour negotiations, under pretext of punctuality, behaviour, and so on.

A third type of pressure tactic which has considerable notoriety is 'bluffing'.[12] Associated with the poker table, its use by experienced negotiators is much more limited than the observer might suspect. A bluff can be defined quite simply as an attempt to impress upon the other party a commitment, threat or any other move that the negotiator does not intend to carry out but which he wants the other party to believe is likely to be carried out. Clearly all that has been said about credibility and commitment applies here with perhaps more strength. Besides, as an experienced negotiator commented, 'Never tell your opponent after the meeting that you were bluffing and never tell your colleagues you are bluffing.' This is because a reputation as a user of bluff is damaging in later negotiations and because, during the use of bluff, the faces of the team members may register fear or betray the use of the tactic.

Specific pressure ploys must also be emphasised and understood because they may repeatedly appear in negotiating situations. They are listed below:[13]

1. The ultimatum, assorted with a deadline, assorted or not with a last offer (which becomes then the 'or else') and/or a breach of communications and threats. It is a ploy to try to force the result of a negotiation all at once.

2. The nibble takes place when agreement is near, many issues have already been dealt with, much time has been invested by all concerned and some concessions have been exchanged. It is necessary that the foremost items of importance have been settled. Then one party comes up with a last-minute additional demand which is new, has never been mentioned before, and is of relatively small size compared with what is already settled. The expectation of the party using it is that the opponent is tired of negotiating, already sees a settlement, and is ready to make immediately a new minor concession rather than going through a new round of bargaining and jeopardising what has already been acquired. A typical use of the nibble is when, after protracted discussion, one party will suddenly ask, 'Will you throw in . . .?' (whatever, a radio clock, white-wall tyres, repainting the garage, insurance costs, full dental coverage).

3. Getting as mad as hell' is capitalising on the power of the irrational. A madman can be expected to do anything, or almost anything. He is not limited by rationality, even his bounded rationality. Not only are his actions not clearly and fully predictable, to a

larger extent than is more or less the case for everybody else, but the range of his possible actions encloses a much wider field than for a 'sane' man. It is a field with very dangerous potentialities. Not only can he hurt the other party, by wrecking the deal for no good reason, by even resorting to violence, or extreme violence, but he does not care in the least if in doing so he also hurts himself. Being mad, he may even want or like to hurt himself in the process. Thus, to appease such a person and to avoid mutually damaging behaviour, a party may be ready to make concessions he would not grant to a 'rational' person. Everyone knows somebody in a family or an organisation who has a reputation for being a 'bad-tempered' person or a 'nasty character', and who, in being so, escapes some constraints or chores falling onto other members of the family or organisation because it does not seem worth the trouble to apply them to these people. The being mad tactic is of the same nature, only emphasised and formalised in the negotiation environment. The difficulties of establishing a negotiating relationship, and of subsequently conducting the dialogue, can be seen in hostage or aircraft hijacks in particular, when highly committed religious or political groups are involved.

4. The 'salami' tactic has the object of presenting a demand bit by bit. Once that or a small part of an item's agreement is won, the party will move its demands to another small part of the item and build upon concession after concession to try to reduce the other party's resistance. As soon as a minor concession is institutionalised as being past practice, the party asks for more on the same item. 'Well you agreed that we share distribution savings at our last meeting, now I want to review the benefits you have had on the manpower side.'

5. The 'false pivot' is a tactic which consists of, during the negotiations, building up an item of secondary or even no importance for a party into what should seem to be a major demand to the opponent, then to 'pivot' by suddenly giving up on that 'major' objective in order to obtain in exchange an important concession from the opponent.

6. The 'balance sheet' technique which involves translating into 'costs' all of the opponent's demand in ways which appear not too heavily loaded but can still be recognised by them. For example, all the points of a trade union wage claim are quantified, down to the last detail of the costs of new lockers for work clothes. Having completed this first stage the negotiator then proceeds to present his demands in the same way. As concessions are made or demands withdrawn a

balance sheet is maintained. The most noticeable effect of this technique is that it relatively quickly results in reduced initial demands. It may subsequently slow down the meeting because an item may have two values, 'cash' and 'psychological', within the other party's bounded rationality.

7. The 'Four Steps' involves the negotiator identifying four sets of potential settlement points and has been identified by J. C. Altmann.[14] Step 4 is a settlement totally disastrous for the negotiator and his side. Step 3 is a settlement perfectly acceptable to the other party but of very little advantage to the negotiator, though marginally acceptable as a fallback, last-chance settlement if nothing better is possible. Step 2 is a solution very acceptable to the negotiator and probably still acceptable to the opponent, although much less advantageous for him than the two involved in the preceding steps. Step 1 is the ideal solution for the negotiator, but involving losses and probably quite difficult to gain the other party's agreement on. The tactic consists of presenting Step 4 in an emotional fashion and in such a way that it appears absurd, unrealistic and totally unfair. Step 4 thus discarded, Step 3 is discussed quite negatively, but in a very technical and unemotional fashion; then the party presents Step 1 as a contrast in order to put the other party on the defensive and offers Step 2 as a potential compromise.

8. The escalation consists in presenting demands that are increased meeting after meeting even though the opponent believes agreement has been reached.

9. The either/or tactic attempts to put the opponent in a situation of choice between two alternatives which have both been set by a party and are both acceptable to him. It involves trying to have the opponent decide between an apparently palatable and a less palatable offer, both sometimes equally bad for him, both always acceptable by the initiator. This tactic overcomes some of the dangers of incorrect assumptions and lack of information about the other party's subjective utilities.

SECTION IV – SOME PRESSURE TACTICS DESERVING SPECIAL ATTENTION

Finally, pressure tactics involve different sets of factors which involve manipulating the costs of agreeing and disagreeing with demands, according to our earlier discussion of bargaining power. They include acting on the costs of the other party, decreasing his costs of agreeing and increasing his costs of disagreeing with one's demands. They also include decreasing one's own costs of disagreeing and increasing one's own costs of agreeing with the opponent's demands. They have been put in these terms because they are actual moves and attempts to influence the resources and constraints in the environment.

(a) Increasing the Cost of Disagreeing with a Demand/Proposed Settlement

In labour relations negotiations:

– The management dismisses the staff on strike and hires replacements.
– The management locks-out.
– The union follows up a strike by organising a boycott of the company products or by extending the strike to other plants not previously involved.
– By selecting the timing of the dispute – unions organising a strike will avoid the period after the annual holiday or before Christmas and select the period before a new model launch.
– The management may seek to choose a period when demand is slack and lay-off would not be expensive. For instance, in the animal feedstuffs industry this would be the summer period when farmers can rely on the fields to support cattle.

In commercial negotiations:

– In the buy-sell situation the store negotiating around one brand of coffee is prepared to de-list all general food products from the same manufacturer.
– A company negotiating the renewal of a contract with a national retailer is prepared to withdraw its product and support a special promotion in a competing chain knowing that brand loyalty is high.
– A whisky manufacturer or champagne distributor may be prepared to withdraw his product in the late November, early December period from the national co-operative outlets because they had previously sold below cost that is, depriving them of sale during their peak period.

(b) Decreasing the Opponent's Costs of Agreeing

This involves some well-known ploys such as:

– It is in fact in your own interests' – for instance: 'This wage increase will go a long way to building the motivation of the service team'; or 'You will be the only distributor of luxury cars in the city and thus will be backed up by our press national advertising which always lists our dealers'.

– Or it is against your real interests – for instance: 'To insist on laying off design engineers and draughtsmen because company X have not confirmed their sub-contract with you. It will take a long time to reassemble that team and other companies are only too keen to hire them'; or 'To ask for such a high raise because we are going to have to fire some people/shut the plant'; or 'If you insist on these terms of trading, in particular payment terms, we will have to reduce both our stock levels and the range we hold. Garage mechanics will take other brands if they cannot get your parts easily'.

– A variation involves 'I can help you with your internal problem.' For instance: 'We are prepared to reschedule our orders so that we receive the total volume by the beginning of December. However, to help you during your annual shut-down we will take six deliveries of 15 000 cases rather than nine smaller deliveries'; or 'If you agree to a 3 per cent overriding discount on our anticipated volumes I am prepared to agree to that price increase. It will establish your new price in the Midlands and our discount arrangements remain private'.

Those ploys always involve showing the opponent that his demands go against his well-understood own interests, and alternatively that one's own demands are in the best interests of all concerned. If the opponent has internal problems, an offer may be a way of helping him solve them and thus decrease the cost of agreeing.

(c) Decreasing Our Costs of Disagreeing and of any Subsequent Conflict

In industrial relations the union will facilitate and support its members' applications to get public welfare benefits for their families or start a strike fund and provide strike benefits. During the British miners' strike it was acknowledged that payments to maintain mortgage contributions were being used to feed families. The building societies recognised this but did not enforce their rights to the money as whole communities were affected. The terms of the mortgages were subsequently revised.

The retailer who decides to reduce his stock of a branded product begins by a search for a manufacturer willing to supply his own label on food. He may then announce his decision to the supplier when the test market arrangements are already under way.

A more sustained effort to reduce the costs of the subsequent conflict may be seen in industrial relations where management organise themselves for the management of conflict by – transferring production, building up stocks prior to the dispute, running the plant with management staff, passing agreements with competitors, who may deliver the company's brand under their own name, or who may compensate the struck employer out of an employer's strike fund (as was the case once in the US newspaper industry, and with the British National Coal Board in the UK during the 1984–85 strikes).

(d) Manipulating One's Own Costs

Also some tactics may deal with manipulating one's own costs, including manipulating one's own cost of agreeing. Probably the most specific case that can be identified in labour relations negotiations is one in which the party makes it more expensive for himself to agree to his opponent's demands: for example, striking firemen who still turn out in emergencies involving the rescue of the elderly in sheltered accommodation despite the fact that the government has mobilised troops as substitute firemen. Clearly such tactics involve commitment but are not limited to it. For instance, in commercial negotiations a weapon system manufacturer goes on with work on a military jet design rejected by a study commission, but before a parliamentary vote. A building company may start intensive work on a site before obtaining the construction permit.

(e) Use of a Third Party

Finally, action on costs of agreeing and disagreeing, whether one's own or the other party's, can be effected through the use of a third party, either to put pressure on the opponent or to concede directly to a party's demands, irrespective of an opponent's actions.

Police, courts, mediators, arbitrators, other parties interested in the results of the negotiation can be used to alter the positions of the parties. In that light, in large-scale labour relations negotiations, the weight of public opinion should never be underestimated.

But the resort to third parties should also not be neglected in commercial negotiations. The weight of a major customer on a contract between its subcontractor and its own supplier can be determinant. This is the case in particular for high technology equipment such as numerically controlled machine tools if the new equipment improves quality and accuracy of the delivered product for the final user.

SECTION V – TACTICS TOWARDS CO-OPERATIVE BARGAINING

Most authors in the social-psychological literature, following the wake of Walton and McKersie, have tended to favour co-operative bargaining and to assume that it produced better outcomes in terms of better joint outcomes for the parties. However, co-operative bargaining faces an enlarged version of the concession dilemma. If one engages in co-operative bargaining, and one's opponent, after the opening moves, practises an extreme conflictual strategy, the results are likely to be extremely damaging for the party because of the elements of trust, of openness, of information disclosure, of unilateral concession-making involved in initiating a co-operative strategy. As a result the opponent is left in no uncertainty, and therefore has a maximum bargaining power and power balance which his strategy indicates that he will use to its fullest extent.

Understandably, openly co-operative bargaining demands very different tactics from give and take or even mixed problem-solving strategies. In Walton and McKersie terms it involves three steps: identifying the problem that both parties seek to solve through negotiation; the search for potential solutions; the selection of an alternative satisfying for both parties which brings the largest degree of joint satisfaction.

In order for parties to engage in that process with a minimum of risks, Osgood[15] has presented an organised set of ordered tactical steps called GRIT (Graduated Reciprocation in Tension Reduction):

- The series of actions must be announced ahead of time as an effort to reduce tension.
- Each action should be labelled as part of this series.
- The initially announced timetable must be observed.
- The opponent should be invited to reciprocate each action.
- The series of actions must be continued for a while even if there is no reciprocation.
- The actions must be clear-cut and susceptible to verification.
- The party must retain his capability to retaliate should the opponent become more competitive during the process.
- The party should retaliate if the opponent becomes competive.
- The actions should be of various kinds, all having in common their co-operative nature.
- The opponent should be rewarded for co-operating back, the level of reward being graduated to his level of co-operation.

Part III
The Interaction of the
Negotiators

Previous chapters of this book have brought together a number of theoretical approaches with the objective of providing a framework within which we can understand the structure and the major determinants of all types of negotiations. Then we moved into putting the concepts into actual operation with the selection of a strategy and the listing of tactics, that is to say, into the process which pits the parties, collective or individuals, against each other. We now proceed a step further towards the negotiating table. In the following pages we will focus explicitly on the individual actors, drawing together material from social psychology and sociology to seek to develop a framework for understanding their negotiating behaviour.

The remainder of this book will deal therefore with what is actually taking place at the negotiating site. The structural aspects of negotiation, and its process, strategy and tactics, must be fitted into a coherent set together with the actual interaction of individual people, the actual negotiators. This set must be established for each negotiation. We have already emphasised that 'how to' recipes or tips on which 'package' works best in negotiation would fly in the face of the premises on which this book is based. The concepts identified in the first two chapters of the book and on which it has been later built clearly demonstrate that each negotiation is unique if only by the bounds on the rationality of the parties involved. An understanding of these concepts, of how they operate and of what has been pointed out on strategy, tactics and style will help each negotiator build himself his specific package before each negotiation. Special attention to the concepts of bounded rationality and bargaining power should be particularly helpful in achieving satisfactory results.

However, our subject does not stop here. Even though it is true that each negotiation is unique, some common features are present in the process of all negotiations whatever the strategies and tactics of the negotiators and the structure of the negotiation.

In order to make the ideas we have developed in the precedent chapter more operational and to move fully into the practical side of negotiating we wish now to address ourselves to the activities of negotiators. By this, we mean the actions taking place at the negotiating site.

Together with tactics actions may be the most discussed area of the field of negotiation. Most of the points we shall review belong to the common lore of negotiating. They are well known by all those who have had a common interest in the practice or theory of negotiation.

Many have already been discussed by several authors under one form or another.

We are going to summarise them as briefly as possible but we shall, however, devote more importance and space to what we think to be essential, or often forgotten, while we shall simply recall and pass quickly over what is already well publicised. If an author has already given extensive and adequate coverage to a point we shall also refer the reader to his work. We shall cover successively the negotiating styles, the phases of a negotiation, and the tasks to be undertaken by the negotiators.

6 Negotiating Styles

SECTION I – DEFINITION

Our starting-point is made of two often-heard questions; the first being, 'What is effective negotiating behaviour?' or 'How do I recognise an effective negotiator when I meet him, either face-to-face or on the telephone?'; the second question being, 'Is one type of negotiating behaviour more successful or effective than any other?' In order to provide an answer to these central concerns it is convenient to use the idea of negotiating style. An understanding of the concept of negotiating style and of its limits can be useful both in conceptual terms and to the practitioner concerned either in developing his skills or coping with a current negotiating situation.

Several efforts have been made to identify and describe negotiating styles. For instance, Sparks[1] by crossing two continua, between trust and disregard and between the drive to control and the drive to defer relatively to the other party, isolates four styles: confrontive (control, trust), restrictive (control and disregard), elusive (defer and disregard), friendly (defer and trust). On the other hand, Mastenbroeck,[2] with a similar process, crosses the continua between co-operation and fighting and along procedural flexibility between activity and passivity. He then also isolates four styles: analytical aggressive, flexible aggressive, ethical persuasive, and flexible compromising. Gottschalk[3] has, through experimental research and contact with negotiators, identified four dimensions of style each with several components and he also introduces a great deal of flexibility into the approach with the concepts of 'core' and 'adaptative' parts of style. We shall adopt his definitions:

Negotiating style is defined as the description of all the behavioural characteristics but only the behavioural characteristics of an individual engaged in a negotiating encounter. This includes both the initial impression and any attribution from previous situations or issued from other independent sources of knowledge as well as subsequent behaviour during the negotiations. The concept of style includes a range of actions, or inputs, which if taken individually might not provide by themselves any practical insight but when integrated provide a framework.

The starting-point is personality. But it is not enough. The linkage between personality concepts as used by the psychologist and the behaviour of individuals in negotiations is at best tenuous and at worst misleading. Even popularised concepts such as introvert and extrovert fail to generate insights because of the interaction between the personalities of the actors and the situational factors such as power, objectives and constraints. Clearly personality variables may play a key role in determining whether people will expose themselves in negotiating situations, but its power to predict the behaviour of the actors in the meeting is limited. However, the basic structures of the personality of a negotiator are at the core of his negotiating style.[4]

Another input into the concept of style must be intelligence. A prima-facie case can be made out that there is a correlation between intelligence and negotiating effectiveness but to seek to quantify this would be hazardous. Testing may have reached a very high standard, as a result of continued usage and modification, but there are no studies which have attempted to explore the direct links.

In addition to personality and intelligence experience suggests that the value system of the negotiator may be another factor in the equation. Individual value systems are both complex and dynamic. In some cases it maybe possible to use simple levels such as 'Christian' or 'Marxist' to describe a broad cluster of values, attitudes and beliefs but in practice there is little usefulness in these broad characterisations. The negotiator will have to find an accommodation between two or more elements of different value systems if he is to reach an agreement.

Besides, the theoretical and practical help that we can derive from the concept of value systems is severely limited when we turn back to our premisses of bounded rationality and the unique package of criteria of satisfaction particular to each individual. This places an individual with more or less clear and defined objectives within constraints and resources and elaborating a strategy to reach his objectives. If we recall this analysis of the situation it is clear that in most cases value systems of an individual will not be the main a priori determinant of their behaviour. On the contrary, instead of structuring the situation in which the individual find himself and his strategy, they will be structured by the situation and emerge as *ex post facto* as a result of the resources, constraints and strategy, in other words they will emerge as a posteriori rationalisations of the behaviour oriented towards objectives.

However, the concept of style is not useless or irrelevant. Goffman[5] has demonstrated that in all social encounters our activity is specifically geared towards influencing the other participants and the audience in accepting our definition of the situation. We aim to control through our behaviour the impression that they receive of the situation. A negotiation is a particularly acute case of social interaction. The concept of style is helpful in categorising the way we project our 'performance' in Goffman terms and the relationships, to be discussed below, within teams.

To the elements resulting from the structure of the personality, should be added the education received and the professional background. But other items are also relevant. Among these probably two important and durable complementary factors of style are the formal task, which the individual undertakes, for example, accountant, production manager, marketing executive, or industrial relations director, and the item or items being discussed. From the formal task, or job title, we may derive some data, or assumptions about the informal educational processes to which the individual has been exposed and which have consequently shaped his behaviour. In some instances the external environment may also impact at this point, that is, in many parts of Western Europe industrial relations negotiators working for major corporations and employers' associations put emphasis on legal training and practice because of the importance and impact of legal regulations on both procedures and behaviours. In both banking and the insurance industry the existence of internal industry professional qualifications, access to them, and employment opportunities for those who have successfully completed them have a major impact on the negotiating style of the individual factors.

The negotiating agenda, what is being discussed as well as what we described earlier as the environment to be analysed, will be of key significance because it is the focus for the meeting, irrespective of its location and the number of persons present. Without issues there would be no meeting. Our individual behaviour focuses around the negotiable item. Is it of high or low value, in financial or psychological terms? The item can have short-term or long-term significance in the relationship between the two parties.

The concept of style is in one sense a convenient way of bringing together a number of factors which otherwise remain both diffuse and separated, though in some situations they may have a critical impact. An introvert, European, Christian accountant working as a tax adviser to a Western multinational oil corporation may have to negotiate tax royalties with a representative of a revolutionary African Marxist government with a developing economy on the tax liabilities for off-shore oil production. The two negotiators as representatives of their respective parties manage themselves in such a way that after a series of meetings in which positions are communicated, concessions and counter-demands are traded, an agreement acceptable to both parties is concluded within known time constraints. Both persons can be said to have managed their negotiating style effectively.

When we accept the idea that our individual negotiating style can be managed to some extent it is only a relatively small series of steps which must be made to operationalise the concept. Initially we must distinguish two parts of our style. The first, the core, which changes and evolves very slowly, and the second part, an adaptative element, which can be managed for individual meetings or parts of a meeting. The core style would include the more stable or longer-lasting elements such as personality, education and intelligence. The adaptative style accommodates the other factors such as the career pattern, the organisational task that the negotiator undertakes, the items being discussed, whether the negotiations involve one person on each side, or several, and where the negotiations are being held. Out of these situationally-based factors there may emerge the process decision issues such as how power is managed, the strategies adopted, the tactics used and the conduct of the meetings.

The core style of a negotiator can change and evolve, albeit slowly. When we enter our first work situation we may be provided with a considerable amount of formal on-the-job training. This, supplemented by the informal acquisition of organisational values, images and language, may all end up in 'the new organisational man'. An example often quoted is that of the IBM salesman. Throughout our late twenties and early thirties this initial learning will form a major influence on the negotiating style of the individual. It focuses primarily on his interaction with one or more people. During our early thirties job changes and promotion may introduce another element – the management of staff or collaboration with other colleagues. This situation now requires new skills – in particular those of team building, the allocation of roles, and leadership. A period exposed to team negotiations may subsequently be followed by a mid-career move. Again the individual's core style may be slightly modified to take into account the fact that responsibility has again shifted from primary concern with one set of negotiations to the management of a series of negotiations held in a range of locations.

both within the organisation and outside. It is at this period that the reality of internal organisational negotiating emerges most clearly in the handling of performance targets, manpower, and financial and other resources. Perhaps ten or fifteen years later a further change will take place concerned primarily with accommodation of career expectations and the process of adjustment to exit from the organisation.

Our concept of a core style accounts for the basis of the behaviour of the other party that we perceive in a negotiating situation. The moves away from that central tendency are made up of the adaptative style. This second element can be changed and managed in response to the situationally specific issues but cannot totally alter the basic responses issuing from the core style. We are all aware that we seek to adapt and manage our behaviour to secure certain objectives. The question that remains is how much. If the reply were one hundred per cent we would only be able to advance a contingency theory of behaviour. Each negotiating situation would involve us in a new learning situation. We could not even be certain that we might not encounter, if not physical violence, then perhaps abuse. However, even if that is not the case we learn nevertheless very quickly to identify the differences between situations. In some cases we may unlearn a previously correct behaviour. For example, internal negotiations over budgets and performance targets by a department head may be characterised by an outspoken bluntness, a direct demand on subordinates, and the combined use of threats and humour. Two days later the same person may be involved in negotiations with the representatives of a Japanese company in which formality is required and requests have to be dealt with in such a manner as to avoid a loss of face. Also our selection of words and expressions takes into account that in internal meetings we share the same national language but that when negotiating with foreigners either we or they are using a second language. Our adaptative style is consciously acquired and managed. It may over time combine with core style in such a way as to be seen to be our normal negotiating repertoire, yet given a sufficiently strong incentive, both in situational and psychological terms, it can and will be changed.

SECTION II – THE FOUR NEGOTIATING STYLES

Having established the concept of style and that two parts can be identified, the core and the adaptative element, Gottschalk adds a further important point. There is no 'negotiator's style' in absolute terms. That is, there is not a style which can be identified as being ideally suited for a negotiator. Within each core style behavioural elements can be identified which could be described as positive or productive as can elements which are negative or counterproductive to the achievement of negotiated settlements. Clearly the behaviours which are positive or negative are influenced by certain situational factors but reflection about experiences and discussion with negotiators have brought out a considerable measure of agreement on what constitutes the positive and the negative behaviours.

Based on practical experience, therefore, four styles can be recognised as being different and identifiable by Gottschalk. There is no behavioural overlap. They are identified with very simple, perhaps dramatic, labels: tough, warm, numbers and dealer. It should be recalled that each style described below is a core style: that is, a style towards which an individual will automatically be carried by the factors having built his style together and listed above. But it should also be recognised that each style at the negotiating table is a combination of an individual negotiator core style (the one towards which he is attracted naturally) and of its adaptive style (the one he thinks fits best with the specific negotiation taking place). It is probably impossible and useless to try to change one's core style deliberately. As described in the case illustrated above it changes very slowly under strong pressures. However, being aware of its nature and of how to adopt the adaptative part is another issue. Deliberate moves can be used purposively.

(a) The 'Tough' Style

The Tough Style

(Dominant, Aggressive. Power Oriented)

Positive aspects	Negative aspects
States position firmly and clearly.	Openly demands his way. Unaware of other party's objectives and unwilling to find out.

Determined to get the best deal. Knows his objectives.	Take it or leave it attitude. Unconcerned about what others think unless he can enforce his views.
Knows what he wants.	Domineering. Aggressively combat-ready.
Likes to take control and keep it. Forceful, presents his case with commitment.	Threatens, bullies, pressures, becomes coercive, tells others how it should be done.
Dynamic 'presence', tower of strength, builds temporary unity by reference to external events, situations, time limits.	Anxious to be respected, listened to. Tends to be pessimistic about individual potential during negotiations.
Does not shy away from conflict.	Becomes angry, upset. Will not let others on the team contribute, and poaches on their territory. 'Do it my way' during negotiations.
Wlling to lead. Prefers to direct. Co-ordinates the work of others.	Quick to criticise, even colleagues. Happy to give negative feedback to own side during adjournments and after conclusion of meeting.
Decisive and quick to act, bold.	Does not listen to others' views or needs.
Seizes opportunities when he sees them. Risk-taking, enterprising.	Takes opportunities away from others in planning.
Competitive, assertive, likes challenge, responds to crisis.	Inflexible, obstinate, proud. Fails to obtain concessions available because of his manner.

| Lots of stamina. | Impulsive, impatient, manipulative. |
| Likes variety, novelty surprises, change. | Likes new things for the sake of surprise, short-term views. |

Our first impression is that of a negotiator who is task and objective orientated. The current negotiations are seen from a short-term perspective. He appears to need to dominate and direct. The other party is held in little regard which may include the range from disinterest to actual contempt. The Tough core style negotiator will ignore his immediate physical environment or control it in considerable detail: his chair, his place. Physically, his stamina shows in his ability to work without breaks or refreshments. Alternatively he may want to enhance his image with hard liquor.

During the meeting he is prepared to be direct, 'This is how I see the situation', and may without clear reason threaten or blame others, 'If you cannot get yourself organised you can expect to lose this business.' The combative element may often be indicated by raised voices, shouting, bad language, offensive jokes about minority groups and other cultures. A master of pressure on the other party he will efficiently use time against them, 'You have two hours and that is it.' Adjournments are used to sustain pressure. The Tough negotiator is prepared clearly to state and explore the differences between the parties with the implication that the other party must make concessions to bridge the gap. Aware of his own authority he is prepared to challenge others, 'If you cannot sign, don't waste my time.'

The Tough negotiator knows what he wants, both inside and outside the negotiations. Results have to be achieved within a specific timetable. As an individual he requires freedom of action and a minimum of detail as his boredom threshold is low. He often needs the personal commitment from co-workers, although he may not handle this particularly skilfully, given his tendency to criticise – 'but they can learn from me'. Within the organisation he needs to receive assignments that are seen to be challenging and difficult. The clear statement of objectives must be linked to a requirement to spell out the limit of resources that he can command. A failure to do this will result in a growing personal empire. As an individual he may need to be helped to develop a more balanced personal response to negotiating situations, in particular, as it regards his tendency to respond in fighting terms, or his feeling underestimated – 'Nobody understands me. I am carrying the whole of this company.'

(b) The Warm Style

The Warm Style
(Supportive, Understanding, Collaborative, People-Oriented)

Positive aspects	Negative aspects
Friendly, interested in other people.	Will not state clearly what he wants. Provides no opposite view.
Good listener. Skilled in asking questions. Concerned about other side's needs. Understands their values and objectives.	More concerned with personal relations than getting the job done.
Emphasises common interests/ goals. Recognises interdependence.	Soft touch – gives the store away, submissive, can't say 'no'. Does not recognise the legitimacy of his own case.
Sets very high standards for himself and others.	Loses sight of own side's interests and objectives.
Eager to respond to positive openings.	Gets disillusioned, disappointed.
Constructive, helpful, co-operative. Supports proposals of others rather than initiates them.	Reluctant to face up to conflict. If threats are used or pressure exerted tends not to be credible, apologises for using them.
Supports colleagues, brings them in. Modest about own contribution and skills.	Reluctant to take responsibility. Too dependent on others. Deferential.

Trusts others and is ready to seek their advice/help. Supportive, optimist.	Becomes unsure and solicits help.
Informative, open, approachable.	Too trusting, gullible, naïve, relies on others in most cases.
Patient, calm, equable. Prefers to reinforce the positive rather than criticise the negative. Power base is not kept in the background.	Apologetic, self-deprecating. Blames himself if problems arise. Hopes that access and time will solve most problems. Not prepared to say no directly and risk consequences. Overestimates reaction of others. Anticipates problems which may not exist.

The first impression is of a negotiator who is people and process orientated. He is friendly and encouraging. His listening skills draw out the agenda and the issues involved. Often one may be unaware that this process of shaping the meeting has been achieved with a minimum of conflict. Positions are indicated and explored in an almost abstract way. The individuals in the meeting are actors who can manage the situation to their joint benefit. The area of common ground, of interdependence, is a foundation on which agreement is built. The Warm core style negotiator wants to find accommodation, to build and strengthen the relationship, he will seek to avoid any loss of face to the other party. A comfortable environment is there to support the process in which both parties can relax and seek to avoid unnecessary personal stress.

Negotiating with a Warm core style negotiator provides examples of behaviours which are often endorsed and appreciated without reference to the objective of the meeting. We meet a person who is friendly and shows his understanding of what he has heard by effective use of summaries. At the outset of the meeting he will refer to the past benefits of the relationship and the anticipated joint gains. If it is a new situation the same objective will be achieved by reference to other situations which both parties may identify without risk and associate with positive outcomes. Throughout the conversation the use of 'we' predominates. Where 'I' is used it serves to bring out incremental, matched disclosure of positive feelings, events and experiences. The meeting appears almost flat, the pace is steady whilst each item is dealt with partially or completely in the time that is required. Changes of topics are confirmed before beginning and time limits jointly agreed. The Warm core style negotiator is prepared to share information almost without regard to the power implications, in particular, if the other party responds by a full and open disclosure of his own perceptions, feelings, needs and objectives. On this basis he can 'help' by making concessions which are of value to the other party because their interests are legitimate and have to be recognised if the agreement is to be both concluded and implemented without subsequent problems. Adjournments are frequently used for the benefit of both sides and are jointly agreed. Often informal contact and discussion continues in order to deepen the quality of understanding and the relationship beteen the parties. This process is seen as joint problem-solving with a premium being placed on openness, trust and knowledge of the other party's needs. The agreement will reflect the quality of the relationship. The balance of power between the parties tends to be de-emphasised because it could if addressed create embarrassment and confrontation. It would not encourage the identification of the factors behind the issues being discussed.

The Warm core style negotiator wants to manage conflict by working either within a developed relationship which exists or to have an opportunity to develop with the other party the framework and procedures in which mutual benefits can be identified and agreed upon. Within the negotiating relationship the Warm core style negotiator maintains a low stance or profile. Issues which are raised are solved because of the quality of the relationships. Both parties should seek to build and maintain psychological and tangible credits with one another. At a personal level the Warm core style negotiator needs to derive satisfaction from the process itself. In difficult situations he needs to be given time to build a cohesive team on his own side. Internal trust and co-operation are important to him even if this involves compromises. In cross-cultural situations he displays considerable sensitivity and can build goodwill effectively. There exists a danger that his Warm style brings in an unwillingness to confront extreme demands.

(c) The Numbers Style

The Numbers Style
(Analytical, Conservative, Reserved, Issue Orientated)

Positive aspects	Negative aspects
Good grasp of facts, logic, detail.	Uncomfortable with people, feelings. Difficulty coping with emotion.
Practical, concerned with the workability of a deal.	Cold to others.
Weighs the alternatives and values his options.	Communication with people is minimal – one word answer
Methodical, systematic, orderly.	'Numbers neurotic' – needs huge amount of information. Will not make quick decision.
Well-prepared, does his homework.	Gets bogged down in detail. Finds it difficult to adopt a problem-solving perspective.
Knows the history of the relationship and situations in detail with speedy access to files and correspondence.	Needs to clarify the words and ideas. Pedantic in words used, suspicious.
Confident in own analytical skills.	Expects others to be convinced by his facts and details.
Valuable team member – technical resource.	Irritated by counterparts who not adopt his perspectives.
Insists on evidence numbers	Doesn't see others' point of view unless expressed in his terms.

Proves the practicality of his counter-proposals and ideas.	Does not give reasons for negative reponses except to question the logic.
Confirms his objectives and ideas with senior management or other external authority/ references.	Unimaginative, inflexible, obsessive.
Persistent, patient.	Prisoner of the past. Pessimist.
Difficult to upset.	Resists changes, new ways. Stubborn, nit-picking. Vulnerable to surprise moves.

The first impression of the Numbers core style negotiator is that of order and predictability. We know what will happen. At the outset of the meeting the key issues will be set out. Each item will then be examined in a methodical way. In some sense the actors are exploring a reality which imposes its logic and structure on the process. The discussion will be precise and to the point, dominated by the use of the appropriate technical language which allows no opportunity for ambiguity. The agenda has to be completed. It provides a structure within which progress can be evaluated. The behaviour and reasonableness of the other party will be judged by their method of working, their technical competence on complex issues, and their willingness to avoid personal involvement in trivial issues. Both parties should have a command of the details and be prepared to spend sufficient time to be thorough and ensure that the subsequent agreement is complete. Nothing should be left to chance. The Numbers core style negotiator is principled, and displays a concern for the technical logic of the situation. Should there be an element of conflict, he assumes that it can be contained by 'being sensible and logical'.

During the meetings the Numbers core style negotiator will present his analysis in detail and expect it to be accepted. If this is not the case he will want to be presented with an equivalent level of structured information which can be examined with the same level of rigour that characterised his preparation either in the meeting or during the adjournment. At the beginning of the meeting the Numbers core style negotiator presents a relatively limited number of options. Alternatives have to be categorised to facilitate their evaluation unless they are to be rejected because of previous analysis. A fairly typical response might be, 'I want to see the figures broken down before further discussion.' The meeting will make reasonable progress because of a concern both for time management and order. A punctual start, a limited number of options which require perseverance to complete are the result of a principled, fair, but reserved approach to the meeting. His logic rules, emotions are controlled and the results are a foregone conclusion as there is no room for alternative courses of action. Although this description is perhaps a caricature of the meeting with a Numbers core style negotiator it should nevertheless provide a starting-point for recognition.

The Numbers core style negotiator appears to want security and the maintenance of the status quo. Precedents, once established, are to be followed and if change is required a long period of time is needed to make the adjustments. In many instances this negotiator prefers to work on issues that have identifiable boundaries or, if unstructured and dynamic, can be dealt with by means of applying known principles that is, of accounting or engineering. As a negotiator he needs to be perceived by his colleagues as being competent and prefers to belong to teams where his regard for them, as professionals, is equally high. When facing a Numbers core style negotiator it is necessary to develop wide areas of interest and to expose him to new situations gradually so that he can build additional criteria for evaluating people and events which are not unidimensional, that is, accurate–inaccurate. To develop his role within a team it is a good idea to provide him with gradually increasing areas of responsibility. To initially simply give him a large, complex task will run the risk of creating an oversimplified response.

(d) The Dealer Style

The Dealer Style
(Flexible, Compromising, Integrative, Outcome Oriented)

Positive aspects   Negative aspects

Quick to see opportunities, angles.	A deal at almot any price. Overcompromising. Can be an underachiever.
Looks for ways to 'make it work'.	Assumes 'everything will be all right'.
Enjoys negotiating across cultural barriers.	Takes on jobs that are not his.
Easy, charming, cheerfully cynical manner.	All things to all men.
Deploys social skills to persuade.	May rub people up the wrong way.
Avoids giving offence (even when saying 'No'). Gives bad news without damaging relationship.	Conflict-avoider, both on interpersonal issues and key items in the meeting.
Adaptable, flexible, imaginative.	Won't stand firm on anything. Goes along even if it does not conform to the better interests of his constituents.
Avoids getting stuck on one point.	Shifts his position too fast, too often.
Timing of adjournments accurate for tension release, or for personal comfort.	Loses credibility of own team and organisation.
Thinks on his feet, fast talker.	Can seem tricky, insincere, phoney.
Effective user of questions.	Fails to prepare, plan properly.
Uses any available argument/fact.	Too clever by half.

Prepared to use 'unplanned' visual aids to support his ideas.	Shifts from issue to issue too quickly.
Won't give up easily.	Links items together only for tactical reasons.
	Too pushy.

The first impression of the Dealer core style negotiator may well be a mixture which characterises negotiating as a social encounter, of fun and risk. It probably gives the closest approximation of its image for the general public. The negotiator may well have an aura of confidence, sophistication, and flexibility. Many of his expressions may suggest that decisions can and should be taken quickly and that in a dynamic environment a failure to respond to opportunities is to invite losses. All of this is captured in the expression, 'This offer lasts for a limited period and is unlikely to be repeated at such a bargain price.' The Dealer is a generalist who displays a broad knowledge and can quickly identify or build convenient linkages between the items being discussed. His imaginative mind is capable of generating many unorthodox ideas, which if they remain unstructured can hinder the negotiations. If systematically integrated by means of summaries and notes they provide a sound basis for avoiding deadlocks.

In the meeting the Dealer core style negotiator does not come across as a primarily logical thinker. Facts are picked up or discarded if this will help the meeting to move to its primary objective – an agreement. He appears to have internalised the salesman's dictum 'Always be closing.' Should he be presented with a direct 'No' his response is to shift quickly to another topic. He will avoid sounding negative, often resorting to 'Yes, but . . .'. If the other party raises an issue they are thanked and if it is a problem its ownership is immediately shared – 'We both need to address this issue.' Should he be unable to agree to a request then the justification is always external, 'Our company policy on this issue has been . . .'. Should the other party refer to his policy constraints the reply is personalised – 'But we need to see how we can resolve this for both of us.' In many instances the Dealer will seek to present alternatives. The issues were identified primarily at the start of the meeting and now the shape of the final package emerges but, in order to ensure that the outcome meets his objectives, sometimes totally new issues are introduced or items bundled together to his advantage. The effective Dealer will seek to ensure that by the time the negotiations approach their end he has established his personal relationships with the other party and that they are sufficiently strong and flexible that understanding and accommodation may prove stronger than the written word. His concern is for the spirit of the agreement not for the letter. This can perhaps best be captured by the humorous Irish observation, 'A verbal agreement is not worth the paper it is written on.'

The Dealer wants social recognition and appreciation as the person who can make things happen, to reconcile the irreconcilable and apparently salvage something out of disaster. Monetary rewards and fringe benefits are regarded as tangible and deserved tokens of acceptance and power. The reality of being regarded as marginal, a loner and self-employed employee, is at best ignored and at worst denied. He requires freedom from organisational controls, the procedures and routines bore him unless they can be manipulated as part of a game. Detail, of all forms, creates a prison which he finds stifling. He needs, in order to become a more effective negotiator and effective time manager, to balance his personal concerns for an agreement with the organisation's longer term objectives. This may also require a willingness to accept closer supervision from his own management and to recognise that his area of freedom in decision-making can be based only upon a mature aceptance of such control. He must be brought to recognise the impact of this short-term behaviour on the viability of his long-term relations.

SECTION III – THE STYLES IN ACTION

We identified above four different and discrete negotiating styles. The description and characterisation of each style was laid out in part to facilitate the identification of those behaviours which could be described as positive and those which are reviewed as negative. The value of these 'lists' of positive and negative behaviour is that they are descriptive of quite broad categories of attitude. The actual words and behaviour used by the participants in the negotiation will depend on the issues, location, and other factors. There are, however, some quite easily recognisable differences in major aspects of behaviour which will aid the processes both of recognising the individual negotiators and of relating their methods to our own behaviour as negotiators.

The effective Tough core style negotiator leaves no doubt that the position he has taken up is one which he will not give up lightly and should he be forced to review his commitment it will only be after the other party has sustained considerably increased costs, financial and psychological. Time alone will not wear him down – 'I am prepared to stay here until we reach what I consider is an acceptable agreement.' The other party's perception of his own position is the target for a continuous process of undermining – 'We are in discussion with a number of suppliers' or 'You may currently be the sole supplier but we are actively searching for an alternative piece of equipment which can meet the same performance requirements.' Often the Tough core style negotiator will block any discussion about the future, trying to increase the other party's feelings that only the short term, here and now, is of importance. If he indicates that a long-term future exists it is only to suggest that it will take place on his terms – 'I am prepared to review our longer term position if . . .'.

In presenting alternatives the Tough core style negotiator often appears to offer the other party the choice between two equally costly alternatives. Should the discussion almost spontaneously appear to explore an alternative which flows out of the discussion itself, the enthusiasm will still be controlled. Caution would clearly be communicated and the examination of ideas would take place with a formal disclaimer, 'I am prepared to look at this but without commitment', 'Do not interpret my discussing this issue as in any way indicating a formal reaction from the company. I am merely seeing if there is a workable alternative to my original proposal.' As the negotiations are concluded the effective Tough core style negotiator is concerned that the other party is left in no doubt as to what is required of him. His duties and obligations within the agreement will be repeated with the assurance that performance will be monitored. The implication is that approval is only grudging and always subject to review: 'Should you fail to live up to your side of the agreement . . .', 'We have a very clear idea of what we are expecting in terms of the quality of service and should this fail you can rest assured that we will take this up at the most senior level in your company'.

The encounter with the effective 'Warm' core style negotiator leaves a very different residual impression. From the outset his commitment to his own position will remain undisclosed or taken-for-granted. He appears to be governed by the maxim that to disclose your own objectives is to either invite conflict or at least cause the costs to increase. 'The sort of thing we are looking for is . . .' provides an indication of the oblique way in which the meeting may start. Clearly the other party may be able to draw on his experiences and therefore to state too precisely one's requirements may be to provoke either conflict or disappointment. The effective warm core style negotiator expects the other party to perceive him as committed to the relationship and therefore as being unwilling to force a particular perspective on the meeting: 'I would like to draw on your experience in this field', 'We have an idea of what the design will look like but remain very flexible on individual points'. The other party's perception will be subjected to a gentle process of redefinition – 'We would like you to see it from this angle' or 'Perhaps we might both look at this from the point of view of our client', 'We as consulting engineers and you as the subcontractor on this equipment might want to . . .'.

The Warm core style negotiator in exploring alternatives will continue the process of generating ideas for as long as those present seem to require it. A summary of the problem signals the start of the ideas/alternatives generating process with an opportunity to check understanding. Often expressions like 'Can I explore that idea?' or 'I would like to build on that point' provides a label which indicates a positive value and contribution. Where the negotiators have established their personal rapport the use of first names becomes quite frequent, as does the acknowledgement of a particular contributor's personal expertise. The alternative may not be accepted or rejected because of expert power but because it fits the wishes and aspirations of those present. As the negotiations move towards their conclusion the communications contain references to both the progress made in terms of the issues which initially separated the parties and the contributions of individuals which marked the steps towards an agreement. Attributions of ideas, insights, and specific proposals which are aimed at securing personal identification with the agreement and its implications characterises the communications of the effective Warm core style negotiator – 'We have listened very carefully to John's (the project engineer's) suggestion and realise that it gives us considerable improvement, both in costs and performance of the equipment on site, so we have no hesitation in going ahead as soon as the drawings are confirmed by the client. In the meantime we will let you have a telex to bring together the points so that you can brief your people. I know I am not speaking only for myself but all of us feel very comfortable about this project and the way we have solved these issues.'

At the conclusion of the meeting the Warm core style negotiator leaves the other party in no doubt that the communication channels have been strengthened between the two parties and remain open for him to use to revise any subsequent issues.

The behaviour of the Numbers core style negotitor is dominated by mental language. It does not have the benefit of warmth and feelings; technical expressions used with great care leave the listener in no doubt of what is meant, provided that he is the equal of the Number core style negotiator in terms of technical training and competence. Should the listener prove that he is no match in the use of the particular technical language, the use of the Numbers negotiator, however, will not cease. He may be used to create a feeling of panic, inferiority and dependency in the other party. This at worst is captured in the expression 'bull and baffle brains'. The other implication of the use of formal language and expressions is that latent or actual hostility, personal feelings, and animosities can somehow be banished. Ordinary language is somewhat vulgar, and imprecise. The Numbers core style negotiator through his use of formal titles creates an atmosphere which is detached from the external environment: 'Let us tackle this issue in what we both agree are its key elements: (1) the agreed facts, (2) the contested facts, that is, uncombated by inspections reports, ship's manifests, bill of lading, (3) the identified/ quantified elements of the claim, and (4) the unquantified elements', 'The argument about liability can be held over till we have a clear feel for the size of the problem.' Having agreed how the meeting is to be conducted the Numbers core style negotiator may even go so far as to indicate a timetable with again both an internal and external justification: the former being that we discuss all the issues; the latter being the need to be able to call on others with relevant knowledge who are not in attendance at the start of the meeting.

A major frustration which the Numbers core style negotiator can create is as a result of his attitude as regards listening and questioning. He will expect the other party to pay detailed attention to his presentation which may involve the use of complex formulas to support calculations, and so on. He, however, may feel that he retains the right to interrupt, to draw attention to imprecisions in language, small mistakes, and more generally to the logical structure of the other party's presentation: 'Excuse me, surely you mean £1840 not £184' or 'I realise that it does not follow so let me draw your attention to it now. I don't want you to feel that I have accepted that point because I did not register my objection at the time.'

The other party will always be invited to be precise, detailed and as accurate as possible – 'Just so we know where we stand.'

In his summaries the Numbers core style negotiator will accurately attribute both the other party and himself with particular statements, claims, suggestions. The summary itself being justified and introduced to either stop the meeting getting out of hand because too many proposals or ideas are being tabled or to deliberately switch the discussion to another item, the logical linkage being obvious.

As the final stage of the agreement begins to emerge the Numbers core style negotiator may signal his enthusiasm by commenting that 'We both realise this is a logical conclusion' or 'these proposals will work and that is the main thing . . . out of this rather messy situation we have managed to build something feasible . . . next time we will know exactly what to do.' The concern for structure, order and precedent will win through.

The conclusion of the meeting is never abrupt. There remains the onerous job of recording the agreement, possibly of signing agreed minutes and notes. Timetables are to be established for the implementation plans and then the relatively formal farewells with perhaps the parting reference to the problem of not being recognised for the contribution being made to the organisation by creating order out of chaos.

The Dealer core style negotiator is a 'natural' communicator who relies not merely on words, but gestures, bodily contact, and, where appropriate, demonstrations and impromptu displays of emotional commitment and enthusiasm. His language shows a high need for acceptance and a wish to avoid rejections. Should the other party be known to respond to certain expressions he will use them.

If the other party with whom the negotiations are being conducted are not working in their first language his own communication will incorporate the appropriate 'foreign words' and expressions to reduce social distance and suspicion. The initial impression will be of a person who enjoys the encounter – the language will be relaxed with early reference to the objective of the meeting: 'I know we have got quite a lot to battle with today – I can't see any big problems and so I have arranged a working lunch here which will give you an opportunity to meet our new Board member for marketing – he is still feeling his way in and we see eye to eye on issues. This evening I thought we would have dinner together' (at an expensive restaurant). The mixture of name dropping, association with higher status colleagues on an informal basis, allusions to real influence on decision-making are meant to be communicated.

The preliminaries disposed of, the agenda will be indicated rather than spelled out. Last minute amendments will be accommodated even if this means discussion without detailed briefings: 'Yes we can certainly add that to our list as long as you don't expect me to be too specific. We can probably leave the nuts and bolts to next time.' The preliminary statement of the other party may sometimes be interrupted on a point of clarification or to show particular sensitivity – 'Yes I appreciate that point, and I discussed the paperwork problems on the telephone yesterday – I have some ideas which will help you with the custom authorities but we can get to that later. 'Should the other party raise a more contentious point he will not evoke a specific response as a direct 'Yes' or 'No' which leaves no room for ambiguity. The operating maxim being: Why say 'No' now, you may not have to say it later?

In some cases the issues will be glossed over or played down with comments such as 'It is not so important' or 'Perhaps the distribution manager has blown this matter up a bit to make certain we deal with it.'

In this initial phase the Dealer core style negotiator will indicate a range of commitments to his demands and avoid absolutes. His ideas will be justified in terms of their benefits to the other party: 'We have undertaken some detailed market research in fully-covered chocolate biscuits and the results show quite clearly that you are losing margin because customers are trading down to half-covered chocolate biscuits which have a lower margin. Our idea is to come in at 8 per cent per packet more than for our fully-covered chocolate finger biscuits.' A proposal has to be sold – it should not create a confrontation. Should the climate change the Dealer core style negotiator will start to laugh and joke. The important issue may be reduced to the level of the banal by pointing out the funny side – 'Well, they are mean in Yorkshire. 'The alternative is to provide a very long rambling and imprecise answer. It never ends with 'Let me summarise – there are two points . . . .'

As the meeting continues the Dealer's style is characterised by its apparent lack of coherence. Items appear and disappear. A problem raised by the other party is dealt with by incorporation and by personalising it: 'Well . . . I am glad you felt you could raise this problem, I regard it as proof that we have got a very open relationship. I would also feel concerned if I were you about the delay in installing the second pump's electrical backup system. If you will excuse me I will phone our people now to make certain that things really are moving'.

At a convenient point the Dealer may begin to summarise. If he is capable of rejecting the other party's inaccurate summary he will also assume equal ownership of ideas and a slightly skewed balance of give and take. He has shown his positive approach by withdrawing certain proposals (not demands). With a casual 'We all know what we have agreed' the meeting concludes. The core style Dealer has moved from issue to issue until the shape of the final settlement has emerged with sufficient time for a pre-dinner drink!

SECTION IV – CORE AND ADAPTATIVE STYLES

The concluding section of this chapter will deal with the relationship between the core style and the adaptative element. One starting-point could be the often-asked question: how much is core style and how much is adaptative? How can one recognise which is being deployed by the other party?

There is of course no possible general answer to this question, it varies with each case, and within the case of each individual, with time.

However, the smaller element will have to be the adaptative style. The adaptative style is one of the other core styles and may be several of these in turn but is the smaller component; it is not built upon the basic personality stuctures and has not been internalised thoroughly over a career span. In that sense it is not 'skin tight' but loose and can be changed on a situationally specific basis. The process of changing our core style is much slower, more difficult to control, for it is largely independent of our will and requires the expenditure of a greater psychological investment, because it is embedded in our personality of which it is a feature. In order for a change of core style to be effective it will require both internal and external reinforcement – for example, a job change, changes in pattern of interactions at work, and changes of people involved in those interactions, as well as psychological help, in some cases.

The adaptative style tends also to be relatively stable, being influenced by the length of the negotiating relationship in which it will be seen, the history of the relationship, and the issues being discussed. Even the 'Tough' core style dealer may over time become the owner and user of a highly effective Numbers adaptative style if the reinforcements, both internal and external, are effective in supporting it. Feeling more and more 'comfortable' with a given adaptative style, a negotiator will tend to use it with more and more confidence. However, it is voluntarily decided upon and acquired and one is never so deeply rooted into it as one is with the core style. In cases of shock, surprise, one will tend automatically to fall back upon one's core style. The factors which are subsumed in the core style such as personality, education, and so on, cannot be discarded.

Of course the core style will be a part of the definition of the bargaining situation by one party. It will deeply influence, through the bounded rationality and the objectives, the understanding of the environment by the party. From then on, he will adopt an additional adaptative component to his style. The effective negotiator will, however, ensure that the behaviours he selects and uses are 'positive'. Having identified a list of positive and negative behaviours there is no advantage in selecting those that are not likely to prove effective unless the objective is to ensure that the organisation does not expose one to such situations in the future.

The selection of an adaptative style will be influenced by a wide range of situational factors – whether we are negotiating alone or in a team, in our own culture or in a foreign culture, in our own offices or overseas, the agenda, the importance of the items, our strategy, our perception of the balance of power, our resources and constraints, the other party, and so on. We may actually find it difficult to switch quickly from one adaptative style to another and should this be felt to be a major obstacle a number of factors should be remembered. Conceptually we have a choice of four adaptative styles – however, one will be the same as our core style. Of the remaining three one of the styles may be seen as 'uncomfortable' or be rejected in terms of our 'self-image'. Our personal strategy as negotiators should therefore be to seek initially to identify the adaptative style that basically we feel the most comfortable with and that we use for most of our negotiations. With a certain degree of candour we can recognise one or perhaps two negative behaviours in our adaptative style which we should seek to control. Subsequently we may feel that a review of the other adaptative styles that we can use may show that they are appropriate for a specific negotiation. From experience, and as a result of discussions with other negotiators, one situation which may trigger the improvement of different adaptative styles will be a cross-cultural negotiation, in particular, when this should require us to cope with language problems. In that situation, if we are working with a colleague, the situational element can easily be used to justify the behavioural experimentation. Should the different behaviours work, our willingness to use them in another situation will also increase. 'Failure' can also be rationalised – 'It wasn't me really.'

We must conclude with a simple but important observation about the negotiator's styles. They cannot be 'dumped' overnight or even at all, totally. An attempt to do so and to adopt fully an adaptative style deemed preferable in theory will only result in loss of flexibility, rigidity in attitudes in the bargaining situation, and discomfort.

A more realistic task for a person involved in negotiating or about to become involved in negotiating is to review the list of positive and negative behaviours and to identify one or two strengths which he can build on. It may also repay us to identify one negative which we wish to control. This can be best achieved in collaboration with a colleague because the process of building on strengths and controlling a weakness requires an opportunity to take on different tasks, to plan more effectively, and to be integrated within a specific strategy. Innovating in a negotiation dominated by a conflictual strategy in which the majority of items are distributively oriented is not the best learning environment!

Finally, obviously, the adaptative component that we select after having identified our core style, and eventually attempted to correct some of its weaknesses and reinforced some of its strengths, must be fitted to our strategy: a Tough one for negotiations where our strategy will be conflictual is obvious, as well as a Warm one for a co-operative strategy. But the other elements of selection of a strategy should also come into play: a negotiation with many items, for instance, may ask for introduction of elements of a Dealer style, or a very technical one for a Numbers one.

7 The Phases of Negotiation

Ann Douglas[1] was among the first to derive from her own observations and from data obtained from the United States Federal Mediation and Conciliation Service a three stage model of negotiation based on labour relations' mediated sessions of bargaining. It consisted of: (a) establishing the negotiating range; (b) reconnoitring the negotiating range; (c) precipitating the decision-making crisis. Speculations, experimental studies, and observations by many social psychologists confirmed the principle of the negotiation moving into 'stages' which are clearly identifiable and often relatively similar in many cases. However, the number of phases which have been identified varies. For instance, Zartman[2] establishes a two-stage model with the first stage concerned with developing a general formula for agreement and the second one dealing with details of implementation. Warr[3] applies to labour negotiations a more general model of group activity including four stages: (a) getting organised; (b) breaking up; (c) accepting a common goal; (d) finding a solution. Druckman's work[4] results in a six-stage model with the following phases: (a) agreement about the need to negotiate; (b) agreement on a set of principles and objectives; (c) agreement on certain rules of conduct (it should be noted that the two precedent phases combined are identical to the negotiation on the rules discussed above); (d) defining the issues and setting up an agenda; (e) agreement on a formula or in principle; (f) agreement on implementing details. Pruitt notes that Druckman's last two stages are equivalent to Zartman's two stages; we can add that Warr's last two stages seem also to play the same function. He also remarks that the role of stages following each other and through which the parties move successively is dual: it organises the intellectual efforts of the bargainers who can think more clearly about the issues and it allows them to deal first with their basic differences and to progress afterwards in order to resolve these issues.

Morley and Stephenson[5] on the basis of Douglas's work and after a full review of the literature, and carrying out their own experiments and careful analysis and observation of case studies, argue convincingly in favour of a three-stage model: A first period of hard distributive bargaining, where the feasibility of demands is assessed, is followed by a period of problem-solving, where proposals are made and evaluated in the light of the opening exchanges, and a third period of decision-making and action, where the implications of possible points are explored, concludes the process. It underlines a remark made by Pruitt[6] that the succeeding phases imply a transition from competition to co-ordination. To a certain degree this seems unavoidable to some extent, because in all cases only 'successful' negotiations that is, the ones ending in agreement) are considered. The agreement may be more or less satisfactory to one or all parties and one party may have fallen victim to very distributive strategy and tactics; nevertheless a minimum degree of co-operation is unavoidable to reach a settlement, however grudgingly it was granted. By definition all other negotiations have broken down at an earlier time, and presumably did so under the impact of competitive or avoiding strategies.

It should also be emphasised that the stages model of a negotiation is fully compatible with our fundamental premiss of bounded rationality: the limitations of the human mind and the uncertainty and complexity of the alternatives make it necessary that a procedure for narrowing down their number and their consequences be employed by the parties. The idea of stages implies a sequential and satisfying model of decision and not a synoptic and maximising one.

In practical terms, the three-stage model that we have retained is the following. The first stage consists of getting to know each other and each other's starting positions: that is, 'the determination of the outer limits of the range in which (the parties) will have to do business with each other'. The second stage is characterised by attempts to establish a range of settlement, through actions taken in an 'official' capacity as representative of a party as well as through informal processes or feelers. The third stage is the one of decision-making. Each party tries to force the other into making a decision.

Beyond the obvious statement that a process has a beginning, a middle and an end, this three-stages model proves itself useful. It emphasises the importance of timing, of adopting a different pace for each of the three periods as well as the need for a degree of synchronism in the movements of the two sides. It has been adopted, with the variations mentioned above, throughout the literature and we can use it by extending it also out of the labour relations field and into the commercial field. It can also be enriched by adding two short sections dealing with what should happen before the negotiaton: planning; and what should happen after: debriefing.

SECTION I – PLANNING

It should be apparent that planning is essential to negotiations, but in practice it is very often neglected, generally with very unfortunate results. There are various reasons for this: lack of time, pressure from other tasks, assumption that one is a 'born negotiator' and that one does not need to bother with unnecessary paperwork, or even simple ignorance. However, the negotiator who has planned in advance is better prepared and better informed and as such, is more likely to get the best out of the negotiation. The ill-prepared negotiator will not have realistic, or clearly formulated, objectives, will know nothing or next to nothing about the issues and the stakes, will totally misread the power balance, and so on.

However, several remarks must be made. First of all, many people do not plan, do not like to plan, or do not plan effectively. It is also true that planning is work, and hard work, that it means that we shall have to be dealing with uncertainty and therefore that it may make us somewhat uncomfortable. Also it can be relatively easily mishandled. Besides, we are generally working under time pressures, and many things other than planning for a negotiation, sometimes much more pleasant to do, call constantly for our attention. Finally, the image of a successful executive does not fit with the tasks normally associated with planning. Brilliance is in many minds associated with on-the-spot sudden decisions. The painstaking gathering and evaluating of information is apparently a type of work which does not fit this image.

On the other hand, there is almost no doubt that a well-prepared negotiator has a definite edge over his opponents.

(a) Flexibility in Planning

It is therefore necessary to plan. However, two remarks should be considered. First, there is virtually no limit to the amount of time and sophistication in quantitave and qualitative evaluation which theoretically could be spent planning. Obviously we must run a cursory cost/benefit analysis and balance the amount of planning to be carried out with the importance of the negotiation for us or our organisation as well as for our opponents and their organisation.

Second, planning can be mishandled. The most common form of mishandling, and one of the reasons why some of us are uncomfortable with planning, is that it is too often confused with rehearsal or a dry run of the negotiation to come. For reasons which clearly flow from the concepts discussed in Chapter 1, accurate rehearsal of a negotiation is impossible, not the least because we cannot know in advance the bonds on the rationality of the other party. Actually rehearsal may constitute the opposite of good planning because, having made up our mind in advance about the succession of outcomes and what we believe will be the behaviour of the other party we set ourselves into a straitjacket. Should, as it will almost always occur, the other party not follow one of the limited number of alternative scripts for his behaviour that we have written in advance for him, and that we are ready to face, we are lost. Taken by surprise, by our own fault, we are then in no better position than if we had done no planning at all. We are locked into a behaviour and tactics prepared in advance for events which do not and will not occur.

Planning for negotiations therefore should not be confused with trying one's hand at clairvoyance. Planning is gathering information, evaluating it, making assumptions, setting objectives, evaluating different strategies, tactics and styles.

Finally, planning should be carried out around issues, not sequentially. The danger of sequential planning, issue after issue, is to create another type of straitjacket for oneself. The order in which the issues will be tackled itself is a negotiable item which we described above as bargaining on the rules. One cannot predict the order of negotiation for more than a few moves ahead and even within such narrow limits with reservations. Therefore planning around issues allows the establishment of tactical links, packages, and is much more flexible. It helps to obtain concessions and brings into consideration a wider range of options. Each issue should be considered with its own logical links to the other issues of our agenda as well as by itself.

(b) Collecting Information and Evaluating It

The first step in planning is collecting and evaluating information. Here the method of check-lists is the most adequate. On the basis of e issues, of what is known about the other party, its constituents, if any, (company or union, members or others) a first list of what is needed can be drawn. This first step involves thinking about what information is needed, what information is already in store, what information it is necessary to obtain before the negotiation starts, where this information is available and from whom.

A second step is constituted of efforts to obtain the information according to plan, review it, evaluate it, and then start the process again. The information should be classified in four categories according to two criteria: how reliable it is and how relevant it is. Here also a matrix can be drawn and the information allocated in four categories: relevant and reliable; relevant but with low reliability; of little relevance with high reliability; and, finally, useless – with little relevance and little reliability.

In the process of collecting, reviewing, and evaluating information we analyse the environment, build a picture of the balance of bargaining power, set up our objectives, decide on a strategy, prepare a tentative array of tactics and build up one adaptative style, as was discussed in the earlier chapters.

However, it is useful to organise the information as it is described below.

(c) Check-lists

The information acquired is to be translated into the form of objectives; for collection and evaluation purposes, strategy, tactics, and style can first be organised under the form of check-lists. An example is given immediately below applied to the managerial side in collective labour negotiations.

1. Descriptive data of the unit covered by the agreement (company, plant, office or other).

- Statistical data: employees by grade, of labour, seniority, sex, age, pay grade, and family status
- Soft data: general attitude of categories of employees (towards union, company, superiors); what are the active factions and relationships between identified groups of employees?; recent changes in operating procedure, effects on schedules, products, new equipment, plant, or other. (In particular the effect on productivity of these changes)

2. The unions

   - Number of unions present on the shop floor
   - Policies of the national unions or federations represented on the shop floor
   - Links of local unions (or shop stewards) with the national unions
   - Influence of each union (numbers of militants, shop stewards, membership, number of votes in elections to work council, and so on)
   - Nature of relationship between the unions represented on the shop floor (competitive, unity of action, open warfare, and so on)
   - Are there minority factions inside the local unions?
   - Influence on non union employees (on work council, other)
   - What are the majority unions among the various grades of employees (blue-collar – unskilled, skilled, maintenance and repair, white-collar – employees, technical staff, research staff, supervisory staff, and so on)

3. Employee representation systems

   - Composition and unions' influence upon the various systems of employee representation if they exist (this depends upon the legal system of the country of operation and the company's policy). It concerns elected employee representatives, work councils, enterprise committees, and so on

4. Bargaining history

   - Summarise and update from past records and the precedent check-list

5. The present climate of industrial relations

   - Managerial input (from the foremen up, interviews for comments)
   - Recent strikes and conflicts in geographical area
   - Recent strikes and conflict in industry, country-wide
   - Outside input (network of personal directors, personal contacts, state or governmental authorities – labour inspectorate, labour courts' records, and so on – whenever applicable)

6. Analyses of past grievances and arbitration awards or personal delegates' remarks or complaints or labour courts' awards (if applicable)

7. Profile of local union leaders and probable members of the other party's negotiating party

8. Evaluation of union's and employees' financial resources (strike benefits, strike funds, availability of alternative work in the area, unemployment compensation eligibility, welfare payment eligibility, alternative sources of income for employees)

9. Probable union demands, broken down by costs

   - On the basis of the analysis carried in paragraphs 4 and 5 above, establish a list of probable union demands in terms of working conditions, hours, schedule, union security, and so on
   - Establish a list of probable demands regarding wages and fringe benefits
   - Cost all demands in one single unit (money/hour of work, for instance)

Note: A spreadsheet is particularly convenient for analysing the consequences of different alternatives

10. Prepare survey of present wage, fringe benefits, and working conditions in industry, area, other plants of the company by using various sources: published data, government statistics, network of personnel managers, chamber of commerce, employers' association, and so on

11. Analysis of recent collective agreements and settlements

   - National, inter-industry
   - National, industry
   - Local, industry
   - Other industries in area
   - Summaries of all applicable

12. Select negotiating team for the company, plant (see below, section on the negotiating team)

13. Can the company sustain a strike in the present economic conditions?

   - Market share and competition
   - Profit margin
   - Strategy and budgets

14. Does the company want to take a strike in the present economic conditions?

   - If yes, for how long at what cost?

15. Preparation of company proposals

   - Suggestion of each supervisor on changes to be introduced and demands to be considered
   - On this basis and considering the analysis carried out above in paragraphs 7, 8, 9 and 11, set up a preliminary list
   - Prepare preliminary proposals with cost evaluations
   - revision and establishment of initial proposals by company
Note: Here also the use of a spreadsheet is convenient

16. Recommendation to management and request for authority

   - On recommended initial proposal
   - To change its content during negotiation (up to a given level specified in advance in absolute terms, in terms of what mix of items?)
   - To take a strike on identified strike issues
   - To obtain information on all forthcoming strategic changes affecting labour relations (lay-off, expansion, relocation, and so on)

17. Strike plans

   * General

   - They must always be ready whatever happens
   - Decision to continue to operate or not (replacements, staff, pickets, and so on)

- Contingency provisions to be taken in order to deal with customers and suppliers
  - warn ahead of negotiations
  - build up stocks (when possible)
  - deliver from other sources (imports, other plants)
  - agreement with competition?
  - impact on public opinion
  - contacts with media and individuals of influence
  - contacts with public authorities

* Safety

- Protection of employees and maintenance of equipment
- Safety provisions dealing with the specific work processes

* Contingency plan

- In case of sit-in
- In case of picketing
- Legal actions – court injunctions
- Pay to non-strikers out of work?

A similar check-list should be established in advance of all negotiations whether commercial or labour, collective or individual, in greater or lesser detail, of course, in accordance with the principle of cost/benefit efficiency outlined above. The illustration we just gave is only – an illustration – and it should not be construed as a model applicable in all labour cases or transferable as such into other domains. Conditions will vary, with the size of the stakes, the national or industrial environment, and so on. A different check-list needs to be elaborated for each case.

In commercial negotiations, for instance, the emphasis will be placed differently on items such as which is 'their' company, who will negotiate on its behalf, and their past record. Information in this case can be provided by trade journals, financial papers, chambers of commerce, commercial courts, corporate registry offices and personnel contacts, including one's own company colleagues who may have already negotiated with them. Beyond these very general points, clearly the focus or the emphasis in planning will vary according to the type of commercial negotiations. For instance, technical preparation will be essential for licensing agreements, may still be important for commercial contracts, but will be less of a point when buying or selling a standard commodity. Product specifications will be instrumental for subcontracting agreements, capital structure, and legal considerations in the case of negotiating joint ventures, and so on.

In many cases the following items should be thought out in advance in commercial negotiations, whether individual or collective:

- product specifications
- quantities
- packaging
- reciprocal trading
- time and condition of delivery (eventually split)
- price and discounts
- credit and interest rate, payment terms (including deferred payment and payment guarantees)
- insurance, transport and customs
- guarantees (including trade record)
- provisions for dispute jurisdiction and arbitration
- maintenance terms
- availability and price of spare parts
- after-sales assistance (including training and demonstrators)

(d) Preparing for the Initial Meeting

On the basis of the information collected it is now necessary to prepare ahead for the upcoming meeting in the framework of the strategy and tactics selected. A four-step preparatory process can usefully focus the mind on what is important whilst keeping enough flexibility.

1. Once the collected information has been assessed, additional information remains necessary; on the other hand, the other party will have gathered information about us and our position and will want to obtain more. Finally, we shall, according to the procedure outlined when dealing with tactical rules, be providing information to the other party. Ahead of the meeting it may be useful to classify the information according to what we want to give and what we want to keep, as well as what we need to get from the other party: what they are likely to give us and what would surprise us if they gave it to us. The following graph summarises this process:

Information

| Us | Other party |
| we want to give | we are likely to get |

we want to give	we are likely to get
we want to keep	we would be surprised to get

Clearly this classification of information needs to be constantly updated, not only between meetings but at each recess during a single session.[7]

2. A second step concerns assumptions. From the information we have acquired we are going to infer a certain number of things regarding the other party and the other party is going to infer a certain number of things about us. These assumptions should concern the bounds on rationality, bargaining power (ours as we believe they allocate it to us, theirs, and the balance), objectives (manifest and latent), strategies, likely tactics, negotiating styles.

We must make assumptions. They are necessary because information will always be incomplete and imperfect. But we must be aware that we are making assumptions and not consider what we think as uncontroversial and proven, which generally we tend to do automatically. Also we should always keep in mind that assumptions are nothing more than assumptions, and are not facts. Therefore they can, and will, sometimes be faulty. In that case what we assume about the other party is erroneous (for instance. we may assume that he is committed to a conflictual attitude whereas he is ready to compromise). However. it may also be that the other party is making wrong assumptions about us, and therefore that he reacts according to his assumptions, and not to what we believe we communicate to him, or what we understand the circumstances to be. This is a direct illustration of the factor of bounded rationality. We should recognise that the bonds on our rationality constrain our assumptions, all in the same direction. One of the basic axioms set up by Korybski, the theoretician of general semantics, sums up the situation neatly: the map is not the ground. From reading the map we assume that it represents the ground accurately, but this only an assumption and it may well be proven wrong: landslides may occur, motorways may be rebuilt, bridges may be closed, hedges may be cut and trenches may be dug, and then the map no longer accurately represents the ground. However, given that we must make assumptions and cannot avoid it, then not only must we be aware that we are making them but we must beware of them and pay attention to the ones which are made about us.[8]

Therefore we must test our assumptions. This can be done either through the use of listening to the other party and looking for dissonances with what we assume, or simply by asking questions, or eventually, at a later stage of the negotiation, by making an assumption public, and therefore known to the opponent, and then observe his reaction. However, we may not want to make an assumption public either directly or through our questions because this could run against our strategy.

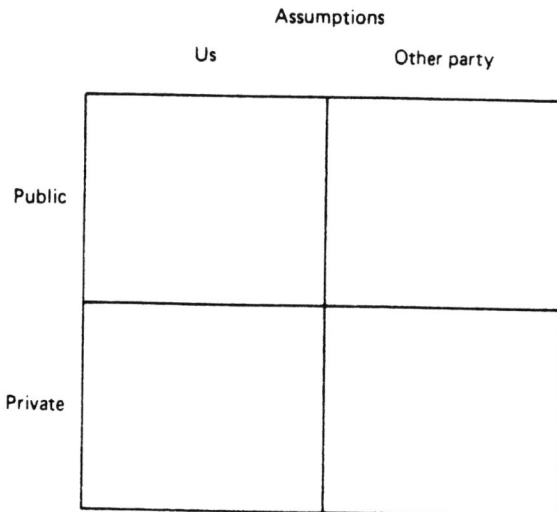

Assumptions

	Us	Other party
Public		
Private		

We must also be aware that the other party is making assumptions about us. We must discover them and eventually influence them. Then again they may not acknowledge or want to acknowledge them. However, we can, if it fits our strategy, probe them more or less directly. This can be done either by referring directly to their assumptions, or by attributing them to a third party, or even by openly stating them and asking the other party to conform or deny them.

An assumption box can be constructed in the same way as for information (see p. 185).

Just as in the case of information, and possibly even more importantly, assumptions should be reviewed at each opportunity.

3. The third step concerns concessions. Within the broad framework of the procedural rules applying to concessions, which was discussed above, it is useful, given the balance of bargaining power estimated and the strategy selected, to prepare for concessions. Concessions from our side as well as the concessions that we hope to get from the opponent's. To put the two in parallel is also a convenient way to summarise the practical consequences of the balance of bargaining power. The same box model can be used then with a further refinement.

Concessions

We	Other party
we plan to make to get what we want	we anticipate them to make
we can make against significant extra gains	we would be surprised (happily) if they made rapidly
we cannot make and would rather remain deadlocked over	they are unlikely to make

Again, as in the case of information and of assumptions, the concessions box needs to be permanently reviewed. A direct effect of the concept of bounded rationality is that what we need from them may not be what they think we want the most from them. In the same way they may not be really interested in concessions that we think that they value highly. In order to try to gain insights into their rationality it is useful to, reviewing regularly, put in parallel another box labeled 'objectives'. It may bring us unforeseen benefits. It should be remembered that the other party may not value the same concession as we do and that our own rationality within our constraints may make us estimate the environment and the situation very differently from the way that the other party does.

Therefore a parallel 'objectives' box can be set up in a similar way. Assuming perfect objective rationality and a maximising and synoptic behaviour on both sides, our objectives should be their concessions and vice versa. In order to account for bounded rationality and real life, the 'other party' sides in the two boxes are two different sets of estimates, two different ways of looking at what we want, and what it seems that they are going to give us. They should be filled as the negotiation proceeds and the discrepancies should provide us with insights into the other party's strategy.

Objectives

We	Other party
need to get	need to get from us
may get	may get from us
unlikely to get	won't get

4. The final step in planning involves contingency action. If deadlock is reached what to do then? And at which point should deadlock be decided upon? As illustrated in the planning example for industrial

relations negotiation described above. contingency plans should be prepared and the point at which deadlock is preferred to agreement decided upon in advance, although, as the box model implies, it can be revised during the process, upwards and downwards. In collective negotiations the negotiators must be careful to get authorisation of their constituencies in case of such revisions.

SECTION II – THE THREE PHASES OF THE PROCESS

(a) Beginning

1. This is the phase where the possibility of a deal will be identified. It is also the first meeting and it is also a social encounter. This is important because a major difference of course should be taken into account depending upon the fact that, regardless of other dimensions of the negotiation, the negotiators might or might not have met before. They may or may not be known to each other. Also, whether they have met before or not, they may or may not trust each other. It is true that a long-term relationship tends to build trust as was discussed above. It is also true that people who have already been in contact with each other, whether these prior contacts were in the framework of earlier negotiations or within other social settings, may tend to distrust each other. The two dimensions are important. Whatever the balance of bargaining power, the strategy and tactics planned and the style of the negotiators, they will give an initial impetus to the negotition.

It can be represented thus:

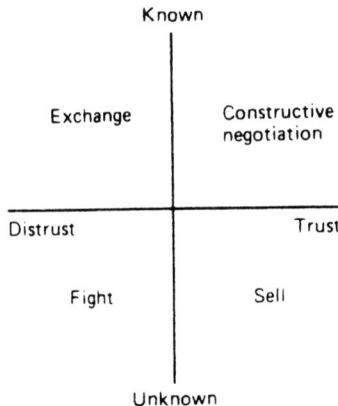

```
                        Known
                          |
                          |
        Exchange          |   Constructive
                          |   negotiation
                          |
                          |
   ―――――――――――――――――――――――+―――――――――――――――――
   Distrust               |           Trust
                          |
        Fight             |   Sell
                          |
                          |
                        Unknown
```

This initial impetus is important because the reciprocal positions are going to be structured very fast. The situation encountered may be very different from the one which was expected during the planning phase, which is why planning must remain flexible to be efficient.

2. This first meeting is important also because it is the one which will establish the agenda. The importance of the agenda has already been underlined when dealing with the control procedural tactics. What was discussed then should be kept in mind at this point. It is the time to include or exclude items. Of course some additional ones may be brought in later, sometimes tactically as an effect of surprise; however, it is much easier then for a party not to agree to deal with these 'latecoming' points if he chooses not to.

Most experienced negotiators prefer to have the other party, when the agenda is agreed upon, make the initial offer. In itself this offer provides information. Maybe our planning was grossly off-target and, instead of revealing it if we speak up first, we may quickly revise our position if the other party speaks first and if we betray no surprise. However, someone has to start. It is customary in some situations that a given party comes with the initial offer: the union with a list of demands or the salesman with a line of products, for instance. Then, usually immediately after, the other party will have to provide some kind of answer, or counter-offer.

Therefore the beginning phase includes the exchange of opening statements. Clearly the opening statement is based on objectives. Our opening statement will provide the other party with information on our objectives and we shall learn about his.

Most of what has been said about objectives applies here and we find the same dilemma. Our opening position will be instrumental in determining what we gain from the negotiation; here also we will not get what we do not ask for. On the other hand, too high an opening position causes the problems discussed in Part I about objectives. Therefore the opening position should be realistic, in our own eyes, defensible, but high enough, with room to bargain added on. It of course depends on the items to be negotiated, but if we refer to our planning for objectives the opening statement should probably be fixed between what we 'may get' and what we are 'unlikely to get'. How high depends on each case, but another saying belonging to the common folklore of negotiating, and often quoted, may be recalled here: the prostitute's axiom which holds that 'the value of services is always higher before they are rendered than after'.[9]

Finally, a decision should be made as to the form in which the opening statement is to be presented: orally, in writing, with a draft statement of agreement, through a visual presentation, and so on.

3. Another important point concerns the use of tactics and adaptative style, whatever the strategy and our style may be: if one opens competitively one may never have a chance to become collaborative later. Therefore if the strategy selected includes some collaborative tactics the beginning phase is the time to use them. They might never have an opportunity to surface again. This is because negotiating has a built-in competitive dynamic. Left to itself the competitive aspect of issues will take over. On the contrary, collaborative aspects have to be consciously introduced. The beginning phase is the best time to do so because it takes place by definition before the conflictual dynamic has a chance to develop. The reasons for the conflictual dynamic are many.[10] In the framework of analysis that we have developed it is clear that bounded rationality will create biases and also that the behaviour of the other party will seem arbitrary, suspect, or unreasonable. Starting competitively will result in a self-fulfilling prophecy, the other party's behaviour is to some extent a response to ours. We think they want conflict, therefore we make them adopt a conflictual attitude by anticipating their actions and adopting conflictual tactics ourselves.

Cognitive simplification makes it such that under the stress of the negotiating we (and they) will tend to see things more and more in black and white. Our position and everything supporting it will be identified as good, the position of the opponent and everything associated with it will be identified as bad (for us). We shall no longer see and identify positive and negative aspects in the other party's tactics, style and behaviour but we will automatically consider it conflictual, and the same will apply from their side. A conflictual spiral is likely to develop.

If we negotiate in teams (to be discussed below) the build-up of hostility will increase. Sherif[11] has experimentally demonstrated, among other results, that when two groups engage in competition, intergroup hostility appears, whilst intra group solidarity increases. Unfavourable attitudes towards the other group emerge, the in-group activity is overvalued, and the out-group activity undervalued.

4. At the end of this first phase the parties should have a rough idea whether or not they are within an agreement or a contract zone, as defined above. A recess is generally useful to re-estimate the balance

of power, re-assess strategy, refine tactics and adaptative style.

Decisions are needed on how to move within the agreement range, and on whether to risk deadlock or conflict to get within this range if the opening positions are too far apart. After each development, information should be re-assessed, assumptions checked, concessions re-evaluated, and objectives checked both for oneself and for the other party.

(b) Middle Phase

Phase 2 or the middle phase is generally concerned with defining a potential deal within the perceived limits resulting from phase 1; or begins by revising these limits. Proposals and counter-proposals are exchanged. Limits on the bounds of rationality are assessed. Critical assumptions about bargaining power are checked, the strategy of the opponent is identified, tactics are used and trade-offs are evaluated. It is then that the flexibility in planning fully pays off for it allows a quick re-estimation and costing of various 'packages'.

Information is exchanged as information tactics are put in play. The time constraints change and timing tactics are used.[12] A search for alternatives takes place as well as attempts to influence and persuasion. Power and pressure tactics are used, concessions outlined and made.

These tactics have already been briefly discussed above. However, some facilitating tactics should be recalled now because their use can be particularly helpful, whatever the strategy employed by both parties.

The first one deals with the use of questions.[13] Questions can be extremely useful. They allow us to know exactly what we want to know. There is a certain natural reluctance in many people to ask questions. We may be afraid to embarrass the other party, or to seem to reveal our ignorance of something which should be common knowledge, or to appear to be unduly 'nosy' and meddling with something which is not our business. However, the result of a negotiation is definitely our business. Besides, it is unlikely that we will be told spontaneously something favourable to us to influence the balance of bargaining power in our favour, if we do not ask for the information. Therefore questions are the way to get information, to check assumptions, to obtain concessions (move towards our objectives), to give concessions, while retaining flexibility: 'What if?' allows us to lead to a concession whilst keeping flexibility and observing the tactical procedural rule of the linkage principle. Questions allow us to probe in detail as well as to call attention to a point that the other party may have overlooked, or to start formulating a deal.

Questions are generally classified between closed (yes or no answers) or open (many possible answers) and directive (focused on one specific point) or non-directive (unfocused and very general).

It is useful to recall here another bit of negotiator's folklore. The list of questions quoted by Kipling in his novel *Kim*, describing the training of an observer, is still quite relevant and useful for focusing our attention on what we want to know, and what questions to ask:

– WHAT – WHY – WHERE – WHO – WHEN – HOW

However it should be recalled that questions may be offensive. Obviously, unless we want, in an extremely conflictual situation, to provoke the other party, questions that we know to be offensive should be avoided. The problem here is that, because of bounded rationality, or cultural norms, we may not be aware that a question which seems perfectly straightforward to us may be offensive to the opponent.

Besides, some questions may also actually reveal our ignorance of a fundamental point or they may weaken our position if the answer is supportive of the opponent's position and would have been better left unspoken, or would have been more effective if brought up by the other party. Therefore some degree of caution should be exercised when asking questions.

The same applies to answering questions: questions should not be answered until they are clearly understood. Counter questions may be used to probe the meaning of a question. Some questions do not deserve an answer, for instance, offensive ones. Questions may be evaded, partly answered, or only simply; an answer may be flatly denied. However, it should be remembered that not answering a question is already providing information. Also too many questions may irritate; the often-quoted practical sales advice of always formulating questions positively and never including a negative, in order 'to positively' influence the other party, may, if exaggerated, reveal itself to be particularly irritating and bring counterproductive results.

A second tactical tool also applicable in the framework of all strategies is the use of adjournments or recesses. They are extremely useful and often necessary. They are used to review what has already happened, get time to think about the process, consider counter-proposals, review and evaluate the information, assumptions, concessions and objectives boxes, and eventually change tactics or even strategy. Practically they may slow down a process which becomes too heated, help to avoid a deadlock and start again the momentum of negotiation, or be used to report back to the constituents.

However, they also should be used with care and timed correctly because they may break the momentum of the negotiations if called at the wrong time. They may also be misunderstood by the other party which might, alternatively, consider them as unwarranted pressure tactics on them, a lack of authority, a retreat from a joint process.

Negotiators may be also changed. This also has advantages; it may break a deadlock, signal a strategic move, allow for compatible styles, bring in specialists of a problem newly raised. It may also be considered as a veiled threat, or a sign of weakness or, if used without due consideration of the process, it may break down the momentum towards agreement.

Finally, the negotiating parties, when negotiating in teams, may break down into specialised subcommittees or study groups whilst the main negotiating teams remain in charge of decision-making. Some issues may be of a particularly technical nature or particularly thorny and impeding progress towards agreement. They may be delegated to subcommittees of specialists or experts. This technique however presents the risk of too much delegation of decision-making, problems of reporting and authority, and is most fruitful in the more collaborative types of negotiation.

(c) End Phase

Phase 3 is the end phase. Generally it is then that the decision is taken upon whether the deal which emerges narrowed down from phase 2 is acceptable or not. It is the time to decide on agreement or deadlock. It is also the last possible time to adjourn. This last recess can be used to measure the present advantages and drawbacks of the best offer from the opponents against the costs and advantages of our contingency plans in case of deadlock.

Relevant tactics have already been discussed above as examples of 'closes'. In the case of an agreement being reached, it is then time to remember that reaching agreement is only part of the negotiating process. Now the agreement will have to be implemented. The implementation process may run a whole continuum. It goes all the way from handing the goods over the counter to a customer who will fly off within minutes, and is unlikely ever to come back to complain or to demand fulfilment of promises, down to the three to five year life of a collective agreement or the construction and creation of a massive industrial complex. Clearly everything we have already discussed about the weight of the relationship between the parties applies here. The process by which agreement has been secured will influence the future relationship, when there is one, and will therefore influence the implementation of the agreement. Therefore two points are of importance when a deadlock is avoided and when agreement is reached.

First, it is advisable to try to secure a degree of commitment from the other party to the agreement, to attempt to sell them the idea that they should be involved in insuring that their side complies with the agreement, and enforces its spirit as well as its letter. In the best of cases it is a question of promoting the idea that the negotiators for the other party be the advocates of the settlement in their own organisations. This is of course impossible if a highly conflictual strategy accompanied by the use of pressure and power tactics has been put into practice. Individuals who feel victimised and played upon can hardly be counted on to contribute to what they will consider to be further exploitation of themselves and their side. On the contrary, they are likely to seize any possible opportunity to renege on the agreement or to re-open a conflict (including court action or arbitration) on obscure points or issues arising later and not fully and clearly dealt with in the agreement. In complex negotiations such issues are almost certain to arise.

However, even in only slightly more favourable circumstances, to obtain the commitment of the other party is not altogether impossible, except in extreme cases such as the one that we have just described. Individuals who have worked hard and for a long time for a result certainly prize this result, and it has been obtained together with the other party. Even if it is not what they initially expected it is something that they contributed to achieve. Therefore they may feel positively about it.

This drives us to our second point: the agreement should be recorded as accurately as possible and as clearly as possible. The final meeting is therefore the time for final clarifications. It can be a costly mistake to agree without probing an uncertain issue for fear of deadlock. The consequences may be extremely long-term and expensive in terms of money, commitment and goodwill. This is only the case, of course, if one does not think confusion is favourable to one's side, but even then it is advisable to think twice and to have very little need of a good long-term relationship as well as secure means to enforce compliance with the letter of the agreement.

SECTION III – THE POST-NEGOTIATION PHASE

This phase is concerned with two important issues. First, the implementation of the agreement of which we have just briefly discussed the circumstances; and second, the debriefing and evaluation of the negotiation. The second issue may be of use for further negotiations and may be even considered as the first step in preparing for a new round of negotiations with the same negotiators or the organisation which was their party or constituents. This is indeed the case for labour relations negotiations but it may also very well apply in many long-term relationships in commercial negotiations.

There is no need to cover again the first issue and we shall only shortly deal with the important points regarding the second one.

The debriefing should be concerned with two aspects: results and process.

Regarding the results it is simply a matter of answering a set of basic questions:

- Did we achieve our objectives and could we have done better? Were they inadequate, unrealistic, too low? Did we concede too much?
- How did we implement our strategy and which were the successful and unsuccessful tactics?
- Which were the problems that we encountered, how did we solve them or not solve them?
- What unforeseen events took place?
- What do we want to do with the relationship with the other party, can we change it, improve it?

A second set of questions should be answered to analyse how the process of negotiating worked and the way our side did handle it:

- How correct was our estimate of the balance of bargaining power?

- How accurate was our information?
- How realistic were our assumptions?
- Was our rate and size of concessions adequate?
- Did we have intra-organisational problems with our constituents and within the different constituencies that they represent?
- Was our style adequate?
- Did we have problems within the negotiating team? (see below)
- Was our planning and management of the negotiating process flexible enough?
- What have we learnt about the style of the other party and their organisation?

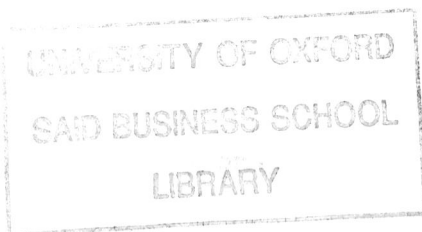

8 The Tasks in Negotiating

We are now, in the final step of our analysis, going to deal with the most practical and pragmatic aspect of negotiating. Balance of power, analysis of the environment, strategy, tactics, style, the management of stages finally have to be expressed, converted into behavioural attitudes. This chapter will deal with actual behaviour at the bargaining table. The multiple aspects of behaviour involved in negotiating involve the following:[1]

- establishing social contact
- sustaining relationships
- communicating
- listening (a little-practised part of communication)
- persuading
- understanding
- signalling
- reading signals
- controlling
- retaining flexibility
- building a climate
- responding to a climate
- providing stimuli
- reacting to stimulus
- expressing feelings
- showing tolerance
- attempting control
- evading attempts to control
- handling conflict
- facing hostility
- making concessions
- following leads
- identifying opportunities
- working in groups (within one team)

Firstly, it should be remarked that the majority of these items are
general social skills. They are used daily by everyone and probably
more often by managers than by anybody else.

It should therefore be realised that they should not be specially
learned or acquired. They are already present in everyone. They can
and should be developed on the one hand, and on the other hand
they should be adapted to the strategy, or tactic selected as well as
used in modes compatible with one's style.

Secondly, some aspects of these behaviours have already been
implicitly or explicitly covered in particular in Part III. We are going
to focus only on the most important aspects. To that end we have
identified several tasks of negotiating: to manage strategic changes,
to communicate, to listen, to record, to manage the meeting.

SECTION I – STRATEGY MANAGEMENT

After the initial meeting it should be relatively easy to check
assumptions and tentatively to assess the strategy of the other party.
If it is not readily obviously identifiable as aggressive or appeasement
or avoidance,[2] as will most often be the case, the accent may vary in
future developments between confrontational, sharing, and collaborative, somewhere in the range between give and take and problem-
solving. Our side's strategy has been prepared and planned on the
basis of the balance of bargaining power, the issues, and all the other
points discussed above. This was done in the limiting framework of
our own bounded rationality. We are now more aware, during and
after this initial meeting, of the strategic emphasis of the other party.
We realise that it issues from their own understanding of the
environment in the framework of their bounded rationality. The
problem we have now to manage is how much we bend our own
strategy and the resultant tactics and style more towards sharing or
problem-solving. We are facing a difficult dilemma.

It is probably likely[3] that the more competitive the relationship
between the negotiators is, the more difficult it will be to reach an
agreement, the less an agreement will be acceptable to either party,
and the less innovative and creative will be its contents if an
agreement is reached. However, it should be recalled that during our
discussion of tactics we pointed out that if a negotiator bent on a
co-operative strategy and tactics meets with a competitive opponent
he will clearly be on the losing end of the deal and compromise his

own objectives and interests or the ones of his constituents. In the same way, if both negotiators have engaged in co-operative negotiating, a sudden turnaround by one party can put the opponent in a disastrous position. This is particularly the case if it happens, for instance, that the party suddenly changing strategy either has gained crucial information (on prices, costs per unit, expected profits for the year, and so on) or has been offered the first large concession; the more so if it was in exchange for minor concessions in order to prime the process of co-operation.

Therefore a negotiator should always keep ready to face a competitive or even conflictual strategy and tactics and to answer to them. To negotiate may mean to have to face a high degree of conflict while keeping the channels of communication open. On the other hand, a negotiator should also be ready to identify co-operative leaning openings from the other party, positive style and behaviour, and to answer it. He should be also ready to enter a co-operative strategy. But he should always try to be able to withdraw immediately without losing ground if the other party switches back to conflictual tactics.

For instance, having entered labour negotiations within the past framework of good relationship and faced with relatively moderate union demands, management may have been admitting that the forecasted sales for the following year are adequate. The union negotiators may then reply conflictually or co-operatively. If they immediately state strongly that 'capitalists can pay' and come up with an additional list of demands and pushed-up costs for their earlier demands, management would be in a damaged position if it had not kept in reserve the possibility of resuming also a justifiable conflictual attitude: for example, it may have mentioned that taxes have increased, as well as personnel costs and raw material prices, and therefore, even though sales have improved, profit can be low or even negative. On the contrary, if the union adopts a more or less co-operative attitude, indicating, for instance, that 'it is good for the company but employees should also have their share because of their contributions', then management, without taking excessive risks, can also reply co-operatively. A slow exchange of constructive information may follow, or a return towards competitive tactics. The management of this process is difficult and the other negotiating tasks listed below may be of help.

In order to manage this strategic emphasis one should take into account one's attitude towards risk and one's own risk profile. Several of the tactical moves listed in Chapter 5 and specially mentioned then can be used.

SECTION II – COMMUNICATION

(a) The Importance of Communication

Negotiating, except in very special cases,[4] requires communication between the parties no matter how imperfect communication channels may be in reality. A failure to communicate effectively will make the process of finding an agreement more difficult. There are also situations in which one party may actually claim that the other party's failure to communicate is a deliberate ploy to slow down the process of reaching an agreement. Diplomatic negotiations between East and West are full of these allegations.

However, in general terms, in the negotiating process communication fulfils four main objectives. The first is to communicate commitment to positions, parties, and interests. The second is to try to persuade the other party to alter their perception of their own previously held position, its benefits and costs, and to alter our bargaining power (which comes of their estimates, as explained in Chapter 1). The third, which continues until an agreement is reached, is the identification of different benefits for one or both parties and the establishment of a relationship capable of sustaining the implementation of the agreement once concluded. The fourth is to convey information to the opponent.

(b) The Process of Communication

We wish to spend some time on the technical aspect of the communication process because it is very often mishandled and it is one of the foremost areas where accumulated and proven, available behavioural knowledge is not used and applied.

Contrary to what we intuitively assume, communicating is not easy and simple. It involves at least three coding operations: putting our ideas into words; having the other party hear the words; having him understand the meaning that we have put into our words. Besides, if our communication has the goal of persuading the other party, we should phrase the meaning we put into our words in such a way that his opinion is altered. Every one of these four steps is loaded with problems. A classic example illustrates the basic communication failures. A well-known game involves a group of children sitting in circle. A first child writes down a message on a sheet of paper which is kept aside, then he passes on the same message vocally to his neighbour, in a voice low enough to be heard only by him, who then proceeds in the same way with his neighbour, and so on. Invariably, when the vocal message has been transmitted a few times and is compared with tne written original, it has taken on a totally different meaning (sometimes hilarious, which is exactly the purpose of the game). It is also true that most people tend to speak inarticulately, often for too long at a time, and sometimes in a way which is unclear or unfocused on specific issues. Finally, most people are also bad listeners.

As far as the first three steps in coding are concerned a few pointers can be of help in improving our communication skills and make them more effective. The first coding operation consists of formulating a message out of our thoughts. The message should be planned ahead and not expressed on the spur of the moment. It should be constructed in very short sentences: only one idea per sentence, and very simple sentences built around a verb, with a few other nouns and adjectives. If an idea is complex it should be broken down into as many separate sentences as necessary. They should be presented one at a time, and the way the sentences are articulated should be emphasised. What may seem simple and evident to us may be new to the other party, not to mention the barriers to communication arising from bounded rationality, theirs and ours.

The message should be prepared. However, except for very particular circumstances, it should not be read. Reading a prepared document tends quickly to bore and bring down the level of attention of the listeners.

The second operation is to be heard by the other party. To that effect we must catch his attention and keep it! To that end we should be brief and concentrate upon the essential part of the message. We should be clear and articulate. This is easier than it may sound if we take the precaution of sticking to sets of short sentences pronounced without haste.

After being heard, the third step consists of being understood. This means that the other party should perceive something other than a vague noise, more or less loud, but quickly dismissed, while he thinks about something else. To that effect the expression of our messages should be timed so that we take advantage of periods when the attention of the other party is freely available. The expression of our messages should be spaced, either by rejoinders or by comments from others. Speaking for too long at a time decreases attention. We should not be afraid to be slow. What seems slow for us, who are used to the ideas we develop, may be much too quick for somebody fighting to get the grasp of one idea and presented with another one while he still has not mastered the first. In order to make sure that our messages 'get across' we also should not be afraid to repeat them. However, too much repetition may be counterproductive and play the part of an irritant for the other party.

(c) Communication and Persuasion

It should be kept in mind that communication during negotiations is not just a conversation. It has a deliberate focus among the ones we identified above. However, as far as the additional objective we mentioned is concerned – persuading the other party – additional problems arise because of his bounded rationality and his unique view of the environment. We noted earlier that pointing out facts whose meaning seems obvious to us may very well fail to convince our opponent who sees them in another light. In the same way our logic, however persuasive it is for us within the bounds of our rationality, may seem to be just additional biases to them. Nevertheless, whatever the difficulty and low probability of fully persuading and convincing the other party through communicating information, some pointers can also be useful whenever it is attempted.

First, one is very seldom convinced by abstract information but mostly by very concrete information that one can immediately relate to one's own situation and understanding of the environment. Secondly, everybody needs time to accept something new or different from what he holds to be more or less certain, especially if that something new is not to his advantage or desire. Time enough should be left to the other party to adapt to the new view of the situation. Third, one can alter the other party's perception of the situation only very early on in the negotiating process. Subsequently, and after a relatively short time of negotiating, the minds are set and the views (of both parties) tend to get more and more firmly held. Fourth, attempts at persuasion should be expressed in words which convey images congruent with what the other party knows, looks favourably upon, and associates with positive items. Negotiating here could borrow a leaf from the book of advertising. Persuading somebody has more chance of being effectively done by using words which are found to evoke attractive images for the opponent. It should be said, though, that the systematic and continuous use of this technique can become a painful irritant when abused.

It should also be briefly added that attention should be paid to language issues. This may include the language in which the negotiation is carried out if it is not the mother tongue of all the negotiators and if some of them are negotiating in a foreign language. Caution should be paid, however well the foreign negotiators master, or believe they master, the language of the negotiation. However, this point may also concern the 'technical' language applying to the specific object of the negotiation, or a specific aspect of the negotiating process when dealing with a given object. This applies to technical language in the sense that it concerns a given technology or technological process in an engineering contract, for instance, but it must also be more broadly understood as including legal, financial, oil, shipping, distribution, or any other lingo. Assumptions about fluency in the language, and common understanding of key words should be checked regularly.

Also it should be underlined that, besides language, attention has to be paid to the medium of communication. We mostly dealt with fact-to-face communications but additional restrictions should be taken into account when communicating by letters, telex or telephone.

(d) Listening

Communicating is by no means one way. It involves receiving as well as transmitting information. Listening to the other party is probably as fraught with difficulties as communicating towards them. However, it is more within our control for it depends mostly on us. Simple experiments, which can easily be duplicated by using a tape recorder and comparing the tape later with what the audience has heard, compared to what was said, show that we listen only to part of what has been said. Any professor is also painfully aware of the obvious fact that average audiences, just after having listened to a lecture, remember very little of it.

It is a fact that most of us are poor listeners, even more than we are poor speakers. We quickly get bored or distracted. Research carried out on selection interviewing has demonstrated that most untrained interviewers make up their mind about a candidate often by listening to him for less than five minutes and then spend the rest of the interview time justifying (to themselves) the rightness of their decision. We probably are worse listeners during a negotiation than in our usual occupations, because we are overly concerned with think-

ing about our objectives, the way to reach them, what we are going to
say next, or the potential reactions of our constituencies to our
present position. This prevents us even more from paying attention to
what has been said. If the negotiations are highly conflictual our
quality of listening will decrease one more degree because now we
are likely to enter into arguments with the other party, in the
conflictual spiral described above, and listen only to ourselves, using
the periods when the other party speaks to catch our breath and
muster stronger arguments for our side, but without the least
attention to what is being expressed.

However, good listening is of foremost importance in a negotiation. There are several reasons for this: once the negotiations have
started it is the best means of obtaining information about the other
party, whether they convey this information intentionally or not. We
have already underlined the primary importance of information
several times. Also it will help us check and refine our assumptions.
Finally, quiet listening helps, or rather is the best means of, answering a question to the point. It helps us find out what the other party
wants. It builds toward a positive relationship and it avoids us getting
into arguments, allowing us to save unthoughtful replies which may
lead us into conflict.

It is, however – again because it depends on us alone – easier to
improve our qualities as listeners, in order to take full advantage of
the potential of good listening in a negotiation. Karass[5] has listed
eleven reasons why we tend to be bad listeners and gives several tips.
Other authors of practical books on negotiating, such as Nierenberg,[6]
attribute great importance to listening. Relevant advice which can be
helpful is briefly summarised below.

First, one should try to pay full attention to what is said. This
means two sets of things: on the one hand, concentrate on what is
said, whoever is saying it, that is, whether or not one likes this
person. Whether he appears to be an impressive character or
somebody we would usually dismiss out of hand, whether we know
him from before or whether he is a stranger, whether we tend to trust
or distrust him. On the other hand, one should concentrate on what is
said, whatever the message is. That is whether or not we like the
contents of what is said, whether or not we may fear its consequences, whether it is in conformity with our opinions and beliefs or
whether it is shocking to us.

Second, we must try to understand the meaning of what is said, and
pay attention to the contents of the message, not simply to the way it
is expressed or to the language, however crude or inadequate.

Third, we should pay continuing attention to what is said. That means putting other concerns out of mind: not thinking (yet) about the consequences on one's position and constituents, not preparing (yet) one's own reply, not bearing judgement on the idea before it is fully expressed, not jumping to conclusions, not trying to outguess what is going to be said (even if one believes one easily can), not getting distracted, and above all not interrupting in order to argue the idea presented.

(e) Signals

So far we have dealt with overall communications where the message is fully intended to be understood as such by the other party. However, sometimes experienced negotiators use the process of signalling. Peters,[7] himself a long-time mediator and negotiator in labour disputes who reflected thoughtfully on his experiences, attaches a great importance to signals. It is a process by which, without fully expressing one move, demand, concession or other, a negotiator uses language or behaviour which implies, if understood accurately by the other party, that he might just initiate action towards accomplishing that precise move if the other party were to let him know that it would respond positively in such an event. This way, without getting in any way committed, one party 'tests the waters' and tries to find out if the other party is willing to move. Signals can be positive or negative. They can be verbal or non-verbal. A full chapter on verbal signals is included in Kennedy, Benson and McMillan.[8] In general, verbal signals are of two kinds. They may be introduced by a hypothetical statement, 'If we were to assume', or a reference to the constituents. They also can be a statement of a position, given certain facts, opening the door to a question probing what would be the change in the position if these facts were modified. For instance, the statement: 'this is the usual price when sold one at a time' is a signal that for a quantity the price may become unusual.

Signals can also be non-verbal. For instance, to ignore a signal is a signal in itself (if it has been understood), to change negotiators is a signal. Silence might be a very powerful signal. We generally are afraid of silence and are culturally used to filling in the voids in a dialogue by jumping in even with small talk or with meaningless or irrelevant interventions. A long time of silence after a proposal or a refusal signals its importance. Non-verbal signals may include also change of speakers or leaving the room.

The problem with signals is that they are of a much more subtle nature than straightforward communications. It should be pointed out that by straightforward communications we do not mean here communications stating the true and candid position of a party; they may include bluff or dissimulation of latent objectives. We only mean communication whose content is the message which is supposed to be understood. We have already discussed the many problems involved in transmitting and listening to communications. These problems are amplified many times when dealing with signals.

A final point to remember is that we may very well give unintended signals to the other party: for instance, smile when we are genuinely pleased, or show satisfaction or disappointment.

(f) Non-verbal Communication

The discussion above introduces us to the subject of non-verbal communication. It should be briefly dealt with. It rests on the premises that our body attitudes carry messages as well as our voice. Some students of negotiation have attempted to decode these messages. Some others have taken strong positions against it.[9] The most interesting work about non-verbal communications has been carried out by Calero.[10] It seems intuitively evident that our body attitudes, gestures, and expressions reveal something about us. We also probably all have experienced feelings of suspicion or distrust or unease when facing someone whose modes of verbal and non-verbal communications were at odds, that is, for instance, a person violently agitated and constantly moving, and speaking in a low, even slow, monotone, or vice versa. Congruence of verbal and non-verbal behaviour relaxes. However, the deliberate use of non-verbal communications towards an opponent may be totally misleading within our limited rationality framework. We may re-interpret such 'messages', to mean what we want them to mean. In other words, we see what we want to see. On the other hand, if we try to 'read' the non-verbal behaviour of an opponent and expect him to be unaware, he may well make us see what he wants us to see. For a trained individual, body signals are probably relatively easy to learn and reproduce. Therefore a degree of caution should probably be exerted here, even though awareness of the existence of non-verbal communication can only be of help.

(g) Recording

Communicating both ways brings information. In order to be able to use this sinformation usefully it should be kept to be analysed later, during breaks, when recesses have been called. We should not rely only on our own memory, already loaded with strategy, tactics, and busy with listening. Most of what is said, all of what is said that is important, should be recorded. Careful notes should be taken. A convenient way to do it fast (which is often necessary for many negotiators may not agree to a recording of the meeting which may prevent all building of trust during the relationship) is to use a sheet of paper divided along its middle, to separate one's own side and their side' and to put in evidence the sequence of important events.

We said	They said
Time	

-------	-------

Break Time	

-------	-------

SECTION III – MANAGEMENT OF THE MEETING

This section covers the aspects of negotiations strictly attached to the behaviour of the negotiators at the bargaining table. Negotiation is structure, process, and behaviour. The first part of this book provided a framework for the analyses of the environment which provides the structure of negotiation; we then attached ourselves to the processes through which the structure and the perception of the structure can be modified to one's advantage (strategy and tactics). Finally, with the definition of styles and stages in the negotiation, we moved from process to behaviour. We now end by addressing ourselves to the expression of behaviour. In doing so we have run the gamut from pure theory to pure practice. Our first concern was with building a sociological, theoretical framework and applying it to negotiation; we have, along the succession of the chapters, provided more and more practical and pragmatic inputs. We are now at the level of pure experimental practice. In other words, we have, chapter after chapter, moved from the domain of knowledge to the domain of know-how.

Developments in the management of the meeting take place within our theoretical framework, but they are inspired by experience. We are concerned with factual issues: management of the negotiating team, management of attitudes, management of the physical setting.

(a) Management of the Negotiating Team

The first decision, prior even to managing the team, concerns of course the choice between negotiating alone or in a team. Negotiating alone presents certain advantages. The negotiator has full responsibility within the limits agreed upon with his constituents, therefore he can make immediate far-reaching decisions such as strategic changes and concessions. It also insures complete privacy. Nobody else but the negotiator (at least on his side) will know what has taken place during the process. It deprives the other party of the opportunity to try to play team members against each other and team members to take different stands and undermine each other's position. Finally, it presents the lowest possible costs in terms of money and time.

On the other hand, when negotiating alone, an individual has to cope with the multiple tasks of the negotiating process: communicating, listening, signalling, and recording, all the while evaluating changes, checking assumptions, and debating on concessions. If one is alone, one, of course, cannot do it all at the same time, therefore one needs to shift one's effort and attention from task to task and one may omit to identify important events and opportunities.

Besides, many negotiations are complex, involving a range of issues which demand a diversity of specialised knowledge, either in labour negotiations (pension plans, economic data, health and safety, wages) or in commercial negotiations (technical knowledge of the product, specifications, manufacturing process). Teams provide the advantage issuing from getting several heads together instead of relying on one. It allows for the tapping of more input, a greater expertise; it also provides mutual support for members during the negotiation, better planning, better listening, and better recording. The tasks of the negotiation process are performed better. There are fewer chances for unnoticed errors. Mistakes which could arise from the mind of an individual left alone are more likely to be avoided. Finally, it demonstrates strength to the other party.[11]

However, it has its drawbacks: a higher cost, not only in terms of money and time needed during the negotiations, but also during the preparation which will be longer and more difficult. It will take the team members out of their normal duties. This is, however, necessary in order to minimise the unavoidable other potential drawback: internal contradiction within the team arising openly in front of the other party because of lack of prepared co-ordination.

The choice between negotiating in teams and alone is therefore not clean-cut. It should depend on the planning for each forthcoming negotiation.

The same thing can be said for the second problem: How big a team and how should it be composed?[12] As far as the size is concerned there is no strict rule but common sense dictates that the maximum limit of the small group be respected. That is, it should not exceed the size where face-to-face contact and effective interaction becomes impossible for the members all together, when they are in planning sessions and in recesses. Another point relating to size should be underlined. There is no reason why the membership of the negotiating team should not be changed: either in keeping the same size and replacing members or in bringing in new members at certain points. It has two advantages: signalling a change in strategy to the other party, on the one hand, or bringing in specialised knowledge (lawyers, technical experts), on the other hand. Then team members should be trained in their respective roles so as to avoid later uncertainty or public squabbling over what one should do, or worse even, should not have done.

What are these roles? Several opinions exist but at least four to five roles can be identified. Of course, in teams of a small size, several roles can be played by a single individual. The first role in importance is that of team leader. He or she is the one who makes decisions and leads the team in cases where the structure of the organisation involved is hierarchical. If the organisation is of a more participative nature, he or she is the one who settles the decision-making process.

He or she will listen to the other members and their opinions but it should be clear from the start that either he or she is the one who has responsibility and authority to decide or he or she sets up the decision-making process. This is particularly why training of the team is necessary, and why training should insist that the team's leader is the one who decides on substance or on the process for making a decision. For instance, if insufficiently trained, a technical specialist drawn from another department and unused to work with the team leader might well take it very badly if his specialised and technically sound advice is ignored by the team leader in exchange for another concession. This could lead to undermining the negotiating position and severely affect bargaining power.

The team leader is also the one, and the only one, who should be empowered to have, in the same two ways, final decision on objectives, strategy, and strategy changes. Tactics cannot be used without his agreement. In particular nobody else but him should be empowered to make a concession, call a recess, accept an offer. Finally, he should introduce and support his colleagues. If they need to communicate with him during negotiations, they should do so in writing by passing notes. Unless there is prior agreement they should not argue with him or with each other. To avoid a potentially damaging bias towards goodwill concessions the status of the team leader should be matched, at least to that of the team leader for the other side. An inferior status could also risk offending the other party. It would certainly open the door for power or people tactics for the other party. The exception would be a tactic of 'limited authority' as described in Chapter 5.

The second role is that of the main spokesman. He should probably be a different person from the team leader. Managing the team and evaluating strategy are enough to constitute a full-time job. The role of the spokesman is to present the case and the arguments. He is in charge of communications. He may be supported by secondary spokesmen who can be called in when their specialised knowledge is needed or when the position that they represent is useful to make a point. For instance, the lawyer is called in to point out a legal impossibility or the financial manager to point out the consequences on profit of a wage demand.

The recorder keeps written track of what is said. He cannot of course take exhaustive notes of everything. He only registers what is important and relevant. In accordance with our earlier developments his importance cannot be overestimated, for we never really recall precisely what was said. Some teams may also contain an observer distinct from the recorder. His role is to monitor the performance of the team as well as what is happening in the other team.

Under the authority of the team leader debriefing takes place at every recess and open discussion follows. But when back in session the role must be assumed again.

Clearly the negotiating styles of the members of the team must be adapted to their roles. However, there is no hard-and-fast rule which never changes. It depends on the balance of power and the strategy adopted. A Tough chairman would be a major problem if a co-operative or compromising strategy was adopted, and vice versa. A Dealer chairman may be ill-fitted to a highly conflictual situation. However, even within a co-operative strategy, a Tough support spokesman can be useful. When the strategy is decided upon, and the tactics selected, the members of the negotiating team must be allocated to roles fitting into the planned strategy by function of their styles. Again there must be coherence in the different steps. But that coherence must be adapted and thought out ahead for each negotiation. A matrix may be built once the strategy has been decided upon.

Role			
	Team leader	*Main spokesman*	*Support spokesman*
Style			
Tough			
Numbers			
Dealer			
Warm			

Clearly this matrix must be reviewed and, if needed, changes be made and replacements brought in at each recess after evaluating assumptions. In general, though, a negotiator with a Numbers style is well used in an observer or a recorder role.

(b) Management of Attitudes

Research has demonstrated that some attitudes are consistently counterproductive and it has been suggested that a given behaviour was preferable and was likely to bring better results consistently. This research will be briefly summarised:

1. Based on their experiences in the Harvard Negotiating Project, R. Fischer and W. Ury[13] have developed and proposed a negotiating method which centres almost entirely on attitudes. Although we believe that this method is better suited to 'integrative' or compromising issues, for it ignores the power relationships at play, it nevertheless contains extremely useful advice on attitudes. This advice is usable in many cases, except when having decided on a highly conflictual strategy. It is clear that negotiation deeply influences emotions. Emotions that we try to repress or to hide come back to influence our behaviour and attitudes. Emotions that we give vent to, like anger, apathy, fear, influence the attitudes of our opponents, and can be counterproductive. Unless one wants to use anger purposely, Fisher and Ury propose a set of guidelines which are useful in controlling emotions. Their method consists mainly of a set of four propositions:

- Separate the negotiators and their relationship from the problem which is at stake. Deal softly with the people but firmly with the problem
- Avoid positional bargaining and 'digging trenches' or vesting too much of oneself in a position, but focus on reciprocal interest which motivates the taking of positions
- Look for mutual gain through innovative options but not at the expense of your interests
- Decide as much as possible on the basis of objective criteria, not on what you, or they, wish

These propositions constitute useful and practical guides for controlling attitudes.

2. Additional research of an experimental nature has been carried out by N. Rackham and J. Carlisle with the Huthwaite Research group, a research and consulting organisation. They have studied in a

sample of experienced negotiators what distinguished the attitudes and behaviour of effective ones.[14]

On the basis of their research, complemented by further observations, two lists of 'dos' and 'don'ts' can be compiled. Effective negotiators tend to practise the 'dos' and avoid the 'don'ts' with a frequency much superior to that of ineffective negotiators.

DO

- Label your behaviour in advance, except if you are going to disagree with what has been said. In other words, give advance warning of what you are going to do (for instance: 'May I ask you a question?' before asking). This has the advantage of drawing attention to what follows, and improves the listening of the other party. It slows the pace and gives the other party time to clear their minds of the previous exchanges. It decreases the conflictual mood and improves the chances of getting the input accepted. It reduces the potential ambiguity and provides for clearer communications.

- Test understanding and summarise what has been said, for purposes of clarity, in order to avoid misunderstanding, and to clarify for oneself the behaviour of the other party. This will also avoid false 'agreements' which would disrupt tentative implementation.

- Ask questions many and often.

- Do not hesitate to comment on your own feelings and internal thought processes. It may or may not be genuine but it tends to build up security and trust, and it is a good substitute for counter-attacks (for example: 'I think I feel uncomfortable with' rather than 'You too. . .').

- Do not hesitate to identify positive aspects in the opponent's statements and build on a common ground on the basis of the other party's idea. It moves towards agreement and it may engineer a better commitment to that agreement.

- Listen attentively.

- Seek information.

- Put proposals forward as questions rather than statements, which are more likely to provoke adverse reactions.

- Use an alternative mode of disagreeing. Give first the reason or an explanation for disagreeing before expressing disagreement, rather than disagreeing first and then explaining why.

DON'T

– Talk too much. It shows embarrassment.

– Argue, debate, or try to score points. It is not the reason for the meeting, and winning the argument but losing the negotiation is useless.

– Be sarcastic or clever. It has no practical use and brings you no advantage, but it is counterproductive for it builds resentment, whatever the object of the negotiation.

– Emphasise differences, or, conversely, gloss over them too fast.

– Use irritators. They may be unfavourable to the other party ('ridiculous demand', 'absurd behaviour,' or the like). This includes all unfavourable value judgements on their attitudes and proposals as well as blame or, of course, insults. They also may be overly favourable to your own position ('very reasonable position', 'extremely generous offer', or the like). It includes all statements gratuitously favourable to one's side without other purpose).

– Make too many counterproposals immediately. It clouds the issue and may appear to hide disagreement without really thinking on the merits of the central proposal.

– Get into defence/attack spirals, it drives to question each other's legitimacy.

– Label disagreement, state immediately the reason for it.

– Dilute arguments and give too many good reasons for support of your proposal or demand instead of one or two excellent ones. Contrarily to what may appear at first glance, giving many reasons to support a point does not build the strength of a position but runs the risk of focusing the attention of the opponent on the weakest reasons for support which will dilute the value of the strong ones.

– Give information about external events, facts, clarifications, general expression of opinion.

3. Several other points should be made about attitudes. The above dos and don'ts and guidelines no doubt have value. However, we should recall that the mode of operation of power, its mechanism, as we discussed in Chapter 1, is, when we want to build it in our favour, to bring uncertainty to the other party. One has power when one controls the uncertainty in the mind of the opponent. If he is certain about you and your likely behaviour, you lose power. If your attitudes become too predictable you build up his power, maybe too much. The dos and don'ts we listed above are what skilled and experienced negotiators do and do not do more often than unskilled

or ineffective negotiators; not what they do or do not do all the time or never; they may sometimes use voluntarily the 'don'ts'. In our theoretical terms this may have the effect of building up uncertainty for the opponent. In the same way the negotiator's attitudes and behaviour should not always be too consistent. Unproductive attitudes should be generally avoided; however, they should remain an open tactical option and be used when called for. One's behaviour should be generally dependable but not too dependable or totally predictable. There should be enough variability in it so that the other party knows that he cannot rely on its permanence whatever happens. There should be some doubt as to what his own attitudes, strategy, tactics, may cause as 'reactions'. Attitudes also should be varied and the variations timed. These variations clearly should take place within a range adapted to each negotiation and adequate to the strategy, tactics, style and roles decided upon.

Secondly, it should be recognised that attitudes are part of the negotiating issues. When dealing with tactics we have already emphasised that goodwill concessions should be avoided as well as exchanging concessions on intangible items against substantive ones. By that we meant giving substantive concessions in the hope of exchanging it against a change in attitude from the opponent. This point should again be underlined here. Some negotiators skilled in pressure tactics can act out changes in their attitudes, especially when combined with high status, aptly enough to extract substantial concessions from untrained opponents, in exchange for simply granting them equal status and legitimacy or recognition. However, this does not negate the fact that some attitudes, particularly trust, legitimacy, and recognition are negotiable issues. But it should be remembered that they are to be traded in kind: against conferring reciprocally recognition, trust, and legitimacy only, not concessions on substance.

The management of attitudes is important. One may feel bad and want revenge after a negotiation where one reached one's objectives but was not treated the way one assumed one should have been.

Thirdly, it should be recognised and we should be conscious that personal issues influence us and our attitudes as well as the attitudes of the other party. Then issues range from familial problems or personal health issues to workplace problems or overwork. We should try to control them and their influence on our attitudes as well as realise that it influences the attitude of the other party. They may be, at some point, reacting to their personal issues and concerns and not to our attitudes, our statements, or our proposals.

(c) Management of the Physical Setting

As in the case of non-verbal communication we do not wish to insist on this aspect of negotiation. Nevertheless it should be mentioned, for some important points are usefully kept in mind.

The first issue concerns the point of knowing where to negotiate: on one's own premises or at the opponent's site? It is of course assumed that we have a choice, for in certain cases the site is dictated by the nature of the negotiations. This is the case, for instance, for travelling salesmen, buying a used car, engineering contracts with a foreign government.

It is probably not a major issue. Many negotiators tend to prefer to negotiate on their own site for reasons of convenience, of lower costs, of availability of help in case of need as well as of ease of communication with constituents. However, negotiating on the opponent's site can sometimes provide useful information on the bargaining power, strategy, or objectives of the other party. A commercial negotiator wants to know if he negotiates directly with top management or at a lower rung. His opponents may want to keep him in the dark on that point for tactical purposes. To that end, some eastern companies provide rooms for the exclusive purpose of negotiating, which reveals nothing of the status of the party negotiating for the company.

In any case, and wherever the negotiation takes place, the party organising the negotiation should take care that suitable arrangements be provided: a conference room large enough and the availability of separate rooms for each team to recess and hold private discussions. These rooms should be suitably furnished including writing materials and materials for presentation of information (blackboard, paper board, adapted writing material, overhead projector and up-to-video monitor if elaborate presentations are forecasted), as well as for communications (telephone, telex, fax). Necessary materials should also be brought: existing contract, product specifications, copies of draft, material already exchanged, and supporting data such as legal requirements, technical standards. Finally, copying facilities and typists should be available when needed. Small details like coffee, refreshments, or ashtrays are more important than it may at first appear. If we draw on our own experience we may remember how useful they may be and how pleasant it is to find them.

Notes and References

Introduction

1. I. W. Zartman (ed.), *The 50% Solution* (New York: Anchor Books, 1976) pp. 20–32.
2. A 1975 American study has already identified more than a thousand articles and books devoted to the subject, apparently in English only; the bibliography has grown limitlessly since. See J. Z. Rubin and B. R. Brown, *The Social Psychology of Bargaining* (New York: Academic Press, 1975).
3. Some other contributions of particular interest to the present book are not listed immediately below and will be discussed later in more detail. Some others are briefly reviewed or discussed in J. Rojot, *International Collective Bargaining* (Deventer (The Netherlands): Kluwer, 1976) from the standpoint of international industrial relations.
4. For instance, F. Y. Edgeworth, *Mathematical Physics* (London: Kegan Paul, 1881); A. C. Pigou, *Principles and Methods of Industrial Peace* (London: Macmillan, 1905); F. Zeuthen, *Problems of Monopoly and Economic Welfare* (London: Routledge and Sons, 1930); J. R. Hicks, *The Theory of Wages*, 2nd edn (New York: St. Martin's Press, 1963); J. Pen, 'A General Theory of Bargaining', *American Economic Review*, no. 42, 1952, pp. 24–42 and *The Wage Rate under Collective Bargaining* (Cambridge: Harvard University Press, 1959), A. Coddington, *Theories of the Bargaining Process* (Chicago: Aldine, 1968), J. G. Cross, *The Economics of Bargaining* (New York: Basic Books, 1969).
5. For instance, J. F. Nash, 'The Bargaining Problem', *Econometrica*, vol. 18, 1950; J. C. Harsanyi, 'Approaches to the Bargaining Problem, before and after the Theory of Games', a critical discussion of Zeuthen's, Hicks's and Nash's theories, *Econometrica*, vol. 24, 1956, pp. 144–57; L. S. Shapley, 'A Value for a N-person Game', in Kuhn and Tucker (eds), *Contribution to the Theory of Games*, vol. II (Princeton University Press, 1953), pp. 303–17; H. Raiffa, 'Arbitration Schemes for Generalized Two-Person Games', ibid., pp. 361–87; O. J. Bartos, *Process and Outcomes of Negotiations* (New York: Columbia University Press, 1974); O. R. Young (ed.), *Bargaining, Formal Theories of Negotiation* (Urbana: University of Illinois Press, 1975).
6. We shall later draw in detail on and make extensive use of the contributions of works in that area of research; they are not therefore listed here and they will be quoted when they are discussed.
7. H. Raiffa, *The Art and Science of Negotiation* (Cambridge, Mass.: Harvard University Press, 1982).
8. D. G. Pruitt, *Negotiating Behavior* (New York: Academic Press, 1981) p. 10.

9. J. E. McGrath and J. W. Julian, 'Interaction process and task outcomes in experimentally created negotiation groups', *Journal of Psychological Studies*, no. 14, 1963, p. 119.
10. Rubin and Brown, *The Social Psychology of Bargaining*, p. 296.
11. I. Morley and G. Stephenson, *The Social Psychology of Bargaining* (London: Allen and Unwin, 1977) p. 121.
12. *The Social Psychology of Bargaining*, p. 297.
13. *The 50% Solution*, p. 32.
14. Rubin and Brown, *The Social Psychology of Bargaining*; J. M. Mageneau and D. G. Pruitt, 'The Social Psychology of Bargaining: A theoretical synthesis' in G. M. Stephenson and C. J. Brotherton, *Industrial Relations: A Social Psychological Approach* (New York: Wiley, 1979); D. Druckman (ed.), *Negotiations, Social Psychological Perspectives* (Beverley Hills: Sage Publications, 1977).
15. C. M. Stevens, *Strategy and Collective Bargaining Negotiations* (New York: MacGraw Hill, 1963).
16. A. Strauss, *Negotiations, Varieties, Contexts, Processes and Social Order* (San Francisco: Jossey-Bass, 1979).
17. S. B. Bacharach and E. J. Lawler, *Bargaining* (San Francisco: Jossey-Bass, 1982) p. 41.

1 Understanding Conflict

1. It will be obvious to the reader that the theoretical developments which follow are heavily weighted towards the method of strategic analysis of organisations as devised by Michel Crozier at the Centre de Sociologie des Organisations. In particular, we are indebted to François Dupuy and the many discussions we had together for the presentation which follows. The responsibility for its exposition remains, of course, nevertheless our own. For the theoretical background from which most of the following concepts are drawn, see: M. Crozier, *Le Phénomène Bureaucratique* (Paris: Le Seuil, 1963) and M. Crozier and E. Friedberg, *L'Acteur et le Système* (Paris: Le Seuil, 1977). Also G. Adam and J. D. Reynaud have applied some of these concepts to the analysis of social change in Labour Relations. See Adam et J.D. Reynaud, *Conflicts du Travail et Changement Social* (P.U.F., 1978). Finally, it should be noted that, with a different perspective and a different goal from ours, a typology of the models and theories applied to the understanding of organisational decision-making has also been developed by Pfeffer. (See J. Pfeffer, *Power in Organizations* (Boston: Pitman, 1981) p. 7–33. This author distinguishes between the rational, bureaucratic, decision process/organised anarchy and the political power models. There are strong similarities between our understanding of organisations as networks of negotiations outlined below and Pfeffer's political model of organisations. However, the focus of our present analysis is totally different but very interesting additional insights can be gained for the study of organisations from Pfeffer's work.

2. See, for instance: Koontz and O'Donnel, *Principles of Management* (New York: McGraw Hill, 1968) which is in the line of Fayol.

3. Chester I. Barnard, *The Functions of the Executive* (Cambridge, Mass.: Harvard University Press, 1938) in particular Pt. III, ch. III, p. 161.
4. See, for instance, Chamberlain and Cullen, *The Labor Sector*, ch. IV, pp. 51ff or G. Bankroft and S. Garfunkel, 'Job Mobility in 1961', Special Labor Force Unit, US Bureau of Labor Statistics, 1963.
5. For a savaging and devastating criticism of the Hawthorne experiments see M. Rose, *Industrial Behaviour, Theoretical developments since Taylor* (London: Penguin, 1978).
6. J. H. Goldthorpe, *Sociologie de Travail*, 1961, no. 1, pp. 1–17.
7. It rightly drew attention to the potential contributions of behavioural science to management.
8. R. Townsend, *Up the Organization* (Greenwich, Conn.: Fawcett Crost, 1970) p. 106.
9. See H. N. Wheeler, *Industrial Conflict, An Integrative Theory* (Columbia: University of South Carolina Press, 1985). The interpretation of the theory is our own.
10. See the references in note 1.
11. *The 50% Solution*, pp. 2–6.
12. *Negotiations, Varieties, Contexts, Processes and Social Order*, p. 2.
13. *Negotiating Behavior*, p. 9.
14. *Process and Outcomes of Negotiations*, p. 3.
15. For instance, Morley and Stephenson attempt to make this distinction, although they end up, after having carefully defined negotiation, defining bargaining as 'the process of negotiating for agreement', *The Social Psychology of Bargaining*, pp. 18–26.
16. Robin and Brown, *The Social Psychology of Bargaining*, p. 2.
17. Ibid., p. 2.
18. See J. E. McGrath, 'A Social-Psychological Approach to the Study of Negotiations' in R. V. Bowers (ed.), *Studies on Behavior in Organizations: A Research Symposium* (Athens, Georgia: University of Georgia Press, 1966) and J. G. Cross, *The Economics of Bargaining* (New York: Basic Books, 1969).
19. W. C. Hamner and G. A. Clay, 'The effectiveness of different offer strategies in bargaining' in Druckman, *Negotiations, Social Psychological Perspectives*.
20. *The 50% Solution*, pp. 7ff.
21. *The Economics of Bargaining*, pp. 6ff.
22. T. C. Schelling, *The Strategy of Conflict* (London: Oxford University Press, 1960) p. 21.
23. Mageneau and Pruitt, 'The Social Psychology of Bargaining', p. 181.
24. *Bargaining, Formal Theories of Negotiation*, p. 5.
25. Cross, *The Economics of Bargaining*, pp. 10–13, has specifically pointed out that the issue must be of value and the process time constrained.
26. This point is illustrated by P. Warr, *Psychology and Collective Bargaining* (London: Hutchinson, 1973) pp. 3–7.
27. Herbert A. Simon, *Administrative Behavior*, 2nd edn (New York: The Free Press, 1965). J. G. March and H. A. Simon, *Organizations* (New York: 1958).

28. Crozier and Friedberg, *L'Acteur et le Système*, notably pp. 267–316.
29. Simon, *Administrative Behavior*, p. 25.
30. Ibid., p.108.
31. See, for instance, G. Allison, The Essence of Decisions (Boston: Little Brown, 1971); Crozier and Friedberg, *L'Acteur et le Système*, pp. 223ff; H. H. Calero, *Winning the Negotiation* (New York: Hawthorne Books, 1979) ch. 4; G. Robin, *La crise de Cuba* (Paris: Economica, 1984); N. M. Fraser and K. W. Hipel, *Conflict Analysis, Models and Resolutions* (New York: North Holland, Elsevier, 1984) ch. 1.
32. On the differentiation of negotiating for rules and negotiating for stakes, see Adam and Reynaud, *Conflits du Travail et Changement Social* (Paris: P.U.F., 1978) pp. 215–29.

2 The Parties, The Environment and Bargaining Power

1. See Leonard Sayles, *Behavior of Industrial Work Groups* (New York: Wiley, 1958), as well as the discussion of his results in Crozier and Friedberg, *L'Acteur et le Système*, pp. 43–5.
2. *The Social Psychology of Bargaining* pp. 130–2.
3. This process, called intra-organisational bargaining, has been put in evidence by Walton and McKersie in a 1965 book which has developed as the source and inspiration for much further analysis of collective bargaining and remains extremely influential. See R. E. Walton and R. B. McKersie, *A Behavioral Theory of Labor Negotiations* (New York: McGraw Hill, 1965). Particularly noteworthy among subsequent efforts is the work of Peterson and Tracy who attempt to enlarge the framework proposed by Walton and McKersie and to test it empirically. See R. B. Peterson and C. Tracy, 'Testing a Behavioral Theory model of Labor negotiations', *Industrial Relations*, vol. 16, no. 1, February 1977.
4. A different grid, but with a similar goal, has been presented by Adam et Reynaud, *Conflits du Travail et Changement Social*.
5. See C. G. M. Atkinson, *The Effective Negotiator* (London: Billings & Sons, 1980).
6. See Section III of Chapter 2.
7. The example is borrowed from Crozier and Friedberg, *L'Acteur et le Système* p. 61 and expanded upon.
8. The notion of raising the stakes and the relevant strategies are very aptly defined and described by Adam and Reynaud, *Conflits du Travail et Changement Social*, under the name of 'Sliding Games', pp. 179ff.
9. Katz and Kahn, *The Social Psychology of Organizations* (New York: Wiley, 1967) pp. 218ff.
10. See Pfeffer, *Power in Organizations*, p. 2.
11. M. Weber,*The Theory of Social and Economic Organization* (New York: Oxford University Press, 1947) as quoted by P. M. Blau, *Exchange and Power in Social Life* (New York: Wiley, 1964).
12. Crozier and Friedberg, *L'Acteur et le Système*, p. 59.
13. R. A. Dahl, 'The concept of power', *Behavioral Sciences*, no. 2, 1957, pp. 201–15.

14. N. W. Chamberlain and J. W. Kuhn. *Collective Bargaining,* 2nd ed (New York: McGraw Hill, 1965).
15. Ibid., p. 162ff.
16. Crozier and Friedberg, *L'Acteur et le Système,* p. 55ff.
17. Bacharach and Lawler, *Bargaining.*
18. On the transmission of bargaining power from a given situation see J. Rojot, *International Collective Bargaining* (Deventer: Kluwer, 1978).
19. The idea of this table to support our contention of subjectivity of bargaining power is inspired by a different example used in R. Fisher and N. Ury, *Getting to Yes* (London: Hutchinson, 1983) pp. 24–25.
20. L. Tracy and R. B. Peterson, 'Differences in reactions of union and management negotiators to the problem solving process', *Industrial Relations Journal,* vol. 8, no. 4, winter 1977.
21. See the discussion above and the application by Warr, *Psychology and Collective Bargaining,* of basic psychological elements to collective bargaining.
22. J. R. P. French and B. Raven, 'The Bases of Social Power', in D. Cartright, *Studies in Social Power* (Ann Arbor: Institute for Social Research, University of Michigan, 1959) pp. 150–67.
23. D. Mechanic, 'Sources of Power of Lower Participants in Complex Organizations', *Administrative Science Quarterly,* 192, 7, pp. 349–64.
24. H. Simon, *Administrative Behavior* (New York: The Free Press, 1965) 2nd paperback edn, pp. 11–12.
25. C. I. Barnard, *The Functions of the Executive* (Cambridge, Mass.: Harvard University Press, 1938) pp. 163ff.
26. T. C. Schelling, *The Strategy of Conflict.*
27. *L'Acteur et le Système,* p. 60.
28. *Bargaining,* p. 41.
29. *Exchange and Power in Social Life,* pp. 115ff.
30. Certain definitions of negotiation by certain theorists even exclude that case. See the developments on a definition of negotiation in Chapter 1.
31. These ideas have been put in evidence by Bacharach and Lawler, *Bargaining.*
32. Crozier and Friedberg, *L'Acteur et le Système.*
33. Those aspects of a negotiating relationship were put in evidence by Jan Pen, see J. Pen, *The Wage Rate under Collective Bargaining* (Cambridge, Mass.: Harvard University Press, 1959).

3 Determinants of the Choice of a Negotiating Strategy

1. *The Social Psychology of Bargaining,* p. 199.
2. *The Social Psychology of Bargaining,* p. 198.
3. J. E. McGrath, 'A Social Psychological Approach to the Study of Negotiation' in R. Bowers (ed.), *Studies on Behavior in Organizations,* pp. 101–34.
4. *The Social Psychology of Bargaining,* pp. 28–33.
5. *Negotiating Behavior,* p. 44.
6. Ibid., p. 42.
7. *The Social Psychology of Bargaining,* pp. 43–55.

Negotiation: From Theory to Practice

8. Ibid.
9. Pruitt, *Negotiating Behavior*, p. 43.
10. These concepts are drawn from Walton and McKersie's 'Area of Interdependency', *A Behavioral Theory of Labor Negotiations*, pp. 37–42, which uses a similar diagram.
11. Ibid., p. 43.
12. Ibid., pp. 37–41.
13. On that point see M. A. Piore and P. B. Doeriger, *Internal Labor Markets* (Lexington, Mass., 1981) ch. II.4.
14. Quoted by Pruitt, *Negotiating Behaviour*, p. 29.
15. Chamberlain and Kuhn, *Collective Bargaining*, p. 182.
16. *A Behavioral Theory of Labor Negotiations*, p. 30ff.
17. *The Social Psychology of Bargaining*, pp. 266–8.
18. *Psychology and Collective Bargaining*, p. 29.
19. *A Behavioral Theory of Labor Negotiations*, pp.20ff.
20. E. Peters, *Strategy and Tactics in Labor Negotiations* (New London, Connecticut: National Foremen's Institute, 1955).
21. *Conflits du Travail*.
22. *The Social Psychology of Bargaining*, p. 130.
23. Ibid., p. 46.
24. *A Behavioural Theory of Labor Negotiations*, p. 13.
25. *Psychology and Collective Bargaining*, pp. 183–9.

4 The Selection of a Strategy

1. The presentation of this diagram is inspired by the one proposed by Thomas, see K. Thomas, 'Conflict and Conflict Management', Chapter 21, in Marwin W. Dunette (ed.), *Handbook of Industrial and Organizational Psychology* (Chicago: Rand McNally, 1976) pp. 889–935.

5 Negotiating Tactics

1. The initial taxonomy of tactics presented below was first established by A. Gottschalk, *Cedep Teaching Note*, 1974, unpublished. It was later completed and developed by the author.
2. J. Pfeffer, *Power in Organizations*, p. 116, makes a similar point when he calls attention to the power embedded in the capacity to control decision premisses.
3. *Strategy and Collective Bargaining Negotiations*, p. 32.
4. *Negotiating Behavior*, p. 23.
5. Ibid., p. 38.
6. As discussed above and defined by Rubin and Brown, *The Social Psychology of Bargaining*, p. 130.
7. *Bargaining*.
8. *Negotiating Behavior*, p. 57.
9. *The Strategy of Conflict*, p. 53ff.
10. 'The Social Psychology of Bargaining', p. 186.
11. T. C. Schelling, *The Strategy of Conflict*, ch. II.

12. Bacharach and Lawler, *Bargaining*, have devoted considerable attention to the use of threats, bluff, and so on, notably in experimental settings. They devised experiments in order to try to predict the use of these tactics from the power balance.

13. Some of these have already often been discussed in the literature on practical aspects of negotiating. See, for instance, H. Cohen, *You Can Negotiate Anything* (New York: Bantam, 1980), or J. Ilich, *Power Negotiating* (Reading, Mass.: Addison Wesley); or C. L. Karass, *Give and Take* (New York: Crowell, 1974). We want here to put them in evidence as related to general categories of tactics.

14. See J. C. Altmann, *Les Techniques de la Négociation* (Paris: WEKA, 1980).

15. Summarised by Pruitt, *Negotiating Behavior*, p. 127.

6 Negotiating Styles

1. D. B. Sparks, *The Dynamics of Effective Negotiation* (Houston, Texas: Gulf Publishing Company, 1982) ch. 12.

2. W. F. G. Mastenbroek, 'The Negotiating Grid', *Journal of European Industrial Training*, vol. 2 (1984) no.4.

3. A. W. G. Gottschalk, unpublished teaching notes, Cedep and the London Business School, 1974.

4. Rubin and Brown, *The Social Psychology of Bargaining*, pp. 175ff., review experimental work aiming to gauge the effects of some isolated personality traits on bargaining behaviour.

5. E. Goffman, *The Presentation of Self in Everyday Life* (New York: Doubleday Anchor Books, 1954).

7 The Phases of Negotiation

1. A. Douglas, 'The peaceful settlement of industrial and intergroup disputes', *Journal of Conflict Resolution*, vol. 1 (1957) pp. 69ff.

2. *The 50% Solution.*

3. *Psychology and Collective Bargaining*, pp. 155–67.

4. Druckman's findings are combined into one model and quoted by Pruitt, *Negotiating Behavior*, p. 13.

5. *The Social Psychology of Bargaining*, ch. 13.

6. *Negotiating Behavior*, p. 133.

7. The author is indebted to A. Gottschalk for all uses of this box presentation.

8. C. J. Nierenberg, *Fundamentals of Negotiating* (New York: Hawthorn Books, 1973), devotes a full chapter to the dangers of assumptions.

9. Several sources exist for this 'axiom'. The earliest one the author has been able to come up with is an anecdote in a French detective story of the 1950s.

10. K. Thomas, 'Conflict and Conflict Management', has listed some of them.

11. M. Sherif and D. W. Sherif, *Groups in Harmony and Tension* (New York: Harper and Row, 1953), and M. Sherif, *Group Conflict and Co-operation* (London: Routledge and Kegan Paul, 1966).
12. Marsh interestingly draws attention to the costs of time, see P. D. V. Marsh, *Contract Negotiator Handook* (Aldershot, England: Gower Press, 1982).
13. Nierenberg, *Fundamentals of Negotiating*, Chapter V, devotes the full chapter to questions and their use.

8 The Tasks in Negotiating

1. A. W. Gottschalk, *Cedep Teaching Notes*, 1974.
2. The terms refer to the figure presented in Chapter 3, the selection of a strategy, first strategic choice.
3. See Walton and McKersie, *A Behavioral Theory of Labor Negotiations*, pp. 161ff for supporting data.
4. See Schelling, *The Strategy of Conflict*, Chapter 1, Section 3, for examples of tacit co-ordination and bargaining.
5. C. L. Karass, *Give and Take* (New York: Crowell, 1974) p. 100.
6. Nierenberg, *Fundamentals of Negotiating*, ch. 1.
7. *Strategy and Tactics in Labor Negotiations*.
8. Kennedy, Benson and McMillan, *Managing Negotiations* (London: Business Books Ltd, 1980) ch. 5.
9. Karass, *Give and Take*.
10. See, for instance, G. J. Nierenberg and H. Calero, *How to Read a Person Like a Book* (New York: Hawthorn Books, 1971).
11. This problem, as well as the precedent one, has been widely discussed, see W. P. Scott, *The Skills of Negotiating* (Aldershot: Gower, 1981) p. 155; Marsh, *Contract Negotiator Handbook*, p. 207; Sparks, p. 24, who devote a chapter each to his subject.
12. However, it should be said that in certain cultures negotiation by teams is prevalent, in Japan or in Eastern Europe, for instance.
13. The method has been published in R. Fischer and W. Ury, *Getting to Yes, Negotiating Agreements without Giving in* (Boston, Mass.: Houghton Mifflin, 1981). It is part of the ongoing Harvard research project on negotiating.
14. The results of that research have been published in N. Rackham and J. Carlisle, 'The effective negotiator', *Journal of European Industrial Training*, vol. 2 (1978) no. 6, pp. 6–12 and vol. 2 (1978) no. 7.

Index of Authors

Subject Index